THE TRUTH THAT KILLED

GEORGI MARKOV

The Truth That Killed

TRANSLATED BY
Liliana Brisby

WITH AN INTRODUCTION BY
Annabel Markov

TICKNOR & FIELDS *New York* 1984

First American edition 1984

Copyright ©1983 by Annabel Markov

With grateful thanks to the *Bulgarian Review*

Library of Congress Cataloging in Publication Data

Markov, Georgi, 1929-1978.
The truth that killed.

1. Markov, Georgi, 1929-1978—Biography.   2. Authors,
Bulgarian—20th century—Biography.   3. Dissenters—
Bulgaria—Biography.   I. Title.
PG1038.23.A74Z474   1984   891.8′133   84-20
ISBN 0-89919-296-3

Printed in the United States of America

S 10 9 8 7 6 5 4 3 2 1

CONTENTS

INTRODUCTION
Annabel Markov

My husband Georgi Markov is buried in an ancient and beautiful country churchyard in the West of England. So old are some of the tombstones in that little churchyard that their inscriptions have almost disappeared. Those which can be read indicate that nearly all of those whose bodies lie there were local, and that most lived long and perhaps relatively uneventful lives. But my husband's plain white headstone proclaims that, in every way, his life was different. He was born in another country, Bulgaria; he met his end unnaturally, before his time; and he died, as his stone says, 'in the cause of freedom'.

It was on 7 September 1978 that Georgi was attacked by an assassin on London's Waterloo Bridge, some time between the early afternoon and evening. As he passed a bus stop he experienced a sudden stinging pain in the back of his right thigh and, turning sharply, saw a man behind who bent to retrieve an umbrella and murmured 'I'm sorry'. Georgi noted that the man sounded un-English and that when he almost immediately hailed a taxi its driver seemed to have difficulty in understanding him. But so relatively unimportant did the incident obviously seem to Georgi that when he came home that night he did not mention it. He had, it is true, mentioned it to a fellow emigré and friend shortly after it occurred. But he had not been sufficiently alarmed to call a doctor, and neither had he gone to the police. It was not until the early hours of the next morning, when his temperature had risen suddenly and alarmingly, that he at last said to me: 'I have a horrible feeling that this may be connected with something which happened yesterday....'

But even as Georgi told the story, and displayed a small puncture mark on his thigh, I did not feel he really believed that what he had feared had at last happened. Yet this was a man who, for nine years, had felt himself to be in danger; and who, for the past nine months, had lived with the certain knowledge that his enemies planned to kill him.

Until 1969, Georgi Markov was one of Bulgaria's top novelists and playwrights, his work known throughout the Eastern bloc. He was a member of the privileged élite and an acquaintance of the President, Todor Zhivkov, even travelling to the West, on one occasion, as cultural representative of Bulgaria. Then in 1969, after just one performance of a new play, *The Man Who Was Me*, he defected. Writing in English in a diary long afterwards, Georgi said: 'Whenever I look back to my past, it seems to me that the most essential part of it is locked between two events, which I still cannot connect.' The first of those events took place in 1962 after the publication of Georgi's first novel *Men* when, as he wrote in that same diary, 'I awoke to find myself a literary star.' The second was on the day seven years later when, in great haste, he left for ever the country he loved.

To begin a new life at the age of forty, having to adjust to the foreign ways of another country, is difficult enough. To do it as a writer, transplanted from everything that went into forming an experience and a talent, unable any longer to communicate in the natural medium, is almost impossible. Yet it is a measure of Georgi's essential optimism and courage that he was determined to succeed as a writer in the West also; and, despite the enforced haste in leaving Bulgaria, he was careful to take with him proof of his talent. There was *Men*, which had been translated throughout Eastern Europe and made into a film that opened the first week of Bulgarian films at the National Film Theatre in London. There were other novels like *The Women of Warsaw*, *Portrait of My Double*, and the manuscript of a novel which had been banned, *The Great Roof*. There were plays like *The Cheese Merchant's Good Lady*, with which Georgi had made his debut as a playwright in 1963, and *Let's Go Under the Rainbow*; and there was also *The Assassins*, a play which had been singled out for censure in an article signed by Todor Zhivkov. In that hastily gathered collection, indeed, could be seen Georgi's development as a writer over the past seven years: from *Men*, which had made him a favourite of the Party, to the novels and plays which had become so outspoken against the system that they were no longer permitted to be published or staged.

When Georgi drove out of Sofia for the last time, he felt, he later described, as if he were attending a funeral. But at that point he did not know if it was he who was, in a sense, dead, or if it was everything that he was leaving behind him. It was soon apparent what the Bulgarian regime felt. Within ten days there was an article in the

Party newspaper *Rabotnichesko Delo* criticizing Georgi's works and describing them as 'alien to socialist society'; within two months all his plays had been taken off the stage; and within a year he was being described in the Bulgarian press as a traitor. Three and a half years after his defection, a special court in Sofia sentenced Georgi *in absentia* to six and half years imprisonment and his property was confiscated. 'We hope,' a Party hack wrote, 'that in the West they know how to bury dogs.'

But those books and plays and short stories and film scenarios – fruits of a prodigious creative output – were not all Georgi had brought to the West. He had also brought his memories and, because he had led an extraordinarily eventful life, they constituted both an unusual and a very complete picture of life in contemporary Bulgaria. For Georgi had observed the present system from its inception, at every level. Not only had he suffered greatly from it (the prisoner in the chapter 'The Justification' was himself), but he had also reaped all the benefits it could offer. Born in 1929, the son of an army officer, Georgi grew up in pre-revolutionary Bulgaria and saw the Communists take over in 1944 when he was still a schoolboy. Subsequently, as a student, he was imprisoned for his political beliefs and this episode left a profound impression on him. Georgi later said that it was at this point when, half-broken by the system, he decided to be as successful as he possibly could within it. After surviving both meningitis and tuberculosis, he qualified as a chemical engineer, running the metallurgy factory referred to in the early part of his memoirs, before finding himself, at thirty-three, one of the country's top writers. As such, Georgi got to know everyone of influence in Bulgaria and, along the way, observed at first hand the corruption of absolute power. In 1975, in a series of weekly talks broadcast by the Munich-based station Radio Free Europe, he began to share his memories with those he had left behind.

By this time, Georgi had established himself in England and managed to achieve a measure of success as a writer. He had joined the Bulgarian section of the BBC's External Services; he had also started to write for the German radio station, *Deutsche Welle*; and he had adapted old plays and begun to write new ones. *The Archangel Michael*, the first play Georgi wrote after coming to the West, won a prize at the Edinburgh Festival in 1974; and Georgi was about to begin a literary collaboration with an English friend, David Phillips, that resulted in what was intended to be the first of several novels. That could have set the pattern of a new phase of life spent concentrating on capturing a new audience in a new environment. But Georgi missed his old audience and, above all, he was a committed writer. He was elated when he learnt that his broadcasts for Radio Free Europe were being listened to by an estimated audience of five million (more than half of Bulgaria's total population), and he laughed when he heard a joke currently circulating in Sofia to the effect that the subjects of some of his broadcasts, the party leaders, were regularly tuning in to hear all about themselves. His amusement did not give way to apprehension, either, when news came that no less a figure than Zhivkov was enraged by the memoirs (and most particularly by a series of talks in which Georgi described their meetings).

During the period when the memoirs were broadcast, Georgi would sometimes receive telephone calls from Bulgarians visiting the West who wished to express their appreciation. Then, in January 1978, there came a very much more sinister call, the purpose of which was to warn Georgi that, if he continued to write for Radio Free Europe, he would be killed. Similar warnings recurred throughout five months and then, in late May, the Bulgarian who had delivered the warnings, who professed to be a friend, came to visit Georgi personally. The decision to kill had been taken by the Bulgarian Politburo, he said; and the means with which the murder would be effected had already been transported to the West. Georgi would be poisoned with a rare substance which would be undetectable (and had, by the way, been tested in Moscow), and he would develop a high fever before his death, which would be put down to natural causes. Everything the Bulgarian said, incidentally, led Georgi to believe that his enemies would attempt to administer the poison orally, and this may have been intentional.

To know that powerful enemies have planned your death in detail would spiritually destroy most people. Not so Georgi. In nine years of living in the West, most of them in England, he had never been able to sleep in an unlocked room, had always taken care with whom he ate and drank, had kept secret any plans to travel abroad. In what were to be the last months of his life he took even greater precautions, but still managed to live as generously and as fully as he always had; and our last holiday together was not really spoilt when he received a telephone warning saying that an attempt on his life was to be made there and then, as we tried to relax with our baby on an Italian island.

I now believe that Georgi's enemies always knew exactly when they would try and kill him, and that specific threats were issued and then not carried out as part of a deliberate policy both to terrify him and eventually to make him drop his guard. ('They're playing with me,' Georgi said, when he returned unscathed from that Italian holiday.) In Georgi's memoirs he stresses the importance of 9 September in the calendar of Communist Bulgaria. It was on 9 September, the anniversary of the imposition of Communist rule, that Georgi, by now in hospital, suffered a terrible collapse from which he was only saved through the efforts of doctors and his own great will to live. He survived for two more days, believing that he would be able to talk with Special Branch officers, who had by then been alerted. But the poison in his system was impossible to resist.

For just a few hours after Georgi's death on the morning of 11 September, it was purely a tragedy for his family and friends. By the end of the day it had become a public sensation also; and, within three weeks, the world-wide rumours that he had been murdered were confirmed. Scotland Yard announced the finding of a minute precision-made metal pellet in his thigh: exactly the same weapon as had been used in an unsuccessful attempt on the life of another Bulgarian defector, Vladimir Kostov, in Paris. At the inquest into Georgi's death the coroner ruled that he had been killed unlawfully, and the poison used to fill that pellet was identified as ricin, rare and exceptionally deadly, which is known to have been extensively researched in Eastern Europe.

It is very clear whose interests were served by Georgi's death; and a wealth of circumstantial evidence exists which heavily implicates them. But because of the nature of the weapon used, which allowed the assassin to get clear away before murder was even suspected, it is unlikely that murder charges can ever be brought (though the British police continue their investigations). What does exist for all to see, however, is the motive for the crime: and these memoirs must be almost unique in the whole field of literature from Eastern Europe in that their author paid with his life for writing them.

I remember very well the general disbelief immediately after Georgi's death. It seemed impossible to many of those born and brought up in the West that a man could be murdered for a series of broadcasts. They were lucky indeed in not appreciating what a closed society involves. Georgi was murdered because he told the truth. Not only did he question the underlying values of Bulgarian Communism, and therefore Soviet Communism also, but he took a cool fair look at Zhivkov, who has now been in office longer than any other East European leader. To look at a man who has encouraged a personality cult around himself as an ordinary mortal was apparently unforgivable. Indeed, the chapters in this book on Georgi's meetings with Zhivkov have been described by at least one Bulgarian emigré as 'dynamite'.

These memoirs have already been published in Bulgarian by means of a special fund and have received considerable acclaim. They have moved some of Georgi's countrymen to describe him as 'Bulgaria's Solzhenitsyn' and, over and over again, I have been told how true they are. 'We have an author in his own right and talent among the greatest in our language,' wrote one Bulgarian who dared not sign his name. Georgi's theme is 'the unimaginable tragedy of our people', as that same Bulgarian put it, and yet, in parts, this is a very funny book. That does not surprise me, having lived with Georgi and known him, and neither does the book's highly subtle and flexible approach. All these qualities single it out among dissident literature, as does the fact that it is the only such work to come out of Bulgaria, the Soviet Union's closest satellite state.

Spanning as they do the years from 1947 to 1969, Georgi's memoirs are, *in toto*, roughly twice the length of this English translation. Hence there were considerable problems involved in selecting the right material for a Western readership. The names of those who would mean nothing to non-Bulgarians have been cut in places, and the chapters on Zhivkov himself have also been reduced in length (we have indicated where cuts have been made). I think Georgi's authentic voice comes through loud and clear in this English translation: and, in so far as it can, so does his rich and striking use of language which so many Bulgarians have commented on. It is very clear from this book how much Georgi loved Bulgaria: not the country it had become, which he said he never missed after 1969, but the true Bulgaria where he was born and shaped and which he never forgot.

Georgi's only child Sasha does not remember her father very well because she was only two when he died. But she helps me when I put flowers on his grave and she asks about him a great deal. 'Why did Daddy write those things if he loved us?' she said not long ago. I told her that Georgi believed that the Bulgarian authorities would never dare risk the scandal that might ensue if they killed him; and I told her that, above all, Georgi was a man who could not compromise or be dictated to. Through this English translation, Sasha will know the father who adored her. It is therefore dedicated to her as well as to those many, many Bulgarians for whom Georgi is a national hero.

Georgi was a man who passionately loved life and understood how it should be lived. That he was prepared to put himself in a position of great risk indicates just how greatly he believed in individual freedom. He died defending it.

This book is intended for all those who say:
'This does not concern me!'

PROLOGUE

Two conflicting desires have accompanied me throughout my journey – from the moment, six years ago, when I saw the sun on Mount Vitosha for the last time to the present, when I sit looking out on a quiet London street.

The first is the desire to forget everything that has been, good and bad. To throw away the past like a heavy, useless burden, to sever firmly and at one stroke forty years of my life, to make a new beginning. Not a new chapter, but a completely new book, in a new language and with a new subject. I have always been attracted by the idea of complete rebirth, which is perhaps peculiar to those who have suffered a lot, or sinned a lot. This desire prompts the question: What was the point of leaving Bulgaria if you are to continue to live with what you have left behind, if you will populate the future with ghosts from the past, if your conscious or unconscious comparisons transform your present life into an elegy for the past? What was the point, if you give in to sentimental exaggerations about beauty long gone, if you seek in the past the justification for everything present or future? This desire reminds me of Goethe's thought, that my fatherland is where I am happiest; it impels me to move to new countries, to meet new people, to learn a new language, to try to think and live in a new way.

But the other desire is that of the boy in the fable about King Midas and the ass's ears. This is the uncontrollable, almost painful urge of a man to express himself, to unload everything the years have deposited within him, to pour out what suffocates him because it has had to be kept in. This desire tells me that the past is more real than the present because I have been born in it and have come to know myself through it, that it is an indivisible part of body and soul, that even though I dwell in another world I remain intact over there – at the foot of Vitosha. And everything there is more alive, more resonant, more colourful than my surroundings here. This desire commands me not to give up my Bulgaria to those who happen to have been born there and who live there by accident and who will vanish by accident, because they neither know the country, nor love it, nor care about it, because they are blind and ignorant servants of an alien will and an alien country. This desire clearly tells me that there is sense in being here only if I continue to remain there, that I have the privilege and the duty to describe that life, as it is. This desire points to the deadened Bulgaria which is represented by the faceless official writings of the regime and the desperate mediocrity of many of those who speak in its name. It points to the travestied Bulgaria, portrayed in the illiterate and patronizing writings of foreigners. Over and over again behind the painted picture of a featureless existence, that simulacre of contemporary life devoid of real happening, behind the provincial calm of a Soviet backwater, my protesting consciousness sees people and events which embody in a vivid, biblical way the true character of the times, incomparably richer and more colourful than those which their alien master has displayed in the socialist show-case.

This desire compels me to tell what I know, exactly as it was, so that people the world over will understand that Bulgaria is not merely a beautiful tourist country, exporting tomatoes and grapes, a sovereign republic without sovereignty, a popular democracy without democracy, a lifeless social existence numbed by heavy-handed police methods, a grey submissiveness steeped in the ancient wisdom 'it's no good kicking against the pricks', a faceless literature and a crippled art. The Bulgaria I want to describe is a land of unceasing effervescence, a land where gestures and words have many dimensions, where everything is accompanied by its negation, where strength and weakness, love and hatred, wisdom and stupidity, courage and fear go together – denying and confirming each other. Under the apparent calm of the Bulgarian sea there runs the strong constant current of conflicts which echo the most important questions of our time and embrace everything: philosophy, politics, morality, religion. When I make involuntary comparisons between the life of a normal citizen in the West and the life of a normal Bulgarian, the difference seems so great that the life of the Westerner could be represented by a child's simple drawing whereas in the life of the Bulgarian reality is inextricably mixed with the symbolic and the abstract in a quite bewildering way. We are subjected to the impact of far more factors and forces than the Western citizen can imagine. While the citizen in the West is constantly striving to acquire ever more, our main instinct is to preserve what we have.

Today, we Bulgarians present a fine example of what it is to exist under a lid which we cannot lift and which we no longer believe someone else can lift. We have no faith in the United Nations Charter or in international diplomacy and politics, in humanitarian aims or sympathies. We exemplify an existence without the right to choose and sometimes we marvel that this, too, is possible, that one can live in this way despite the consciousness of being doomed people whose shadows are immured within the walls of our prison. Life under the lid has no horizontal dimension. Everything is ordered along a ladder with a dual destination – up or down. On this ladder is enacted an endless carnival of the power of man over man, a demonstration of climbing, pushing, hitting and jostling, of headlong ascent and violent descent. On this ladder, plots are woven, battles are fought, forces are regrouped, ambitions and primitive instincts are fanned and every flicker of nobility and dignity is extinguished. And the unending slogan which millions of loudspeakers blare out is that everyone is fighting for the happiness of the others. Every word spoken under the lid constantly changes its meaning. Lies and truths swap their values with the frequency of an alternating current. We have statesmen who have no state, personalities who have no personae, politicians who have no policies, shops in which nothing is sold, writers who do not write, elections in which there is no choice, courts which are themselves condemned, thefts which are called privileges, and privileges which are called thefts, matches whose results are known before they are played and crimes which are unmasked before they have been committed. The graph of our development is the most incredible labyrinth. If you are a hero today, you may be a traitor tomorrow, hanged the day after tomorrow, and rehabilitated with a monument erected to you the day after. Everyone on the ladder can do anything which comes to mind, without any responsibility but with one overriding justification – that he has done it for the Party. Under the lid, 'the Party' is the most real but at the same time the most abstract concept. Real, because everyone feels its weight like a strong increase in atmospheric pressure; abstract, because no one has seen its face. If, universally, Macbeth, King Lear and Richard III are stage characters, at home in Bulgaria they are the citizens with whom we live and who play the most active parts in our lives. In the streets of Sofia you can meet comrade Caligula, followed at a respectable distance by comrades Talleyrand and Fouché, while Ostap Bender* is in command of

* Hero of the comic adventure novel *The Twelve Chairs* (1961) by Ilya Ilf and Yevgeny Petrov, first published in Russian in 1928.

the parade. We have no present. We have only a 'terrible' past and a 'wonderful' future. While many citizens in the West spend their lives in constant communion with cats and dogs, we live in the closest contact and in utter interdependence with other humans; we exist through others and others exist through us; each is against everyone else and each is with everyone else because this is what the law of survival dictates. In this unbelievably tight proximity we feel the warmth of each other's bodies, our slightest shivers, our least movements; we have become accustomed to read each other's faces and we can converse for hours without speaking a word. Yet our hours are longer than Western hours because they contain a huge and continuous expectation. Our nights are richer because they are filled with sleeplessness as well as darkness. While those in the West know the many nuances of the seven colours of the rainbow, we are past masters at recognizing the two colours of conflict – black and white – in all their shading.

And that is why, when Western revolutionaries shout about radical change in the world and a happy future life under socialism or Communism, we want to tell them: 'Come join us, under the lid; come live your happy life here!' They do not know the meaning of the words they mouth and they become intoxicated by their infantile fantasies. We know the meaning. We have paid the highest price to learn it. Behind the uplifting slogans of the Revolution we have seen both big and small opportunists on the march, hungry for power; we have seen the front line of idealists inevitably replaced by a band of ruthless power-seekers, avid dictators, agents of a foreign state who, once they have reached the top, establish the most oppressive police state and turn back the spiritual development of their people by several centuries at least. We have seen how personality vanishes, how individuality is destroyed, how the spiritual life of a whole people is corrupted in order to turn them into a listless flock of sheep. We have seen so many of those demonstrations which humiliate human dignity, where normal people are expected to applaud some paltry mediocrity who has proclaimed himself a demi-god and condescendingly waves to them from the heights of his police inviolability. We have seen how the only aim in the life of these comrades is ruthlessly to hold on to power, how their only interests are those of their own megalomaniac existence, how the only happiness for which they struggle is their own happiness, and how the only function they have is to serve a foreign state – the owner of the lid. They remember that they are Bulgarians or forget that they are Bulgarians according to the current directives of the alien Ministry of Foreign Affairs which has appointed them. They are such great patriots that more than once, having caused complete chaos and got utterly lost, they beg their masters officially to annex Bulgaria and turn it into the next Soviet province.

But it is not only these people I want to talk about. They are merely one side of the coin. It is the other which compels me to write. Looking back, I see an epoch packed full of characters and events. I see hundreds of faces of ordinary Bulgarians whom I have met in the course of my profession as an engineer and my prolonged stays in hospitals and sanatoria. Hundreds of faces of writers, actors, producers, public personalities, generals, ministers, high Party dignitaries – society's élite, where my career as a writer landed me. I was fortunate to meet and work with rich and interesting personalities who, despite the corrosive mediocrity of regime and atmosphere, managed to preserve their identities. I witnessed dramatic incidents, when the ugliness of the times was suddenly illuminated by the noble acts of individual people. Both as observer and participant I was able to witness the complex ambiguity of our relationships, relationships rendered even more complex by the dialectic of our time, as if we were a transitional generation after which everything would be clear and either paradise or hell would descend on earth.

I see before me the sad eyes of Ivan the machine operator who used to say: 'When you're in pain, start doing something with your hands, try to make something and it will pass.' I can still hear Julia's deep voice repeating: 'Just because someone is a rat, that's no reason for us to behave like that!' I can see the faces of the students in the labour brigade at Malyovitsa who asked me: 'How do you reconcile your convictions with the privileges you enjoy?' And the mocking face of Radoi Ralin†* reciting an epigram about the brotherhood of man. ... And the distraught expression of the former first lieutenant who cried in front of me: 'Have you ever killed a bound man? What do you know?' And Christo, who used to say that the only way to resist was to declare your position publicly at every occasion. ... And the meeting with the young prostitutes summoned to the Directorate of the Militia for a pep talk: 'Surely, comrades, the body is not what really matters?' And the midnight rendering of the old Bulgarian national anthem '*Shumi Maritsa*' in honour of Vulko Chervenkov. ... And the trembling voice of the actor Kosta Kissimov: 'Why the hell don't you write about Mother Bulgaria?'

* Names marked with this symbol (†) are to be found in the Biographical Notes.

Before I left Bulgaria I was obliged to burn my diaries which I had kept for fifteen years, but many things have remained as fresh and clear in my mind as if they had happened yesterday. I shall attempt to describe it all, because one day someone might need my testimony.

I

From 1947 until 1952 Markov was at Sofia's Polytechnic, studying chemical engineering. It was during this period – between 1950 and 1951 – that he was imprisoned for his political beliefs. During the seven years after he left university, he worked at a metallurgy factory, at one stage running it.

ECHOES FROM MY
STUDENT YEARS

The decisive and fatal change in our country occurred during my student days. When my contemporaries and I entered the Polytechnic in 1947, we lived in one kind of world, but by the time we had finished our education in 1952, we had become inhabitants of a different world. It may or may not be symbolic, but that period saw our transformation from 'Mr' into 'comrade'. The entrance exams we had passed still reflected to a large extent 'bourgeois' notions of objectivity and fairness; indeed, only the most able candidates were accepted. But barely five years later, no trace of an objective competitive system was left. The reign of 'connections', of knowing the right person, had arrived; to this day it remains the chief method of selecting people and the main qualification for securing any personal advancement. It was during these five years that the centuries-old structure of the people's moral scruples was demolished; the very idea of applying objective criteria was abandoned forever.

However from the very beginning there appeared amongst us freshmen the colourless faces of young people who not only had not sat any qualifying exams, but who had not even completed their secondary education. They were imposed on the university through some secret and unimaginable privileges. And although they had little use for the subject which they were supposed to study, the faces of these strange colleagues soon began to acquire a special importance. Quite frequently one could see the outline of a gun under their overcoats. Their manner towards us ordinary students was one of inexplicable hatred and constant suspicion. Their hatred was particularly virulent towards the more brilliant student or the more distinctive personality. They often cut lectures and gathered at long secret sessions which lasted well into the night. We saw how they followed us, how they listened to our conversations and how their expressions became more and more threatening. They were the organizers of every kind of political initiative and they abused us by saddling us with tasks which had nothing to do with our studies. They dragged us off to meetings, demonstrations and 'labour' brigades and demanded that we chant their slogans. They organized special study groups for the scrutiny of party propaganda material. Although their academic equipment was mostly nonexistent, they managed, in a mysterious way, to pass their exams. A few years later, when I myself was teaching a university course, the mechanics of that kind of examination became clear to me. A deputy minister in the Department of Light Industry simply telephoned me one day and ordered me to give a pass mark to an incompetent girl student who, as he put it, was 'one of our children'.

'Ours' and 'enemies' – these were the two most important categories and they occupied a central place in our lives during those years. It was then that there began a merciless sorting out of people, which surpassed the cruelty of racial discrimination because it condemned the victims to suffering not merely for the duration of a war but for a lifetime. It was explained to us that this division followed Stalin's formulation about the intensification of the class struggle in the transition period. In a country like Bulgaria, where there has never been a class system or a class struggle, nor indeed rank social inequality, Stalin's theories brought about the artificial fostering of class conflict which will remain one of the absurdities of the time. 'Every Bulgarian can find the clogs of his grandfather in the attic' goes the popular phrase, which exactly reflected the classless character of our country in the past. At first, this savage division of people was carried out in a manner as peremptory as the marking of cattle for slaughter. But while even cattle are branded according to some standard, the marking of people was done with unbelievable arbitrariness. A great many people, branded as enemies, had to pay dearly. However, if I thought then that some of the cases were the result of error, it became obvious to me later that justice and injustice had nothing whatever to do with the matter. The important thing was the process of separating people out, for it was aimed at instilling universal fear and confusion. Moreover, the concept 'ours' proved to be highly relative. In order to remain one of 'ours', a person had to furnish daily proof. The dichotomy between 'ours' and 'enemies' provided the pretext for the cruel punishment of an entire nation, for the breaking up and destroying of natural human ties, for the setting of each against the other. Years later I was to see documentary evidence of how the Soviet security service and its Bulgarian agents organized and performed on the public stage the satanic play that Joseph Stalin had written, in which the whole nation had parts.

And when, in 1948-9, we were engulfed by an unremitting wave of student purges, when the State Security vans were waiting at the university gates to pick up students who had just been expelled, it became obvious to all of us what subject our sinister colleagues had been studying all along. Suddenly and senselessly, it transpired that the most able, the most gifted, the most outstanding students had to abandon the studies for which they had a vocation. I shall never forget the mass meeting in the assembly hall when we listened to the roll-call of those who had been expelled from the various student organizations (which in itself meant automatic expulsion from the Polytechnic). Nor shall I forget the barbarous silence in which victims and survivors voted with deadly unanimity 'for' the expulsions. I now think that we were so frightened by the arrests, the beatings and other cruelties, perpetrated throughout the country, that no one dared speak out. And yet my fellow-student Pavel, who was one of the most brilliant mathematicians of our year and had a politically 'stable' past, could not bear the spectacle of this universal humiliation. He got up and amidst the deathly silence he said firmly: 'What you are doing is shameful! You are expelling the best students. What is it all for? I must tell you that I feel ashamed to remain a student.' He had scarcely finished when somebody proposed that his name should be added to the list. Everyone voted in silence. Pavel's impulsive act cost him three years' manual labour. I am not sure whether, had there been more like him, things would have taken another course. Pavel's action was noble and beautiful, but one of the most characteristic features of Communism is its complete lack of sensitivity to moral beauty, to any show of nobility. The noble gesture, the honourable action of the enemy fail to move them. Their response to the gesture of the knight who throws down his gauntlet is to clout him over the head with a rod or hit him with a stone in the back of the neck.

During that winter of 1948-9, the rest of us were already 'comrades'. Our comradeship was expressed in silent submission, fear, servility, and participation in all manner of mass activities such as political agitation, labour days and study groups devoted to the biography of comrades Stalin or Georgi Dimitrov†. We had to repeat phrases in which nobody believed, nonsense like 'leader of incomparable genius', 'father and teacher of all progressive humanity'. Our intellectual individuality was degraded to the extent that we began to resemble bleating sheep, trained to obey. But we were still painfully conscious of the situation in which we found ourselves. We could see that our professors also – amongst whom there were learned men with international reputations, people of great authority – had retreated into their academic shells and were in the grip of ever greater fear. Most of them pretended that they were entirely devoted to their specialities and had no interest in real life. Others quickly conformed and accepted the new political religion, and this in turn stabilized their position. The leaders of the youth organizations within the faculties had greater authority than the university administration. The notorious lists for the expulsion of students prepared by these leaders were not their own work – they were dictated to them by the State Security and the Party committees. It was not unusual for individual students to be summoned before their faculty organizations to be questioned in order to elicit from them information about fellow-students or instructors. Imperceptibly, an atmosphere of continuous spying was created, in which the smallest foolish step could have momentous consequences. Gradually, our instinct for self-preservation developed to such a degree that most of us acquired sombre expressions, so that during the second half of our studies it became difficult to distinguish us from the real 'comrades'. There was a tragicomical competition for each to show himself to be more Catholic than the Pope, in order to allay any suspicion about himself or his family. There was a time when each one of us assiduously searched his family tree for any examples of anti-bourgeois, anti-monarchist, antifascist activity on the part of some relative. This was the period when many people simply invented 'progressive' biographies. If you take the trouble to read the endless memoirs that are published in our country today, you will be amazed by the descriptions of millions of exploits against the authorities of the Third Bulgarian Kingdom. The fabrication of heroic Communist biographies became commonplace; all the more so as the Politburo members themselves, generals and other leaders, set the tone by inventing non-existent feats. In this frantic search for heroic acts, everything was greatly inflated: harmless arrests for drunkenness became acts of political defiance; the passing of a note from Peter to Pavel became the daring mission of a Party courier; a five-jointed star scribbled on the wall of a public lavatory was hailed as the equal of the broadside of the *Aurora*;* technical errors due to sheer incompetence were described as sabotage. If one was

---

* The Baltic fleet cruiser which bombarded the Winter Palace during the October Revolution and thus helped the Bolshevik victory.

acquainted with a genuine Communist activist, this was regarded as more precious than one's mother's milk. I could tell really funny stories about the writing of progressive biographies. But as the present was even more important than the past, truly theatrical performances were unleashed on the public. Often they exceeded all credibility and we found ourselves in the position of the good Soldier Schweik, who carried out his orders to the letter. When the newspapers published a picture of the Stakhanovite* textile worker, Marussya Todorova, who had started to weave on twenty-five or fifty looms, some of my female colleagues immediately began tó do their hair like hers. Trilbys and Homburgs had disappeared, and almost everyone wore ordinary caps or peaked ones like Stalin. It also became the fashion to affect rough, virile manners because this was presumed to be proletarian. At public meetings, two-thirds of all speeches contained the expression 'as Comrade Stalin teaches us' or 'as our beloved leader, Comrade Dimitrov, says'. Often the quotations were quite untrue, but no one dared interrupt the performance, for this was a struggle for survival. Prisons and concentration camps were filled to capacity. Countless people passed through the militia stations, which were conducting a full-scale campaign against 'enemies'. All human relationships were based on the suspicion that your neighbour wished you ill. The most acute national paranoia took root and flourished in the belief that anyone could be an agent of the State Security. There can hardly be another police force in the world which has struck greater terror into people's hearts than our own State Security during those years. To this day, the expression 'a DS man' (the initials denoting a member of the Bulgarian State Security) provokes a powerful reaction: people immediately change colour. Denunciations also flourished. One of the methods applied systematically by the various police authorities was to summon a citizen and question him until he had said something about another citizen. Then the second citizen was called in and confronted with what had been said by the first one; and because it was untrue, this provoked a violent reaction and the second citizen in turn 'implicated' the deeply unhappy first citizen who, summoned again, now volunteered abundant true and false information about the second one. The objective of the new rulers was to crush the people, to incite one against the other. Years later I was able to observe this consistent and meticulous application of 'divide and rule'. This,

* Stakhanovite: a worker who increases his output to an exceptional extent, and so gains special awards.

in turn, led to the desire to become someone's protégé: everybody tried to take refuge under the wing of a powerful person whom he could serve. The divisions existed not only at the bottom of the scale, but also up at the top, where a life and death struggle raged between the different party coteries and, above all, between the Soviet agents imported from abroad, headed by Georgi Dimitrov and Vulko Chervenkov,† and the local party leaders. Later on, this struggle was to assume another form, but it was never to subside because its aim was that no one should feel safe and all should be afraid.

Very soon, from naïve and innocent young people, linked by normal human ties of friendship, full of love and faith in people and the world, we were turned into shadowy figures full of suspicion, fear and mutual hatred, a branded herd, with each trying to displace his neighbour in order to win a few minutes' respite for himself.

We had truly become 'comrades'.

During the summer of 1948 all the students from our faculty had to take part in a forty-five day labour brigade on the banks of the Danube where we made bricks. It is from that time that there stems my most vivid memory of the first flagrant injustice, which later on was to become a fundamental party and state principle. Whilst we, ordinary students, had to work twelve hours a day at a crippling pace, the party comrades who had been appointed (on whose authority no one knew) as 'commanders' lounged about all day long and played volley-ball. There was something cynical in the contrast between the exhausted girl students running around carrying heavy hods full of bricks and, in the background, behind wire-meshing, the self-satisfied faces of the 'commanders' playing volley-ball. The work was extremely hard, so much so that some of us paid with our health. That same autumn I was sent to the sanatorium for tubercular students near Vladaya. And from that time, too, dates the memory of my strange meeting with Georgi Dimitrov. Those were hard years and many people died of tuberculosis. But in the student sanatorium, the atmosphere was always optimistic and gay. In the evenings, all those who were able to leave their beds descended into the lounge where they sat playing backgammon, chess or cards. Most of the time we played bridge, but on a friendly basis, strictly for pleasure - gambling was totally unknown. Early one evening, I don't remember the exact date, it was snowing lightly and about forty of us students, girls and boys, players and onlookers, had gathered round the tables. Everyone was engrossed in the game; there was the usual din, interrupted from time to time by a fit of coughing. Suddenly the door opened. I was facing it and I saw that the man who had entered was 'the leader and teacher of the Bulgarian people'. He was accompanied by his bodyguard, who was known, I think, as Kolyo the Sailor. Dimitrov stopped for a moment, looking around as if prepared for the customary noisy reception, the clapping and rhythmical chanting of his name. His face had acquired the condescending expression of a man who is used to acclamation. But strangely, nobody even looked up from the tables, as if the man who had just entered was Nikolai the doorman. I realized that the students were so absorbed by the games that not one amongst them had noticed him. I seemed to be the only one observing him with intense curiosity. He remained standing by the door, as if unable to believe that his appearance had provoked no reaction. The man whom the regime's propaganda machine called 'the greatest Bulgarian', who was always accompanied by the relentless echo of his own name, who clearly thought himself a super-hero or a demi-god, was suddenly faced with cool indifference. Had he been an ordinary citizen, it would not have been difficult for him to guess that the people in the room had simply not noticed him. There were a fair number of Communists among them. But his paranoia ran wild. I noticed how his face changed colour, his Adam's apple started to jump up and down, his eyes blazed and the next moment he shouted in a high-pitched piercing voice: 'Students! What kind of Monte Carlo is this? Gamblers! Card-sharps! Shame on you! Is that why the nation has sent you here? You are playing cards with the people's mone-e-e-ey. . . .'

He continued to yell like a madman, totally out of control, and looking at him, I kept thinking how insignificant and petty this man was, who could erupt with such hatred because of a genuinely unintended slight. His face was twitching, his hands were trembling, his whole body was shaking. All the students immediately turned round, many of them jumped to their feet, one of them with more composure tried to make an excuse, but the Leipzig lion* roared away until his voice gave out, after which he ran out slamming the door behind him. Afterwards it was said by some that he had been drunk. But from that moment, the student sanatorium, in which I was fated to spend long months, was the only medical institution in the country where

---

* An allusion to Dimitrov's trial in 1933 after the burning down of the Reichstag, when he was celebrated for having stood up to his Nazi judges.

introducing playing cards into the building was considered as something akin to treason.

In fact, this was the second time that I had seen Georgi Dimitrov at close quarters. The first time was during the elections for the National Assembly. On that sunny Sunday, he arrived at the polling station in the old reading room at Knyazhevo. I saw him square his shoulders proudly and enter briskly, accompanied by several people. After about ten minutes he reappeared in a most unexpected way surrounded by his supporters who were trying to calm him down, while he, ablaze with fury, was shouting words like: 'Scum! People's enemies! Fascists!' Waving his arms about, he was threatening someone who had remained inside. What had happened? Many elderly Knyazhevo inhabitants remember this scene and can recount the details. On entering, Dimitrov had been welcomed with deference by the entire staff of the polling station who rose to their feet.

'Who is the representative of the opposition here?' he asked curtly.

'I am, Mr Dimitrov,' replied the agent Vassil, who, like the rest, was standing to mark his respect. Vassil was an architecture student, a war hero, one of the most honest and courageous people known in Knyazhevo, but he had not been allowed to finish his studies.

'You?' Dimitrov shouted, swaying slightly. 'Do you know that you are a traitor! Do you know whom you are serving and where you will answer for it!' Suddenly the 'great leader and teacher' started to pour forth a stream of disconnected abuse. Clearly he was very drunk. At this point, Vassil suddenly raised his voice and said severely: 'Mr Dimitrov, on this day, when the destiny of Bulgaria is being decided, when the voters are not allowed to drink, how can you, a parliamentary candidate, dare to come in here drunk! Will you leave immediately!'

Completely losing control, Georgi Dimitrov hurled himself at Vassil, but the sturdy Knyazhevo peasants intervened and he was obliged to leave. Ultimately, this encounter nearly cost Vassil his life. There followed long years in concentration camps and prisons, in which his youth wasted away.

But we students of the Polytechnic were obliged, quite apart from our academic work, to study the biography of this unwanted guest from Moscow. We had to repeat his empty phrases and to wonder what he had in common with us, with our lives, with our Bulgaria. He, the pseudo-hero product of carefully directed propaganda, could not withstand a meeting with an ordinary Bulgarian hero. That is why he reacted as a vindictive little man who had been somebody's servant all his life. Never, not for a moment, had I experienced the slightest positive feeling for this Soviet citizen, with whom the tragedy of our country really began. One must be either totally blind or completely corrupt not to see that Dimitrov brought to our country the Soviet style of government, where power is directed against ordinary people. He was the man who introduced the degrading ritualistic deification of leaders and imperial conceits such as even Napoleon had not permitted himself. He was the one who introduced the black limousines and drew their heavy curtains between himself and the ordinary people, and he was the one who allowed his country to be ruthlessly robbed and ruined by those who had sent him to colonize it. He introduced methods and practices about which many generations of Bulgarians, even ten centuries from now, will read with the same feeling of shame with which we read today about the corrupt and lawless kingdom of Boril.*

At about the same time, I also saw Traicho Kostov† at close quarters. When they stripped him of all his posts, he became for a time Director of the National Library. It was said jokingly that he had started to translate the novel *Far from Moscow* by the Soviet novelist Vasily Azhaev. The novel was later translated by someone else. The demoted Traicho Kostov came to live in the villa of Goldstein in Knyazhevo, which was next door to our house. I saw him several times when he stopped to talk to my grandfather. He looked pensive and oppressed, as if he foresaw what awaited him. I shall always think that in his gestures and in his voice there was something very different from the other Politburo members, who now seem more to me like Madame Tussaud's wax-works. My grandfather would complain about how hard life was and Traicho Kostov would reply with a sad smile that this was a transitional time and things would improve. A few months later they hanged him. Years later eye-witnesses at his trial told me how the examining magistrate had kept hitting Traicho Kostov on the nose. . . .

While he was being tried, an orgy of meetings was organized throughout the country, at which everyone called Traicho Kostov the most disgusting names. In the hospitals we were driven from our beds to attend meetings which ended with the chanting of demands for 'Death! Death!' Few things have filled me with greater horror and revulsion than these orgies of human hatred and vileness. And the

* King Boril, who ruled during the Second Bulgarian Empire (1207-18), usurped the throne and forced the rightful successor, Ivan Assen II, to seek refuge abroad.

Bulgarian newspapers which at the time poured their rivers of filth over Traicho Kostov never found the slightest courage to apologize later. I have often wondered how people can continue to read these newspapers, which belched forth lies and deceptions and sent innocent people to their deaths, sang hymns of praise to the greatest crimes and worshipped criminals. How can *Rabotnichesko Delo** continue to exist when in its issue of 21 December 1949 the name of Stalin was mentioned no fewer than three hundred times...?

But what struck me particularly at the time was the extent of the savagery of our comrades, the 'activists'. There were so many who proposed the most cruel punishments for a man whom they had deeply respected only the previous year. I had the feeling that their violent hatred of Traicho was for them a personal organic necessity. They had this need to hate, and Stalin satisfied it. When the news of his hanging was announced, there were some who started dancing. An insignificant doctor, who within a year would rise to be the head of the government hospital, walked along the corridor of the sanatorium declaring that this was the happiest day of his life. This was no fanatic madness, but rather a necessity dictated by his servile instincts. For it is noteworthy that all these comrades hated Traicho Kostov *publicly*. They hated him when others could see and hear them. They hated him because such hatred was richly remunerated, it was rewarded like a heroic deed. Do not think that the great majority of them believed in his guilt. If any of these people who were so full of hatred says that he did believe in it – he was either infinitely stupid, or he is simply a liar. I could see that they knew Traicho to be innocent, but they seemed to be engaged in a mad competition in which everyone lied to everybody else claiming that he was guilty.

The 'enemy' mania raged with a murderous force. Perhaps many were intoxicated by it because it liberated them from all human inhibitions. At least, let us not lie to ourselves today by conveniently blaming Stalin for everything. The tragic truth is that Stalin was not alone, that Stalin would not even have existed if it had not been for the little Stalins, the thousands upon thousands of his followers, nameless criminals.

Historians and psychologists will say that the interaction worked both ways, but I believe that it was not Stalin who created them (as many still maintain), but that they created Stalin and through him gave the most contemporary name to evil – Stalinism. If I had to give

* *Rabotnichesko Delo* ('Workers' Cause'): daily newspaper of the Bulgarian Communist Party.

a precise description of the little Stalin of my time, I would say that he was a petty, energetic, ambitious, spiteful and essentially lonely creature, for whom the giving of orders, the bullying, the threatening and the terrorizing of other human beings was a psycho-pathological need. The little Stalin wanted to be taken notice of, he wanted the world to see him, to hear him and somehow to pay homage to him. And since usually he lacked the qualities to be a good farmer, tailor, artist or craftsman, since he did not have the capabilities of an ordinary working man, he was filled with envy and hatred towards all who possessed these qualities, towards the good human harmonious world of tolerance and love, in which there was no room for irrational fury. For our own little Stalins in Bulgaria the Revolution was never anything else but a convenient pretext to give free rein to their base passions and instincts, and to the diabolical satisfaction of their painful inferiority complexes. The brutal crushing of another man's will became for them the triumph of personal superiority. The Party, socialism and Communism were the justification. And amidst this pack of wolves we had to live and keep our faith in man.

I know of no other political religion which has had a stronger impact on the baser human instincts and passions, which has given such encouragement to human vice generally, as the Communist ideology. A time had come in Bulgaria when men were expected to express themselves solely through the commission of evil deeds, which were justified as a dialectical necessity of the Party. And it was precisely through the practice of that evil, by causing pain and suffering to others, that some people in Bulgaria now saw that they could cut a figure in life and society, better themselves, perhaps even gain a place in history. I know of a high-ranking officer in the State Security who had once lived as a humble employee in a forestry enterprise, and who in normal times would never have left it. But his entry into the militia, followed by a long series of arrests, interrogations, torture and testimonies extracted by force, had pushed him up the ladder of promotion to a most powerful position. In a dramatic confession, he told me once that his career began from the moment when he was sent to arrest his closest friend of whose innocence he was totally convinced.

I know of many people who made brilliant Party and State careers and rose to positions which they would never have reached in a free society - solely by manufacturing evil for all those who happened to stand in their way. The capacity to do harm proved to be the most useful talent of the Communist epoch, since the *evil* done to individuals always turned out to be *good* for the policies of the Party. Figuratively speaking, people were not allowed to hold out a hand to help each other, but were given every opportunity to exchange cruel blows. When we talk of the 'enemy-mania' which raged in all the spheres of our society and became a fundamental element in the Communist mentality, we must not forget that not only the Party but also many citizens felt a need for it. Through it they found themselves and discovered a purpose to their lives, they lived in order to seek out, hate and fight enemies, as if the existence of the enemy justified their own existence. Actions against the enemy were at the same time actions of self-approval. The reward was two-fold: on the one hand, the gaining of Party recognition, and, on the other, the achievement of personal self-confidence and gratification. That is why this 'enemy-mania' acted like a powerful bellows fanning into a blaze fiendish feelings and ambitions that otherwise would have remained locked in the cold silence of an untapped human coal seam. If, throughout the centuries, men have felt a need for the existence of God, king or leader, in our time many people felt the need for an enemy. Nothing is more important to the life of a Communist society than the existence of an *enemy*. Voltaire's claim that if there were no God, men would find it necessary to invent him, had its perfect application in our society, with its need for an enemy. Without this enemy, ideology, Party and regime became a ridiculous nonsense. Through the enemy, everything found some sort of justification. The enemy justified the terror regime and all its violence; the enemy was the excuse for the immense failures and mistakes of incompetent leaders; the enemy explained economic reverses ... and in the most cynical way the enemy was used to defend the need for the privileges of the élite. This gigantic, terrible, dastardly, indefatigable, constant and ubiquitous *enemy* was the magic key to the Communist regime's existence. Most public activity in Bulgaria at that time was directed against various enemies. All secret or open meetings and sessions of Party organizations or individual groups of Party members were directed against some enemy; ministerial and managerial councils were transformed into headquarters for the struggle against the enemy; the whole atmosphere in the country was fraught because of the unceasing war against the enemy.

I shall always remember an incident of a slightly later period, which nevertheless sums up the blackness of that time and the two faces of 'enemy-mania' – the public and the private.

It was, I think, during 1958. My friend K and I were queuing for bread outside a bakery near the tram stop in Knyazhevo. Everything was calm and normal. The baker took the bread out and about ten of us began to shuffle forward. At this moment, a Major appeared from somewhere – I learnt later that he was from the barracks at Gorna Banya. He was about thirty-seven or thirty-eight, with a reddish face and dark eyes, and he moved with marked self-confidence, hitting his boots with a small crop. Instead of joining the queue, the comrade Major tried to jump it without even an excuse. The people at the front, obviously frightened, meekly made way for him. But my friend K, who could not stomach this triumph of impudence, ran forward and placed himself between the major and the bread.

'Take your place in the queue, if you please!' he said.

For a moment, the Major seemed amazed that somebody had dared to challenge him; then his face grew dark red and he yelled: 'Who are you to tell me what to do?'

'Instead of showing people an example, you behave intolerably!' K replied firmly.

At this, the people in the queue took courage and started to heckle the Major, who, seeing that he would not be allowed to have his own way, flew into a rage.

'I'll teach you who I am!' he shouted at K, turning away and quickly walking off into the main street. The people heaved a sigh of relief and a pleasant animation set in as if every one of them had won a victory. But those of us still queuing shuddered when we saw the Major returning after a minute with two militiamen in uniform.

'This one here!' he said, pointing to K.

Nearly all of us in the queue tried to explain to these representatives of law and order what had happened, and that if anyone deserved censure, it was the comrade Major. But without listening to us, the militiamen seized K and, accompanied by the Major who looked at us with triumphant fury, they marched him off to the militia station.

I immediately rang K's parents, and his father ran around trying to do what he could, but was not able to achieve anything that day. K spent the night in the Knyazhevo militia station and was let out only the following evening. When he came to us, his face was unrecognizable – it was covered with ugly bruises and two of his front teeth had been knocked out.

He told me that when they brought him to the station the Major and one of the militia officers who was clearly a friend of his had pushed him onto the floor and brutally beaten him up.

'So you're not going to let *me* have bread, are you? *Me! Me!*' yelled the Major, kicking my unfortunate friend.

But this was the end of only the first Act. In the evening, they took K to the chief of the militia station himself. He listened silently to the story of my friend and even pretended that he sympathized with him.

'If you really are one of us, the Major was clearly in the wrong,' the station chief said, whereupon he suddenly asked: 'But are you one of us?'

My friend did not know what to reply, and the chief added: 'Remember that whatever you say will have to be proved!' Then he looked at him meaningfully and said: 'Now, tell me the names of your friends!' K cautiously mentioned a few names of friends who had a certain political weight.

'And now, tell me who your enemies are?' the militia chief demanded.

K thought a while and replied: 'I don't really know, I don't think I have any enemies.'

'No enemies!' The chief raised his voice. 'Do you mean to say that you hate nobody and nobody hates you?'

'As far as I know, nobody.'

'You're lying!' shouted the Lieutenant-Colonel suddenly, rising from his chair. 'What kind of a man are you, not to have any enemies? You clearly do not belong to *our* youth, you cannot be one of *our* citizens, if you have no enemies! We are surrounded by enemies, and this man here claims that he has none! Where do you live? On what planet?'

Afterwards the police chief reeled off approximately the following speech: 'The man who doesn't hate isn't one of us! Because one cannot live without hating! It is not possible for a citizen of ours not to have a proper attitude towards the enemy. Even in his time Christo Botev† used to say: "To love and to hate strongly!" And if you really do not know how to hate, we shall teach you! We shall teach you very quickly!'

And, indeed, they wasted no time teaching him. K was offered his immediate release on condition that he would become a secret informer and regularly report whatever he heard to the militia. Merely in order to get off, he signed several declarations on oath promising to serve them. After this incident, he suffered from a prolonged nervous fever and kept repeating to me that he no longer wanted to live in Bulgaria. Finally, he fled abroad.

However, what impressed me so greatly, and what I never forgot, was the diabolical declaration by the militia Colonel that 'You are not a proper man if you do not hate!' Probably without being aware of it, this servant of the 'people's democracy' had formulated precisely the basic moral tenet of Marxist–Leninist–Stalinist ideology. Hate was the main engine, the motor of all relations between man and Party, man and State, and man and man. Only a few years were needed by these professors of the art of hate to turn fear and hatred into the main emotions of the period.

Look at any newspaper of that time, read any speech, examine the workings of any department, enterprise, co-operative farm, school or university – and you will inevitably discover the corrosion of hatred. We students of that era were expected every day to hate Nikola Petkov,† Traicho Kostov,† Tito, Franco, Chiang Kai-shek, American imperialism, German revanchism, Yugoslav revisionism, the black Fascist past, the Church and the clergy, bourgeois remnants, the émigrés – and so on. In reality, this abstract hatred took on concrete forms: you hated your colleague because he was more gifted than you, you hated your friend because he had more success with women, you hated your chief because he was above you and you hated your subordinate because you suspected him of wanting to take your place, you hated the greengrocer and the baker because they had not kept you anything under the counter, you hated your powerful relative X because he did not let you have a passport to travel abroad, you hated your wife because she wanted a life of her own, you hated your children because they did not obey you. In the end, you hated yourself, because you could not become what you wanted to be.

Nor did this hatred remain merely an open or undeclared feeling; very often it was translated into powerful actions to which the cultured Western world referred euphemistically as 'violations of the law'. The better name is 'terror'. It seems to me that there is no closer link on earth than that between hatred and terror. And since both needed enemies, when no more enemies existed they had to be invented. In principle, everybody could be an enemy; absolutely every Bulgarian citizen had done something, however innocent, for which he could be declared an enemy at a given moment. If somebody had done nothing, then this was an even stronger reason for treating him as an enemy. I am convinced that if one day, somehow, enemies cease to exist and there is no way of inventing them, people like our Lieutenant-Colonel will die out, for they will have nothing to live for.

I must confess that I don't remember anything bright or uplifting in all my student days. I don't remember one single moment which was not hideously deformed by all sorts of fears, or threatened by someone's hatred.

The power of the lugubrious colleagues who had been foisted on us grew all the time. From the university it spread to our homes, to our private lives, even to our intimate thoughts and feelings. God help you if you failed to turn up for a brigade, a day of labour, any organized action, or even simply for a meeting or a literary circle. God help you if you were friendly with people who were considered to be enemies, or if you dared behave more freely with your friends, or if you told jokes. Our relationships, our conversations, were crippled. Everything was accompanied by an unavoidable black question-mark, which turned our attempts at sincerity into mockery. We got used to lying to each other with straight faces, to talking in official phrases while trying to give them a double meaning that would find a corresponding response in more quick-witted interlocutors. 'When you say something, always leave a door open behind you through which you can retreat if necessary.' This was and remains a guiding principle. We were forced to submit to circumstances, and so we were not honest in our submissiveness. We voted for resolutions that we could not have signed honestly, we read newspapers without really reading because we did not believe a word in them, and we learned the trick of talking to one another while saying nothing. Indeed, we took such pains to hide our own personal truth from others that sometimes we hid it even from ourselves.

THE WORKERS' REPUBLIC

The 'Victory' factory consisted of a sprawl of formless buildings sur-rounded by the strange kingdom of the *Dunovisti** with their wooden huts and little gardens full of fruit trees. In the summer of 1952, this was still an unspoilt world. The wood, which King Ferdinand had planted, reached almost to the factory fence and we all liked to walk through it on our way to the tram stop. On the other side of the factory, the gardens of a popular swimming-pool looked idyllic. Only ten years later, this peaceful sunlit landscape would be changed out of all recognition. Ugly apartment blocks and private houses and garages with their noisy occupants would put an end to the morning ritual of the bearded *Dunovisti* celebrating sunrise and to an existence in which people and nature seemed to live in mutual contemplation. On top of the hill the 'Palace of the Pioneers' would rise and the quiet of the wood would be shattered by strident slogans shouted by marching children with red ties.

Before nationalization, our factory was called 'Iskovich-Levy' and was famous throughout Bulgaria for producing a shoe-polish called Imalin. At the same time, it had the best department in the country for plating sheet iron, which later enabled it to become the most important centre for the manufacture of tins. In fact the export of canned goods absolutely depended on the Victory factory. I was fated to start my engineering career in this factory, and to form long lasting relationships with its workers. My appointment was not quite in order, as my specialist knowledge should have singled me out for duty in a heavy metallurgical plant. But a universally applicable law of our social order then, as now, decreed that a huge number of people should devote their energies to work for which they were not suited. Under this law, which led to the most inexplicable and impossible

* The *Dunovisti*, a small sect of sun-worshippers named after their leader Dunov, were a familiar sight with their flowing white robes and long hair.

appointments, colleagues of mine who were specialists in rubber were sent to produce glass, specialists in glass found themselves in the pharmaceutical industry, while food experts ended up in heavy metallurgy. All this was partly the consequence of an almost hysterical scramble to remain at all costs in Sofia, where with good reason life was considered to be better than in the provinces. Those active in the Communist Youth League, of course, secured places for themselves as lecturers and assistants in the Polytechnic and the University. Thus my landing in Victory was part of a cunning move to remain in Sofia.

The managing director of the factory was Manya Encheva, a Communist with a brilliant record in the underground and an imperious and rather insubordinate nature. She was the wife of Colonel Docho Kolev, who became the commandant of Belene concentration camp.

On my arrival at the factory, I found the atmosphere very tense. It transpired that a ruthless struggle was going on between two Party groups. One was that of Manya Encheva, the other was made up of Party members supported by the district committee of the Ministry of the Interior and, therefore, by the Security Service. The struggle was for the post of director and had a purely personal basis. However unlikely this may seem in retrospect, Manya's enemies were making every possible effort to undermine the work in the factory, particularly as regards productivity and export plans. During that time, I was able to observe the ruthlessness and greed of these power-hungry Party members whose behaviour exactly reflected the general character of relations within the Party. They arrested specialists whose work was vital to production and sent them to concentration camps; they detained others under temporary arrest and, finally, they went over to open sabotage. I shudder to this day when I remember how an unknown hand released the huge flywheel of a big machine which shot over the heads of forty female workers and which, had it but flown only a few centimetres lower, would have caused a massacre on the shopfloor. There was another extraordinary incident when the district security service arrested several workers on a particularly crucial day for production targets. It was then that Manya showed her courage, which I still admire, by ordering the seven factory guards to open fire on the people of the Interior Ministry if they tried to force an entry into the factory. Manya was one of the rare examples of genuine Communist fanaticism and idealism, which made her an attractive person in my eyes. At a time when the whole country was tearing itself apart in all sorts of struggles and purges, she felt quite instinctively that what was important for a factory was that it should produce, and that, as far as production was concerned, many of the so-called 'enemies' were more useful than the Party's own loafers. Manya was also one of the few Party members who did not exploit her public position for private gain. Years later, amidst the general corruption of the Party aristocracy, I would remember Manya as a lonely island of old-fashioned honesty.

Walking up and down her office, she gave me my first lecture on industrial life. 'First,' she said, 'forget what you have learnt in books and what you've read in newspapers. True, we now have workers' rule, but you should never let the workers step over the line that divides them from us. Hold yourself aloof and never let them even think that they are your equals. "Every frog should know its bog." The best workers in this factory are not our people, but the enemies. They know that they are enemies and the only way they can make us forget their record is to work hard. Try to take advantage of this.'

The 'enemies' were specialists whom she had extracted, with the help of her husband, from concentration camps and police stations, where they had found themselves thanks to the senseless actions of the militia.

The country's best lithographer came from a camp, the best chemist was also brought to us from Belene, the most experienced worker in the metallurgy shop was a sergeant-major from the former Royal Army. The worst placed 'enemy' was the senior engineer Christov, who had studied in Germany and now had to work eighteen hours a day for several years in order to prove that he was no enemy. Even so, Manya never trusted him, which in the end ruined his nervous system. I think that she went too far with her obsession about 'enemies', and even the bitter lessons she learnt when her Party rivals struck at her factory did not help to soften her attitude towards some people. The director had her own intelligence network. It was customary in all offices and enterprises for the boss to have a whole web of informers. I was unpleasantly surprised when, a few days later, the director let me know that she knew everything I had told the workers on various occasions. The trouble was that, more often than not, the informers' reports, far from revealing the truth, only reflected personal ambitions. Nevertheless, they were entered on the personal file of the employee in question. Later, when I became director, I was amazed when factory employees came to me in the morning to report all sorts of things – from the behaviour of the senior personnel down to that of the lowest worker, often with intimate private details. This was a kind of institutionalized secret gossip, with the political element quite overshadowed by love affairs, family dramas and financial questions.

In our factory, as in so many others, the leadership had appropriated the right to meddle in the private lives of the workers. Often the boss took part in important personal decisions like marriage or divorce. About ten years later, when I was visiting the director of the 'Black Sea' mine, I witnessed a scene which I later described in one of my novels.

It transpired that the mine's best shock-worker,* a Turk, had abandoned his wife and two children for the love of another woman, who had also left her family. The director ordered the worker either to return immediately to his wife, or to leave the mine. Rather touchingly, the worker tried to explain that he had not acted on a whim, but out of a deeply rooted love. 'Comrade Director, haven't you loved too?' the worker asked. 'No, I haven't!' he shouted. 'Either you go back to your wife, or I'll sack you!' I think the worker left. Another director from our industrial complex tried to prove to me that organized spying was necessary – not because it served him, but because it helped the work. 'Does the State have its intelligence service?' he asked me. 'It does! So why shouldn't I have one too? My factory is my State!'

During that time I learned another unwritten rule too. 'It is not important to finish your work, the important thing is to render an account of it!' This rule led to all sorts of production tricks, the gist of which was to report on work which had not been carried out. In order to report an over-fulfilment of the plan, the production targets were deliberately set well below the capacity of the works. Precisely in order to put an end to such subterfuges, the accounts department of the enterprise was inflated beyond belief. With production only a little lower than ours, the former private owner Iskovich-Levy had employed a single man as book-keeper, cashier and accountant, while now our accounts department alone employed twenty-four people. In Iskovich-Levy's day, only seven people out of the whole staff were not directly employed in production; now we had over seventy. The nationalized industry represented a bureaucratic jungle, in which one worker in production supported a dozen non-productive citizens who controlled his work in one way or another. Nor did our bureaucracy mean organization; quite the reverse – it was characterized by the complete disorganization of people who did not dare and did not want

---

* Shock-workers: a body of workers engaged in particularly arduous tasks who aim at record output.

to shoulder the smallest responsibility. Long exhaustive letters were written for the most ludicrous trifles, and interminable correspondence dealt with subjects as trivial as a bag of nails. My most disagreeable memories are of our long meetings. We conferred all the time and about everything, without ever taking a decision. These meetings deprived the factory of its senior staff and foremen as a result of which the work became shoddy and slapdash. The whole point of the meetings was to decide on whom to place the responsibility which everybody shunned like the plague. I had one colleague whom I always remember carrying a big book under his arm. When he received some instruction, he wrote it down carefully in the book, and then presented it to his superior with the words, 'Sign here to show that you have given me this order!' Then he would go to the relevant worker, pass on the order, then offer him the book, saying, 'Sign here to show that I passed on the order!' It may seem funny now, but in those days it was all-important to be on one's guard, for after the various political enemies ran out, a campaign was launched against the economic enemy and economic sabotage.

From the point of view of modern technology, we worked in the most impossible, primitive manner. The initiative of engineers and technicians was completely paralysed by the total lack of incentives and by the reluctance to take risks. The Achilles' heel of our production structure was the rigid and ill-conceived system of remuneration. According to the Labour Code, the salaries of engineers and technicians could not exceed the average worker's pay by more than 6 per cent. But in practice, almost all engineers received considerably less than the workers. This bred indifference and affected work morale. Later, many attempts were made to find a solution, but the problem remains unresolved to this day. In general, good work was not encouraged as it should have been. The titles and awards we gave to shock-workers were quite insufficient and far too unfair to kindle a serious interest in productivity. Taking into account the poor qualifications of the general mass of workers, it becomes clear why we could not even begin to compare in productivity with the former capitalist business. The quality of our production was abysmally low. The shoe-polish we released on the market all but burnt holes in people's shoes. Old workers used to tell me indignantly that Iskovich-Levy would never have tolerated such a state of affairs. Many of them remembered with nostalgia the period before nationalization. Indeed, they had signed a petition demanding that their enterprise be denationalized. Yet, we continued to exist, we continued to produce, because we had no competition whatsoever. Good or bad, we were the only, monopolistic, enterprise.

However small our factory, it reflected to a high degree the entire life of our society, its ethics and the way in which it worked. The characters of some of the people whom I knew then were typical of the whole period.

The newspapers then, as now, kept repeating Maxim Gorky's famous phrases: '*Man*, there's your truth. M-A-N – that has a proud ring.'*
I don't know exactly how the word 'man' sounded to Maxim Gorky, but from personal experience and observation I can say that it had no meaning at all for the rulers of both my country and Gorky's fatherland. But whereas in the Soviet Union the utter contempt for the individual had deep historical roots, in Bulgaria even at the time of the worst Turkish outrages there was a certain consideration for the individual person. The whole of our epic poetry is a vivid demonstration of respect for the individual. Read folk proverbs and sayings and you will be convinced how strongly developed that democratic and tolerant attitude was, even towards hated enemies: 'He, too, has been born of a mother', 'He, too, has a soul'. Until the Communists came to power, we never knew cruel exploitation on a massive scale, whether of peasants or of workers; nor did we have capitalist or working classes. All Bulgarians are more or less peasants or direct descendants of peasants. And perhaps it is the character of our peasant, moulded by his closeness to nature and his traditional sociability, which has given Bulgarians their conscious tolerance and respect for man. Another's suffering, misfortune or death has always roused deep emotion and sympathy in a true Bulgarian.

Alas, the Communist Party, which ideologically is opposed to the ordinary person and aims to transform him from a many-sided, independent and proud creature into a puppet, created an atmosphere of brutal disregard and contempt for the individual human spirit. In all its policies since coming to power, the Communist Party has unerringly followed its basic principle: 'Man is only a means in the struggle, but has no value whatsoever in himself.' This is the same principle which, in the first days of the War, justified Stalin and Timoshenko ordering a cavalry corps to attack a German tank division. I have seen documentary photographs of this madness, when men with horses and sabres attacked tanks, only to be completely destroyed.

* From Maxim Gorky's *The Lower Depths*.

The attitude of the Communist Party towards Bulgarian workers more or less reflected this battle: sabres against tanks. For it should be remembered that in the so-called 'black bourgeois past', the workers had, through their trade unions, managed to pass a law which proscribed what is now called 'work according to norms'. The workers' leaders of the past were quite right in believing that the pursuit of norms or targets for the sake of more pay was unfair on the workers, driving them to exhaustion and ill-health. This law was considered – even by pre-war Communists – as a great victory for Bulgarian workers. But when the Communists came to power, this did not prevent them from introducing exactly the opposite – the Soviet, inhuman, anti-worker practice of standardized work by norms. All enterprises now had their 'norms' departments staffed with norm-specialists instrumental in effecting this unprecedented exploitation of the workers. In order to force the worker to chase higher productivity his basic wage was pitched so low that he had to strain to fulfil and overfulfil the norm. But the norm was not something permanent: as soon as it was overfulfilled by 10 per cent, that was the signal to raise it. In this way the stronger and more skilful workers annihilated the weaker and more clumsy ones, because with their efforts to earn better wages they established norms that the others had no chance of catching up with and thus doomed them to penury. Later many managers of state enterprises personally took it on themselves to do away with this cruel injustice by forming labour brigades composed of various categories of workers, with productivity bonuses shared by all. In many cases where the official fixing of the norms was kind-hearted (as in our factory), a whole system of tricks was used to allow the shock-workers to be paid more without having to raise the norms to an impossibly high level. Our technical and engineering staff, for instance, felt great sympathy for individual workers and tried to help them with all sorts of stratagems when fixing the norms, dividing the work-force into categories, especially when launching new production lines. But the regime's policy of total exploitation of the workers remained unaltered. One of our deputy ministers once expressed it thus: 'Let the norm hit their heels and you will see how they run!'

And since these were lean and hungry years, people struggled for every bit of money. Most of our workers came straight from the villages with unpolluted natural air. But once they arrived in our chemical hothouse where the atmosphere was saturated with turpentine and various noxious gases, many of them contracted tuberculosis. We had a really good health service and the treatment at our clinics produced satisfactory results, but what was the point of opening pulmonary cavities in people and then having to pay over many years for their medication! I have seen workers fainting over their machines. Two of our press operators, Nadka and Dancheto, had achieved such perfect mechanization of their hand movements that they managed to score 20,000 strokes in eight hours, which must be far above any world record (the average is 8,000 strokes for eight hours). Even the most fabulous circus tricks have not impressed me as much as the incessant movement of the hands of these two girls, feeding the sheet iron into the press....

One of my workmen went out of his mind. He was a newcomer, but he could not last out and tried to commit suicide. Later, in the psychiatric clinic, he made a second attempt on his life. He told everyone that he did not want to live. When I went to see him, he received me with a meek half-smile and begged me to arrange that he should be left to die in peace. I tried to talk him out of it and, amongst other things, I asked why he did not want to live. He stared at me and said in a voice, which still sends shivers down my spine:

'There is no order to live, comrade Markov! There is no order to live!'

I thought how right he was. There were orders for work, service, sacrifice, suffering, death! But there were really no orders to live. Life had been deprived of all beauty, nobility, meaning. The Party's attitude to sheep and cows was essentially no different from its attitude to people. In times of war, they were cannon-fodder, in times of peace draught animals.

A trades union to defend the interests of its members did not exist. The 'trades union organization' was exactly the reverse – an instrument to facilitate the repression and deprivation of rights imposed on the workers.

The president of the trades union organization in our factory was nominally elected, but in reality he was appointed by the managing director. The same was true of the Party secretary of the local organization. In my experience at least, these two public officials were always chosen by the managing director, a procedure that saved him possible disagreement and trouble. The trades union leadership had a voice in the nomination for rewards, the use of the central factory fund for entertainments and the distribution of vouchers for the trades union holiday homes. Beyond that, the trades union organization had no say on the main questions which should have been its main concern working conditions and pay. The Central Council of the trades unions was – and remains – a sinecure to which Party members known for their zeal but useless on the production line were sent to idle the time away for services rendered. I don't recall a single case in which the trades union stood up for the interests of the workers, just as some years later, as a member of the Writers' Union, I never witnessed a single case in which this body defended one of its members who was under pressure. Where production was concerned, this allowed the management of a state enterprise to infringe even the Labour Code if it found it expedient. When we fell behind in our plan fulfilment schedule, we more than once forced the workers to clock up overtime which was neither accounted for nor paid. In the face of such injustice, the workers' vengeance expressed itself in alienation from factory and work. The outrageous system of the norms affected the workers' morale and their mental attitude towards labour and production. When a worker was put on 'general work', that is without a norm, then the devil himself could not have forced him to do his job well: 'just so much money – just so much work'. Nevertheless to foster some sort of artificial interest in the work, various competitions were constantly being organized. Workshops, building sites and brigades signed solemn promises and swore oaths to fulfil and over-fulfil their production tasks. These promotions were repeated several times a year until people got sick and tired of them and apathy overcame even the liveliest interest in winning awards. If I were to define the attitude of the ordinary Bulgarian non-Party worker towards production, I should say that 90 per cent of his working time was spent being apathetic.

None the less, with sweat and anguish, production kept going. In every enterprise, there were a few people who were good workers, liked work and worked because that was what made sense of their lives. The majority of them were old workers, former artisans, who really knew their jobs. I have always admired the great technical proficiency of these self-taught experts from the people, who showed a natural talent for grasping the most modern technological plans and did their own work with a feeling for aesthetic perfection. Our expert foremen, Ivan, Georgi, Iliya and others, epitomized a conscientious attitude towards work, or as one of them put it to me: 'If the state has renounced its conscience, I haven't renounced mine!'

They used to arrive at the factory early, before the start of work, and were the last to go home. They planned their work with exemplary efficiency; their sections shone with cleanliness and order, and no matter how much we insulted and humiliated them, they never degraded themselves by lowering their standards. When I want to think of the best in Bulgaria, I think of their hands, calloused, scarred, with fingers missing. They were the pillars of our enterprise. We could have done without everyone else but not without them.

How different from the new generation of workers! Poisoned by the general irresponsibility of public life, they had an irresponsible attitude towards work and state property. For them, work was drudgery, they felt victimized, they hated the work itself, hated workdays, hated the whole enterprise. Very rarely one of them showed real keenness for his job and a wish to learn its finer points. While the older foremen, who had been nurtured in the old Bulgaria, were proud of what they knew and could do, the new workers were permeated by the spirit of the times: they lived from day to day, or as one of my neighbours in Dragalevtsi used to say: 'They carry on, as if the world were going to end tomorrow!'

In vain we organized various training courses and proficiency exams, in vain we attached young people to old foremen and tried to train them as their successors. The results were mediocre. Once the Minister of Light Industry asked me what was lacking in their work. I replied: 'Passion!' I don't know whether he understood my answer, which neither moved nor interested him. I lost count of the times I was told: 'I don't want manual work, give me a white-collar job!'

I deliberately stress the difference between the two types of workmen - the old and the new - to contrast the labour ethics of two different worlds, so vividly reflected in the workdays of our factory. Both had come from the same nation, with the same traditions, but how different they were. With the passage of time, the factory grew, its capacity expanded, new machines and new technology were imported, but I think that the workers' fundamental attitude towards labour has not changed significantly. Later I had the same experience in other factories, and not only in industrial production, but everywhere: slapdash work, just good enough to pass muster, to discharge a tiresome obligation. It was the same in agriculture, in trade, in educational establishments, in administration, and even in literature and art.

KIRO AND THE OTHERS

The first time I arrived at the factory, the porter telephoned somebody. After a while I was confronted by a short stooping little man with prematurely white hair and a face whose sharp features were to be a permanent part of my days in Victory. As they signed my pass, he stood there with his legs apart, twirling a little watch-chain on his forefinger and staring at me with his head imperiously raised. There was an amusing discrepancy between his tiny build, the unnatural tilt of his head and the defiant severity of his face. This was Kiro, the factory's Party secretary and, at the same time, chief security official. The smaller enterprises did not have regular Party representatives, and thus Kiro was able to fill the position for which he seemed to be cut out. He was a pure Shop from the surrounding villages, though I often thought that he must have had some other blood as well. He spoke in a strong Shop dialect, but tried in so far as was possible to pronounce his words in an educated way, with the incredibly comical result of a salad of newspaper clichés in Shop disguise, foreign words and home-grown Shop curses.* His voice was sharp and high-pitched and seemed perfectly attuned to his intolerant character. He lived in a whirl of ceaseless activity, which was reflected in the speed with which he twirled his chain. He walked quickly and energetically and spoke excitedly, swallowing half his words.

Kiro had become a Party member after 9 September 1944 and when internecine Party strife in the factory led to the disgrace of the former Party secretaries, he had suddenly, on Manya's initiative, found himself in this post. He was very attached to her and followed her about like an obedient and faithful dog. Everything the managing director said was law to Kiro. One could only guess at the state of mind of this half-literate, intellectually and physically limited man.

---

* This mixture, superbly caught by the author, defeats this translator. Shopi are peasants from the Sofia region.

The great power which had fallen into his hands through his responsibility not only for the security of the factory but for all its Party activities had clearly crazed the poor man's faculties.

During my time at the factory Kiro was in his element. The Party propaganda line, which claimed that enemies lurked everywhere plotting sabotage, conspiracies and uprisings, had brought Kiro to a state of almost hysterical vigilance. On his initiative, security measures were in force which transformed the innocent shoe-polish factory into something resembling a fiercely guarded centre for atomic weapons. He doubled the number of regular guards, ensured the supply of reserve weapons for extra protection, skirted the whole fence with new wire and enclosed some open spaces with barbed wire. He had set up a complex internal security organization which was often put on red alert. Every morning Kiro came to make his report on security and the behaviour of open or hidden enemies. He was a typical instrument of 'enemy mania' and his most constant feeling was suspicion. At our meetings, he often vetoed an appointment, saying emphatically with narrowed lips: 'I think that there's something fishy about that man.'

Manya accepted his goings-on but did not always take him seriously, which hurt his feelings and made him say: 'You don't believe me, but wait till the enemy burns down the factory!'

Kiro was particularly strict and intransigent with the workers. This was the era of almost daily meetings. The workers were obliged to stay on after hours, but since most of the women were mothers with children who had to be fetched from school and had many other domestic chores, they tried to slip away. But at the door a determined Kiro barred their exit. I used to hear his strident voice rising even higher with fury:

'I'm telling you! I won't let you go home! Not before you've gone to the meeting!'

'But, Kiro,' the women pleaded, 'the children are hungry, they are expecting us.'

'I am hungry, too, but I am staying,' Kiro replied.

The women scolded and swore, but like a vicious sheep-dog he herded them back into the large hall of the canteen where meetings usually took place.

'You don't want to go to meetings!' shouted Kiro. 'But you want to eat! No way! I tell you, not possible! And when I tell you not possible, then it means not possible!'

Another of his manias was to suspect all the workers of theft. When they left the factory, he positioned himself at the gate and expected each one to empty his bag or carrier on the table in front of him. The whole thing was absurd because there was nothing in our factory worth stealing. To avenge themselves, the women used to fill their bags with plaster and then empty them in front of Kiro whose face and clothes became white like those of an old miller. All in all, there was constant warfare between Kiro and the workers.

'If I wasn't here, you'd go to the dogs!' Kiro would declare and sometimes he complained to me: 'I am fed up with guarding them, comrade Markov! They have no conscience! No conscience.'

Kiro was in his element, however, where the reinforced security watch was concerned. To this day the Communist regime believes that the enemy is likely to be particularly active during holidays or other great events. Therefore, at the approach of May Day, 9 September, the October Revolution, New Year and a motley assortment of congresses, the authorities decreed intense vigilance. This meant that the regular watch was reinforced by several other workmen and white-collar workers whose loyalty was above suspicion. The strengthened guard, armed with rifles, took up its position for four hours on end, especially during the night, and guarded the factory from the presumed enemies who would attempt to disrupt the celebrations. The extraordinary guard duties were a great nuisance and everyone tried to shirk this senseless and silly task. Indeed, the only privileged ones in the factory were the 'enemies' themselves. The others could not escape the irrepressible Kiro who promoted himself into a kind of commander-in-chief. He deployed his troops round the factory premises, he relieved them, he reviewed them, while he personally stayed up all night during these periods of alert. This was his finest hour. Bent over the map of the factory area, he plotted the path of all sorts of imaginary enemy infiltrations, setting up his secret posts and ambushes accordingly; no doubt he would gladly have mined a whole field, had he been allowed to do so. He declared various targets 'top secret' and had them guarded especially. Many will not believe this, but the employees of the factory can bear me out. We had some reservoirs for turpentine which were empty and next to them stood one single tank full of vaseline, left over from the period before nationalization. Kiro suddenly decided that these reservoirs and the vaseline tank were exceptionally sensitive targets, likely to be attacked by the enemy, and so he surrounded them with a triple wire fence plus some extra wire-netting, and appointed two members of the reinforced watch to guard them. It was the winter of 1953, a period when, I forget on what pretext, the need for 'intensified vigilance' was proclaimed once more. Kiro had deployed his guards as usual. But it so happened that the couple who were to keep watch over the vaseline tank were two who did not in the least share Kiro's madness. They were my colleague, the engineer Bobby Zakhariev, and the canteen manager Anton Karavulov. Both were kind-hearted, jolly fellows with a taste for drink, food and a pleasant life. Their shift was from midnight to 4 a.m. It was bitterly cold and a snowstorm was blowing. The two decided that it was an insult for intelligent normal people to obey absurd orders and guard a tank full of vaseline, which no one in the world was likely to want either to steal or to bombard. They abandoned their post and went to the canteen, which at that time also served as a restaurant and stocked alcohol; there they took a case of red wine and half a crateful of pork chops and pickles, left money, and went into the baths next to their post. In the baths it was warm and pleasant; they leant their rifles against the wall and made a start with the wine and the pork chops. One by one the bottles were emptied and the two began to think that it wasn't so bad to be posted on guard. But around four in the morning the door suddenly flew open and there stood Kiro. He was almost unrecognizable, his whole face was bloody and lacerated, his clothes torn and covered in snow, his hands frozen.

'What the hell are you doing here?'

And while they were struggling to find an answer, he yelled at them with insane rage:

'Do you realize that I had to fight my way through the wire!'

Poor Kiro! In order to test the vigilance of the guards, about whom he had had his doubts from the beginning, he had tried some time after midnight to breach his own barbed-wire fence from outside; and, what with the darkness and the blizzard, he had become hopelessly entangled and had managed to squeeze through only with the greatest difficulty. But imagine his frustration when he found not only that nobody had witnessed his exploit but, what is more, that there was no guard by the tank.

'Well, if you're crazy enough to creep under the wire when there's a perfectly good door, that's your look-out!' Anton replied with his mouth full.

Kiro could not bear such insolence. He let out an impotent roar and ran away. Next day he reported in a frenzied hysterical tone:

'I struggled for three hours with the cold and the wire. And when I got through – nobody there! But instead of me it could have been the enemy! This is a gross lack of responsibility; I'm flogging myself to death while they eat and drink in the baths. Comrade director, I want them punished, so they will remember! It's either them or me!'

Nothing could have wounded Kiro more. He was beside himself with anger and bitterness and to placate him the two culprits were given some kind of punishment. But what became a more serious punishment was that they had won a lifelong enemy.

Years later, at a dinner with important personalities and their wives, I told this story which, incidentally, had kept the whole factory laughing. At the table, a few of the guests laughed too, but the wife of a member of the Party's Central Committee turned to me reproachfully and said:

'Why do you laugh? Can't you see that this Kiro was a real poet!'

It wasn't worth arguing with her, because the difference between poetry and the triumph of silliness is quite clear.

Unfortunately, Kiro was not unique, or the only one with such obsessions. But there was no doubt that he exemplified in a most typical way the effects of our political and social environment. I am even inclined to believe that years before he was contaminated by this environment, Kiro was a good-natured man with a normal intelligence. The madness had come from the disparity between himself and the power he had been given. This power had deluded him into thinking that his place in life was special, that he was an important element in the pattern of things, that he personally could determine and decide the fate of other people and that much depended on him.

It is difficult not to smile at the efforts the puny Kiro made to fill the large stature which the authorities had conferred on him. How he tried to look important, mysterious, the bearer of fateful secrets! Over and over again I noticed how, when someone's name was mentioned, Kiro's eyes would blaze with prejudice, suggesting that he knew something which others did not. At the same time, I sensed that he instinctively tried to imitate those he admired, like, for instance, the local security chief, one of the deputy managers and even a deputy minister. Kiro copied their gestures, their gait, their tone of voice. For the technical intelligentsia he felt disdain, though he showed us a certain consideration, while he had nothing but contempt and scorn for the workers. In his eyes, the ordinary workers had no distinguishing characteristics: they were no more than a mass that had to be led and ordered about.

For the workers, in turn, he was a tiresome person whom they tried not to take seriously. When he overdid it with his security guards and vigilance initiatives, they took their revenge with small jokes and pranks. They either filled his pockets with shoe-polish, or called him on the telephone on behalf of the area authorities to send him on 'special missions' – to the top of Mount Vitosha, for instance – or simply involved him in unlikely conversations and made fun of him. They would not accept that he was more important than they and tried to belittle and mock his authority, which mightily offended him. His eternal watch-chain became the symbol of parasitism in power.

'Anyone can do it with a chain' was one of the workers' refrains.

With the passing years, Kiro and his methods became obsolete. And when the time came for him to give up his place to ambitious new Party members, he suddenly found himself a lonely wretch, needed by nobody, who could give orders only to his wife.

THE PARTY AND WORK

One morning D came into my room. He was a thirty-five-year-old Shop with a kind face and ungainly movements, one of our best electrical fitters.

'What shall I do today?' he asked with unusual solemnity.

I looked at him with astonishment, because work was always allocated at the beginning of the week and he should have known what his duties were.

'You will do exactly the same work as yesterday!' I replied rather curtly.

'O-o-oh no!' he contradicted me, gently but firmly. 'You must find me something else.'

'Why?'

'Haven't you heard? Yesterday I became a member of the Party!' And he smiled like a man who knew a thing or two.

'So what?' I was perplexed.

D leant over my desk and said pompously:

'I didn't become a Party member in order to work. Find me an administrative job. I, too, want to walk round the factory twirling my watch-chain like Kiro. When you're in the Party, you're in power. If you're in power, you don't have to struggle so hard! Let the others struggle!'

This declaration from our electrician made a great impression on me. It may have been crude, but nevertheless it was an absolutely genuine reflection of the real attitude of ordinary people to Party membership. Subsequently I was to come across more and more examples of people joining the Communist Party on the strength of this simple opportunistic logic. I know many people who are Party members without even sharing Communist ideals, let alone ideology, and who are motivated purely by a desire to be aligned with those in power. Otherwise, the fantastic increase in the number of Party members, who in only the five years after 9 September 1944 grew from a few thousands to nearly half a million, would indeed have been a miracle. It was not difficult to guess at the real motives of all those people engaged in a headlong race to become Party members.

However, in the early 1950s, the Communist Party purged its ranks and imposed stricter selection criteria for Party membership. This selectivity was directed against the country's intelligentsia. Following the example of the Soviet Party, our own Party felt great mistrust towards the intelligentsia, and more precisely towards anyone who tried to think for himself. According to one ruling, we engineers, as well as other administrative officials, could not be accepted as Party members. The new Party ranks were recruited exclusively from the workers and those who had come to the capital from the villages.

Again, copying the Soviet model, people from the furthest provinces were placed in leading positions. Uneducated, half-literate and intellectually insignificant citizens suddenly found themselves occupying important posts purely because of local Party connections, and yet entirely in the spirit of over-all Party policy. Innumerable times in my own work I collided with unbelievably mediocre and entirely inadequate directors, heads of sections and ministerial department chiefs. My colleagues still remember their legendary inanities. Incapable of thinking for themselves or taking decisions on complex questions of production, they were utterly obedient, blind instruments of those who had appointed them. The life they were enabled to lead far surpassed their wildest provincial daydreams. They had power, they decided the fate of people who previously would probably not even have bothered to talk to them, they worked in luxurious offices, they were given modern homes, they enjoyed privileges, they were somebody. And all this they owed to the Party. Without it, if history had taken its normal course, they would have remained forever where they were. That is why they served the Party, or rather, its leaders, with all the loyalty and fanaticism with which they defended their own prosperity. More than once, I heard sincere declarations like 'The Party has elevated me, the Party made something out of me, who was nothing! Without the Party I am a nonentity!' Or: 'All I possess was given me by the Party!' This was the pure truth. At the same time, these people became examples for imitation. Just as Napoleon's soldiers knew that by following him they could win a marshal's baton, so many Bulgarians of this kind knew which path led upwards to an important career. This was the second big wave of Party corruption. The first was the establishment of the higher Party aristocracy.

The flaw in all this was the fact that loyalty towards the Party was the thing least needed by production. Slogans could not make the machines work, but only clever heads and skilful hands. The newly hatched managers of the Party nurseries, who up to a point were conscious of the absurdity of their position, acted exclusively out of an instinct for self-preservation. Almost their sole aim in their life and work was to keep their positions, to hold on to power and, if possible, to climb higher. Everything they did was governed by this instinct. Like some kind of janissaries of an industrial age, they accepted with uncritical servility all instructions from above and applied them with fanatical persistence, regardless of what was practical or even possible. For many years they ruined whole industries with their incompetence, lack of experience and, above all, dishonesty and selfishness. They were greedy, avid for success and did not spare either people or materials in order to be able to report some supposed achievement, which eventually turned out to be either a fraud or else to have been attained at much too high a price. When they had to take responsibility, they hid anxiously behind the backs of their protectors. I remember one or two encounters with such managements and my horror at discovering that they did not know the first thing about their work. But they were faithful and trusted Party members and this was what mattered. It was years before the Party could grasp that these loyal trusted citizens caused much more damage to the economy and the country than could possibly have been inflicted by any real or imaginary enemies. In the army, the militia and the secret police they could prosper, because there, all that was demanded of them was loyalty and obedience. But in industry, in the economy as a whole, in trade, they were useless. The more intelligent immediately surrounded themselves with experienced technical advisers and specialists, and, with their advice, managed to avoid major mistakes by steering a cautious course between demands from on high and what the factory was really capable of.

To be a Party member was and is a passport to an important post. Today, as then, any serious position demands Party membership. It's bizarre indeed for a specialist suddenly to find he has to answer to a half-literate creature hardly able to sign his name who nods his head at everything he is told – without understanding a word. I remember one of my more honest directors. He was a short and very ugly man, but with a certain natural kindness. When he first arrived, he summoned the engineers and addressed us more or less as follows:

'Frankly, I don't know why I'm here. I've no idea what you're doing, how you're doing it and what it all adds up to. However, as they've sent me here, I'm going to stay. But I don't want us to tread on each other's toes. I shall be the director, but you will work in the way you're used to and as you think fit. Don't ask me questions because I can't tell you anything!'

He did not stay long – he was too honest.

But the subject whole books could be written about, and which inspired my literary researches later on, was the undeniable fact that the Party became an organization for ambitious but incompetent people. Looking around me, I saw that almost all good-for-nothing engineers and specialists, incompetent technical managers and incompetent master-craftsmen had become Party members. What united them was not so much the Party's ideology as frustration at their own shortcomings, which were richly compensated by the advantages bestowed by the Party ticket. I have always maintained that ability means independence, that a capable person acquires an independent and nonconformist outlook. The able person cannot be a member of a disciplined submissive organization. Moreover, it is very difficult to create a union of talented people. Precisely because they are gifted and have self-confidence, they will always disagree with each other, raise objections and act in opposition. By contrast, the strongest and most lasting alliance is between fools. The union or the Party gives them what they can never achieve individually and independently. The advantages of power compensate for the lack of talent. As we shall see, this rule applies particularly in the world of the arts.

Meanwhile, life in our factory reinforced my opinions. I observed the behaviour of newly appointed workers. Everything always followed the same pattern. If the workman was good, liked his work and improved his expertise and qualifications, he showed no interest in Party membership. But if someone arrived who possessed little skill, whose ambition far exceeded his ability, then his eyes inevitably turned to the Party organization, and soon I would hear that he had been accepted as a candidate for membership. Amongst us engineers, it was quite usual to say about various workers: 'Pavel has become a good machine operator. Ivan will make an excellent turner. Christo will be a Party member.' It was evident that Christo had not come to work but to climb. After a time we would see the Christo in question engrossed in trades union and Party affairs, calling people to meetings, organizing study groups, keeping an eye on those who did not attend demonstrations, until finally we saw him ensconced in the Party office with the right to meddle in our affairs.

Again in our factory, I met with another example of corruption through power. A young man, whose name was Angelov, came to us straight from his military service, as an electrician. He was of peasant stock, modest, hard-working, with the natural desire of every man to make a better life for himself and his family. His modest and pleasant behaviour with everybody won him the goodwill of the whole management. But the boss, who wanted to fill the Party organization with his own people, decided that Angelov would make a good member and pushed him into the Party. As the only Party member in his section, Angelov was immediately promoted to be head of section, which did not quite accord with his experience. And it was as if the first taste of power awoke unsuspected ambitions in the boy. He abandoned his normal work and threw himself into frenzied public activities. After two years he became a member of the Party bureau, after yet another year Party secretary, then member of the district committee, and so on. The pleasant inquiring physiognomy of the young man changed as if by magic. His features tightened, his expression became coarse and stern, he acquired the habits of the typical Party leader – when speaking, not to look people in the eyes, when listening, to hear only what suited him. His gentle manners were also completely transformed. He was imperious, emphatic, used crude expressions, swore at the workers and treated them with undisguised contempt. At the same time, he toadied to every more important person, always agreeing with them, all the while spinning an amazing web of contacts and friendships. He played the informer for our director, then informed on the people in our factory to the Ministry; he wove a mass of intrigues and plots and I marvelled at this sudden flourishing of a singular talent. He organized impressive initiatives which the newspapers reported, he uttered sonorous pledges at solemn public meetings, he did everything according to the best recipe for a promising career. And he succeeded. Even in my time, our factory proved too small for this indefatigable and unscrupulous climber, and his new friends found him a higher place.

Years later, when I was creating one of the main characters of my novel *Men*, this Angelov was one of my models. Subsequently most of the critics remarked that the portrait of Mladen (Angelov) was a gem. For my part, I thought that this character was one of the most striking stereotypes in Bulgarian life.

TO ENDURE SOMEHOW

Recently I happened to see a new Bulgarian novel on a working-class theme, written by a former friend. Quite apart from the novel's qualities or shortcomings, I must say that it represents yet another written proof of the prevailing ignorance about the situation of workers in Bulgaria. One more literary work joins the series of syrupy fantasies about the happiness of our working class. For more than twenty years our authors have been producing books in which the portrait of the worker is painted more or less as follows: an attractively rugged fellow, whose common talk is larded with wit, and whose rough manners contrast with his surprising professional dexterity. He combines in a mysterious way the consciousness of his own dignity with a proper public spirit. Usually, he experiences two conflicts: first, he wavers between personal interest and selfless service for Party and society; and, second, he wavers between two women. All is solved with the help of a highly principled Party comrade. The worker discovers his real, important, place in life, throws himself with renewed fervour into his work, accomplishes wonders, is decorated and lives happily ever after with his beloved job and the beloved woman. Nowhere else have I read or heard such frightful unsophisticated dialogues between workers as in the pages of Bulgarian works focusing on their life. But I have also felt anxious that this trite literature is beginning to influence and devalue the simple, sensible and sometimes very expressive vocabulary of our workers.

In my days as a worker, we were as far removed from this danger as we were from the spurious worker's prototype presented by our literature. Indeed, we hated the loads of verbal rubbish offered to us daily. For the life of each of us was determined by a very simple and sound principle – to endure somehow. No doubt this is the principle of a man who realizes that he is a victim of unalterable circumstances. It is the principle of minimal hope and of minimal resistance. Almost every Monday we were obliged to attend political meetings, which took on a variety of forms. But almost everybody had accepted that they were compulsory and went to them feeling rather like Muhammadans might if compelled to attend Christian prayers. . . .

Our workers lived with a healthy realistic attitude towards life. In these early years their honesty was so unblemished that they blushed deeply when they had to repeat parrot-like, in front of everyone, the words that others had written for them to declaim: 'In honour of comrade Stalin's birthday, I pledge to work with all my might and overfulfil my personal quota by 20 per cent.' They knew these were not their own words. They knew they were lies. Each of them was well aware that he would have achieved this 20 per cent in any case so as to secure the bonus which he had already included in his budget.

During the seven years I worked as an engineer, I did not meet a single worker who toiled for the sake of the Party or achieved a labour record for it. Nevertheless many production successes were ascribed to Party inspiration and dedicated to Party events.

It is not at all in the nature of the Bulgarian worker to boast about his work and achievements. Almost all the good workers I have met were modest. They did not like to show off about their accomplishments, although they had a noticeable self-confidence. Somehow it seemed absurd to have to offer solemn pledges and take part in labour competitions. I remember old Iliya reading a slogan put up by someone in his workshop: 'In honour of 9 September we promise to produce quality work!'

'The devil take them!' exploded Iliya. 'So the rest of the time they needn't produce good work! What are they paid for? They make them promise to do what should be their duty!'

But if the workers did not like politics and political questions, because they were placed in the position of primary schoolchildren made to repeat and learn alien phrases, they stood unreservedly in awe of the Party. Everyone felt that essentially the Party was his or her employer. Just as prisoners in every prison experience feelings of fear and subordination towards the prison governor, so our workers felt fear and subordination before the Party, whoever its representative appeared to be. The basic feeling of self-preservation made almost everyone try to be on good terms with the members of the Party bureau, with the Communist activists, with the director and with the Party organization of the neighbourhood in which he lived. Everyone was particularly careful to be on good terms with people known or suspected to be working for the secret police. Although on the one hand the workers tried to have nothing to do with them, on the other, they had to appeal to them for various services. This question of relations between the secret service employees and the ordinary people looms very large in Bulgaria.

My underlying feeling, looking back, is that the Party created nothing new, in the constructive sense of the word, where the workers' attitude to labour was concerned. In time a new relationship developed, but a negative one; it was generally felt that work was drudgery, that only fools worked, while those with a bit of sense twirled watch-chains on their fingers.

It took the Party quite some time to destroy the natural sense of responsibility towards their work which for years was innate in our workers. Anyone who knows something of the life of Bulgarian workers before the Second World War will agree that negligence, shoddy work and irresponsible attitudes were rarely encountered. In those days, workers used to feel it as a personal insult and disgrace if they slipped up in their work. There was a feeling known as professional pride, which is not much in evidence in the world of today's Bulgarian workers.

The Party managed very convincingly to impress on the workers that good work alone would not be enough to help them earn more; they also needed the protection and power position and connections can give. If you are a Party activist, you may not work very well but you will nevertheless be promoted and given a good post. If you are a creature of the management, its ear and eye, you need not try so hard at your machine. Whatever mistakes you may make, they will be covered up. If, however, you have powerful and influential relatives, you will very soon be able to abandon your manual work and be placed in a departmental job despite your lack of qualifications and ability. Instead of evaluating the labour of the workers by the results, unacceptable and sometimes absurd criteria were applied.

We promoted someone merely because he was protected by the district Party, we gave awards to people merely because they were in our good books. Woe to him who dared criticize the management! No matter how good a worker he may have been, or how much he may have applied himself, promotion would never come his way. I remember how once, when I put forward three workmen for awards, Kiro said at the meeting:

'The first - not possible, because he talks too much!'

'The second - not possible, because he never opens his mouth!'

'The third - not possible, because I can't make him out yet!'

To begin with, our workmen are paid very badly. The comparison with their counterparts in the West drives one to despair. That is why they are so aware of promotion, bonuses and awards, which are vitally important to augment the meagre wage. There were countless occasions when workers came to me and said awkwardly and with great bitterness: 'I know it doesn't depend on you, I know it's a put-up job, but I've come to tell you: it isn't right! I work like an ox, for years I've never slipped up, I know my work inside out, and yet you've appointed Stefan as brigade leader. He's utterly incompetent! It's a disgrace!'

The sense of injustice was strongly developed in our workers in those years when, on paper at least, attractive ideals were preached. The future, it was said then, belonged to the workers, to those who toiled. With the passage of time, this deceitful flirtation with the workers subsided, giving way to the cruel law of what was perhaps the most terrible injustice in our history – socialist feudalism. As we lost our illusions about dignity, equality and justice, the production process became a struggle for position which had nothing to do with genuine labour. Even in my time pride in good work started to sink into a mire of toadying, unprincipled behaviour, because this is what was rewarded and well paid. It is no exaggeration to say that the structure and relations of this society began increasingly to transform the workers into doomed serfs.

But I must stress that everything bad, corrupt, demoralizing, humiliating, everything repugnant and shameful, came exclusively from one direction – from above. The corruption of labour was a consequence of the moral corruption fostered by the highest leadership. Those at the very top were lackeys and demanded a lackey's submission from their subordinates, who in turn passed this attitude down the ladder. The press, radio, television, theatre, literature – all demanded and spread cringing servility. Once I was telephoned by one of the deputy ministers of Light Industry, who asked me to find him a room where some newly imported machines from abroad could be stored. I told him that I had no such room. He then ordered me to dismantle the working machines in one of the workshops and to empty it, which was sheer madness as this particular workshop brought in large profits. Moreover, basic machinery could not be dismantled without the permission of the bank which financed us. I explained this to him.

'I take the responsibility and I order you to dismantle them!' he shouted down the telephone.

'It's the same as setting fire to the factory,' I replied. 'If you were the managing director, would you burn it down?'

'And how!' he replied. 'As long as someone else took the responsibility, I'd burn it without batting an eyelid!'

This was the attitude propagated by a feckless and arrogant leadership whose one concern was to cling to power. What was encouraged was sycophancy, spinelessness, gossip, calumny, informing, string-pulling and especially envy. Often people were treated like dogs; a position was dangled in front of them and they were told: 'If you help us to topple X, the post is yours.' Gradually the ugly, cynical, diabolical face of our future began to take shape.

The moral roots of our workers were firm because they were still deeply embedded in peasant soil. They had not yet been poisoned by the bitter class struggles which workers in the developed industrial nations have known. The relationships and characters of our workers were considerably milder, more human; they had a strongly developed feeling for mutual help and compassion. But the Soviet chemicals of ruthless demoralization and moral corruption, which the Party and State leadership deliberately poured onto our native soil, acted with increasing effect.

OUR WORKING DAYS

In those days we got up before daylight and the tram-car was full of sleepy people going to work. Dozing children hung on the shoulders of tired mothers who would leave them in some nursery and fetch them at night. Salaries and wages were pitifully low and every family member who was of age had to go to work. For the first time, women began to work on building sites, in mines and in stone quarries. Women's equal rights meant the denial of their physical capabilities. Women stirred concrete, pushed wheelbarrows full of plaster, loaded stones and bricks, built walls, dug ditches and canals. Children who could not be found a place in a public nursery and happened to have no grandparents to look after them were left to themselves. The older ones and the primary school pupils spent their time on the streets and years later the adverse educational effect of the street was recognized. The normal working day was eight hours, but for the great majority of workers it was much longer. Because work in the factories was badly organized, while production plans became more ambitious every year, many managers broke the law by keeping the workers after hours. The workers did not complain, because the fulfilment of the plan meant some meagre bonus for them. Add to this the uncomfortable transport, the long journey to work, plus the various meetings, conferences and study groups after working hours, and the result was that home became merely a place to sleep in. Engineers and technicians throughout the country worked on the basis of the so-called 'non-standardized' working day, which more often than not meant twelve hours.

Then came the long and depressing queues. Food supplies were then at their very worst. This had less to do with bad harvests or genuine shortages than abysmal mismanagement. The state supply apparatus was enmeshed in its own bureaucratic web and we knew many hungry days. There were whole periods when one could eat only in a restaurant or in the factory canteen: public supplies were given absolute priority over the private needs of the citizens. The food shops were almost always empty except for a few jars of jelly or jam on the shelves. Imported goods were out of the question. The greatest paradox was the lack of popular Bulgarian produce on the market. Bulgaria was a country famous for its vegetables and fruit, but in the markets there was a constant shortage of them. One can judge the real performance of the system from this striking fact – there was always a crisis in the supply of the necessities of life. Over and over again we told ourselves that if in peacetime the regime was incapable of satisfying the people's elementary need for food, God alone knew what awaited us in wartime. I was convinced that in no more than a month, and without the use of any nuclear weapons, we should have died from starvation. The situation did not improve significantly in the following years, though there was a period when it appeared to. Only a few months ago an Italian complained to me that he had driven round Sofia all day long looking for meat. He didn't succeed. The reason for all this terrible muddle is rooted in the system itself, starting with the appointment of incompetent people to responsible positions and ending with the general feeling of inertia towards any systematic work.

Those years were the hardest. The only compensation was that people could count on free treatment in hospitals and sanatoriums. In the battle for survival, we became champions of queueing. We queued for everything: meat, bread, vegetables, fruit, shoes, clothes, firewood, coal, cement – everything. Imagine the deep misery of our lives when, after a full working day, we had to start queueing. Queueing became a national talent. Some people were specialists at it: they brought their folding chairs, knitting and sewing, and one political agitator actually organized his meeting in a queue. A funny story went round about a man who happened to stand on the pavement outside a door reading his newspaper. When he looked up after some time, a fifty-metre queue had silently formed behind him. Whenever a necessity became available anywhere, it disappeared with lightning speed. We often played a rather sad game: we thought of something we needed and were sure we had seen in the shops only two days ago and so we started looking for it. Of course, we never found it. The words 'not available' and 'sold out' made up 90 per cent of the vocabulary of shop assistants. Countless times, dog-tired after work, we had to join several queues to make sure of our dinner. But for the regime and the comrades in power ordinary people's time did not count. The people themselves did not count. The Party and the State were cold and merciless in their attitude to the individual.

While ordinary mortals in the country suffered from this shameful mismanagement, the comrades at the top lived a very different life. Many of them did not know and did not want to know the reality. They existed separated by wealth and luxury like Bulgarian reincarnations of Marie-Antoinette whose phrase 'Let them eat cake' was not so far from their attitude. In Sofia it was said that the wife of an important Party official once boarded a tram-car (probably for the first time), gave a five-leva note to the conductor and went in. 'But, comrade, the ticket costs only twenty stotinki,' the astonished conductor shouted after her. 'So cheap!' exclaimed the wife of the leading comrade. Indeed, many of those at the top and their families had never taken a tram-car. They used large black limousines with little curtains, at first Soviet Chaikas and later German Mercedes.

We witnessed too the most vulgar demonstration of inequality in the whole of our history – the 'special supply system'. I shall not be surprised if one day historians categorize the members of our Politburo, a large number of our Central Committee, and their hangers-on as a strange 'man-like' species. For how otherwise can one explain the fact that while eight millions suffered, starved and went through daily trials and tribulations, the élite had built itself a real paradise. The vans of the special supply service delivered the choicest food, the best produce of our country, to the homes of the important comrades. In our meatless days they ate roast lamb and roast pork, Bulgarian sausage, special salami and cheese made of pure butter, not to mention how they enjoyed wines, clothes and luxury goods beyond the dreams of ordinary people. Moreover, as if further to emphasize the notion of 'Communist fairness', they obtained all this for a symbolic price – that is, they paid nothing. Nor were Politburo members required to settle private bills in restaurants and other public places. Sometimes they threw a few scraps to their drivers or servants which gave us an idea of the life they lived: I knew the chauffeur of a Politburo member who once or twice brought me something that he had obtained from a special supply van. I still do not understand how Vulko Chervenkov and his heirs could indulge in gluttony while the whole country went hungry. Perhaps this explains why they built high walls to enclose their houses, which they surrounded with heavily armed guards to protect themselves from 'the love of the people' whose 'beloved leaders' they claimed to be. Subsequently there was a big wave of protests against these special supplies, which were temporarily abolished after April 1956 [the beginning of Bulgaria's 'de-Stalinization']. However, soon afterwards the system was restored and many new items were added to the special deliveries that sped along secret routes towards the homes of the comrade bosses.

The Bulgarian population did not suffer seriously from supply difficulties during the War solely because of the Bulgarian villages, which stood behind us and fed us. Vulko Chervenkov's regime reduced these villages to penury. Those years [1950–6] will be remembered as the most wretched in the existence of our peasants. The enforced collectivization, which caused the disappearance of male labour from the fields, plus the abolition of personal smallholdings, inevitably brought famine to the country. The cruel law of enforced deliveries, which obliged the peasants to sell to the state meat, wool, milk and so on, on the basis of land and produce that existed only on paper, did not help. That was the period when countless peasants ended up in prisons and concentration camps. Thus we townspeople no longer had the reserves of the countryside behind us. Moreover, many peasants used to come to Sofia to buy bread. All sorts of decrees to control the sale of the necessities of life were proclaimed, but few observed them.

It was then that one of the most notorious features of those years – theft – spread throughout the country. Necessity forced people to resort to tricks, sometimes very ingeniously devised, so that they could earn a little extra. It is no exaggeration to say that everybody who had access to the honey licked his fingers. People stole everything and from everyone, but most of all from the State. The main 'heroes' were, of course, managers of restaurants, shops, various trade enterprises, forestry estates and stewards, store-keepers, buyers and accountants. Water played an important part in all this activity – not only were wines and spirits diluted, but we bought moist sugar, watery foodstuffs and thinned-down milk. Each person's moral justification was that he took back what the State had stolen from him. After its complete triumph on the political front, the militia now threw itself into the economic battle. A special economic militia was set up, which arrested and tortured people with terrible brutality. Economic crimes earned the heaviest sentences, including death. As some of the fraudulent schemes to appropriate public funds were impossible to unravel, the militia proceeded to keep watch over people's spending habits to discover who had more money than usual. After that the victim would be caught, interrogated and tortured until he or she admitted something. Gradually the economic militia became a dreaded monster, for many people were victimized for unintentional mistakes. Of course, the economic militia never investigated the huge misappropriations and economic abuses of people at the top.

The cinema and football were our main mass entertainments. However, both were regarded by the regime as ideological areas. This was the period when only Soviet films were shown on our screens. To think what unbelievable rubbish we watched! For many years not one Western film was allowed and I remember that the first sign of a thaw in this respect was the arrival of two Austrian films. They were a great event. Huge queues waited outside the cinemas to see harmless Austrian ballet on ice. The wisecrack from this period was, 'Is the film good or is it a Soviet one?'

On the other hand, football offered a well disguised pretext for expressing one's hatred of the regime. Free to indulge all their whims, the comrades had formed a football team known as the Central Sports Club of the Army, which was to be a symbol of Party invincibility. Naturally this made the vast majority of the football crowds into fans of Levski,* which became a symbol of the old Bulgaria. The matches between the two teams were veritable wars. Sport was controlled by the militia and they took measures to ensure the defeat of Levski. The football pitch was often the scene of fights which were essentially political. I can still visualize a courageous lad from one of the more squalid Sofia suburbs, who succeeded in felling half a dozen militiamen who had tried to eject him from the stadium during a match. At another match between the two teams a Major from the Ministry of the Interior, in charge of security at the stadium, assembled his men and made a speech, the gist of which was: 'Today "our" players are confronting the bourgeois-capitalist rabble of Levski. We shall bring in a whole detachment and if any of their fans gives the slightest trouble, arrest him immediately.' Years later Levski's popularity was destroyed in the most painless manner by making it into the team of the secret service. There was nowhere better to appreciate the Bulgarians' real feelings for Soviet Russia than at football matches. When Soviet teams played against ours, our public, which is known for its fairness, yelled like mad against the Soviet players.

Everything Soviet was a synonym for that which was disagreeable, hostile, or of poor quality. But all the same we lived – and sometimes we even laughed.

---

* This club is named after a nineteenth-century Bulgarian hero of the anti-Turkish liberation struggle.

MONDAY EVENINGS

Monday evening – the time for Party and political education. In the life of nearly all Bulgarians there runs a long grey thread of Monday evenings. Long, because they are really the longest hours of the week. Grey, because one can hardly remember the difference between one Monday night and another.

The scenes which follow each other in my mind are disturbingly similar, as if each Monday night life somehow stopped dead for an hour or two, as if the instinct for self-preservation put consciousness to sleep in order to preserve it from the weekly verbal downpour.

I see myself sitting in the factory canteen surrounded by workers of both sexes who have just taken off their overalls and sunk their weary bodies onto creaking chairs. Facing us is Todor, a former door-keeper at the Party district committee headquarters, who has been sent to us to reinforce the Party contingent. He is tall, with a moustache and dark eyes always ablaze with awareness of his own importance. Todor genuinely believes that if he were not on this earth life would come to an end. And this conviction can be felt in everything he does. He has received only primary school education, but his self-confidence is that of a man with two doctorates. But self-confidence is of no help to him when he talks, because he has a stammer and often stops in his tracks to find the right word, which usually evades him so that his thought remains hanging on an an inarticulate 'mm!'.

Today he is conducting a compulsory political information class on the theme of 'West German revanchism* and the Berlin question'. This is the leader in *Rabotnichesko Delo* and usually 'political instruction' consists of discussing the leading article. We all take part in this educational activity – unless we are engaged in similar activities

---

*Revanchism: a term used by Soviet and other East European Communist propagandists to describe alleged West German intentions to change (forcibly) the European status quo established after the Second World War.

elsewhere. For several such study groups take place simultaneously in the factory – on the history of the Soviet Communist Party, on the history of the Bulgarian Party and on the history of Georgi Dimitrov.† Recently we have all been studying, several times over, the biography of Comrade Stalin. Now, however, it appears that his biography wasn't worth bothering about and we, who knew the life of Joseph Djugashvili by heart, have been at a loss to know what to do with our erudition.

When the district instructor tells us that Comrade Stalin's biography will no longer be studied, Toshko from the metal division asks him: 'Are you sure, comrade . . .?' This confuses the comrade. 'Well, for the time being . . . this is the decision,' he answered. 'Because . . .,' Toshko continues, 'I liked Comrade Stalin's biography very much. . . . His life was so instructive . . . and worthy of imitation. . . .'

The man from the district committee does not know how to react. Nevertheless, he finds the courage to say: 'We decided that it is better to study our own heroes and leaders!'

'Then, why don't we study the biography of Christo Botev?'† asks another whose motives are also not altogether innocent. 'There will be time for Botev too, comrades. We'll get to Botev!' the instructor says.

And so, while the more diligent among us listen and discuss our Party history and the biography of the beloved leader of the Bulgarian people, we are engulfed by the stuttering voice of Todor, who explains to us how and why 'the filthy hands of German revanchism reach out towards Berlin!'

'Who captured Berlin? Them or us?' asks Todor and beats his chest as if single-handed he had planted the victorious banner on the Brandenburg Gate.

No one answers him. Next to me Nadka knits woollen socks for her child. I see how she shapes the heel, completely engrossed in her work. Earlier she had told me that she was hoping to finish the sock because, with his stammer, Todor was likely to go on for two hours. On Nadka's other side, good old Stoyan is slouching on his chair, sleeping with his mouth open. He has been unloading goods the whole day and can hardly stand any longer. Then I see Stanka who has her eyes fixed in front of her and is probably millions of miles away from Berlin. Her husband has abandoned her and since then she has become very silent and self-absorbed. Exactly in front of the lecturer sits Dikran, a sixty-year-old Armenian carpenter with a marvellous sense of humour. Now his funny face is screwed up in almost morbid seriousness and his open-eyed gaze is fixed on Todor. He had told Minko, 'Today, I'll fix Todor. It will be fun to see what happens!'

It is difficult not to laugh at Dikran's pose. I know that he is longing to applaud, but cannot yet find a suitable moment. Todor says, 'The revanchists are baring their predatory fangs....'

Does one applaud for 'predatory fangs'? On my left, I notice that our pretty secretary Reni is trying to flirt with the new planner. She looks at him provocatively, while he blushes and pretends to listen. I bet that if someone were to ask Reni what the lecturer is talking about, she could not even hazard a guess. She is a past master at skipping Monday nights, but this time she did not manage it. Altogether, the rallying of the workers during the day was very peremptory and threatening. The district Party committee had found out that attendance at the political education session was unsatisfactory, and so today the responsible comrade made everyone sign himself in. Todor was firm, even brutal.

'There will be a check-up by the district committee!' he said. And when Parashkeva, who had two small children waiting at home, cried that one of them was not well, Todor replied: 'If you were able to come to work, you'll stay on! Those who want to work will also attend political education!'

This was their strongest argument. Everyone knew that if he stayed away, it would be written down, and that even if they did not sack him – for you could not really sack people for such things – his non-attendance at the political education classes would remain a permanent blot on his whole career in the factory. So many times they refused to give bonuses and titles for over-time to good workers only because of such absences; so many times, when it came to promotions in the factory, these absences were taken into account. There were many ways of punishing the disobedient. And everyone knew it.

'German revanchism,' Todor continues, 'wants to turn the wheel of history back to the terror of the Gestapo, the enslavement of the working class, the destruction of freedom and democracy.'

This kind of political education for the masses started while I was still at the Polytechnic. Soon after the nationalizations of 1947, we were informed through the channels of our student organization that we *must* take part in this type of study group which seemed unbelievably alien to us then. Later, when the purges of students started, the attendance at these study groups – devoted to the biographies of Stalin and Dimitrov, or the 'Short Course of the History of the Soviet Communist Party' – became a decisive factor in every student's political record. Very quickly, we were pushed like mindless chicks into these Monday evening gatherings, where various lecturers explained to us with emotion and enthusiasm what a fabulously good, manly, handsome, intelligent and generous man Comrade Stalin had been, and how, even when he was a small boy, his amazing genius had made him stand out far above young and old.

We were engineering students, young people used to the exact sciences, and such romantic outpourings conflicted with the world we knew. But we had to accept them because, on top of everything else, we were examined on the subject. I think that the mania for quotations dates from this period. The members of these study groups were learning by rote various passages from officially approved works which they recited right and left wherever they could be of use to them. I find it hard to remember any public statement at the Polytechnic, whether it be a speech, a report or any other pronouncement, which was not accompanied by 'As comrade A teaches us . . .' or 'as comrade B says. . . .'

Later on, in every place I worked, the first comrades to get hold of me were those responsible for political education.

'Which study group would you like to join?'

I would look down the menu of courses and then approximately the following conversation would ensue: 'I have already done G. Dimitrov's biography eleven times!'

'Oho!'

'The history of the Soviet Communist Party – seven times!'

'But which history? The new or the old?'

'Both.'

'Very well, but which one have you studied more?'

'The old one.'

'All right, that means that now you must concentrate on the new one . . . every Monday, straight after work. . . !'

'But I have a French lesson on Mondays.'

'Impossible!' he says. 'On Monday night you can't learn French or German, or indeed Bulgarian! Change your lesson to another day! You know very well what Monday evenings are for!'

In the first years under Communist rule, enforced enrolment in various forms of political education was pursued fanatically. There were *Agitpropchiks* and assorted instructors, like our Party secretary Kiro, who considered participation in such activities a supreme duty, while looking on the shirkers as enemy agents and traitors. Later this bigotry became even stronger as the Party ranks were swamped by an influx of opportunists, who naturally tried to be 'more Catholic than the Pope', making it impossible to avoid these obligations. Everyone I knew spent their Monday evenings in this way, which in the case of our Todor meant listening to homilies strongly reminiscent of a sergeant-major's pep talk to new recruits. For people such as Kiro and Todor, this activity was very important, because for an hour or two it enabled them to be at the centre of attention and to hold forth. In ordinary life no one was likely to sit down and discuss any public issue seriously with them, but in the political education classes they were in their element. Kiro, however, was far more interesting. He spoke with absolute conviction and clearly accepted the leading article in the Party newspaper as true Christians accept the Ten Commandments. For him not one single word could be suspect and everything was exactly as it was written. His fanatical tone of voice and the incredible mixture of Party vocabulary and his particular dialect transformed even the most serious theme into pure farce. Very often Kiro digressed from the leading article and tried to explain world events in his own words:

'These days imperialism does all it can to divert our attention. American scientists have apparently spotted saucers flying in the sky! And what if they were saucers, comrades! The working people of America keep craning their necks and looking up and up ... and so they don't see what is cooking down here, on earth. There you have what is called diversion!'

Neither Kiro nor Todor were in the least put out by the fact that amongst their listeners there were people with two university degrees.

Some time later the fanaticism all but disappeared from political education and Monday nights became a matter of mere formality. The chore of organizing and conducting the courses tended to be left to one of the better liked and more respected colleagues, who, in his efforts to enrol us, usually appealed to our feelings of friendship.

'Little brother, both you and I know that all this is nothing but rubbish, but it has been decreed. If we don't do it ourselves, they will send us an organizer from outside, and then there won't be any shirking at all.'

In one of the factories, the workers had agreed to take part in the study groups on condition that they could bring their own drinks and consume them during the lecture. In one department of Foreign Trade, a new element was introduced as a complement to politics: pop music.

But apart from businesses and offices, Party education was brought to the masses in local city and peasant organizations under the aegis of the Fatherland Front. Every year around September, the newspapers solemnly announced the start of the Fatherland Front school year. This primarily concerned pensioners and grandparents. The Mondays organized by the Fatherland Front offered a more varied programme, for instance, 'collective readings of books' followed by discussion, or collective visits to the cinema, theatre or opera, also with discussions. Naturally, the book had to be of unimpeachable political orthodoxy. I have attended many collective readings. . . . But my experience cannot be compared with that of my family. My grandmother, God rest her soul, attended no less than three study groups on Marxism-Leninism, while my grandfather, aged eighty, had to follow a course on atheism. My mother and other women from our neighbourhood used to meet and read aloud appropriate novels; while our neighbour, old Kolyo, who was the private owner of a bull and did not want his clients, the dairy farmers, to take advantage of its possibilities, used to say, 'The bull's not here!'

'But where on earth has it gone, Kolyo?'

'He must be at a study group. Today is Monday!'

At last our lecturer Todor finishes. He declares that as long as we remain on earth, the German revanchists will not get hold of Berlin. Then, covered in perspiration but conscious of having done his duty in an exemplary way, he wipes his moustaches and sinks down on a chair. The chairman now invites questions. He is met by complete silence. From then on everything follows a familiar script. He will ask three times and nobody will get up. Everyone knows that if he wants to be hated by all the other men and have the women refuse to talk to him for weeks on end, he can get up and express an opinion, thus giving Todor the opportunity to detain us for another half-hour. Meanwhile, the study group members already 'have their foot on the accelerator', waiting only for the chairman to say: 'Well, since there are no questions, let us thank comrade Todor and go home!'

Now Dikran starts applauding noisily and we rush to the doors. An hour or two have been taken away from our lives. Every Monday evening. If you calculate that four million or even two million people are forced to waste this time, economists would be horrified. Because in fact no one has learnt anything in these study groups. The point is merely 'to do your bit for the sake of peace'.

'Look here,' says one of my colleagues as we hurry towards the bus stop, 'if they take it into their heads to make us learn the telephone directory by heart, do you suppose that we won't do it? Of course, we'll learn it, and with a vengeance! Whatever tune they choose to play, we'll dance to it! They make the music – we simply supply the feet!'

STALIN IS DEAD

The news that Stalin was ill caused real excitement throughout our factory world. The main reason for this was surprise. It had been drilled into us for years on end from all sides that Stalin was the wisest, the most courageous, the greatest man on earth, the meaning of our paltry existence, the movement of our planet and even of the universe, and eventually we, like the propaganda, had accepted unquestioningly that he could not fall ill, let alone die. On the eve of the news of his death one of the old workmen from the carpentry shop told me knowingly: 'Stalin cannot die, do you understand! Even if he dies, they will resuscitate him, and though he is seventy-three now, he can start again, perhaps at thirty, what do you say!'

It was the view of the secret service and of our Kiro that the enemy could take advantage of the situation to strike, so the watch was reinforced once more, sentries were posted at all ends of the factory and sudden nightly checks made sure that the patrols were not asleep. Meanwhile the weather had turned very cold and the ground was frozen. We had planned some office dance, but everything was put off and Anka from the Party bureau said in everyone's hearing: 'Who dares laugh now?'

Which was true, because no one dared venture even a smile, although at least a dozen people in the factory had suffered at the hands of the dying comrade's regime and secretly exulted.

While, for most people, Stalin was part of an unavoidable reality which had been forced on them - like evacuation during the wartime bombardments - for the regime's creatures and their opponents, he was the symbol of an immutable order under which they had prospered. The greatest agitation, bordering on complete confusion, was amongst the Party activists. All of them felt that Stalin's death would bring changes, and nothing frightened them more than possible change. Some Party comrades even expected the Americans to seize this chance to attack. Although discipline in the Party apparatus under the command of the secret service was strict, things began to creak from the moment the news of Stalin's illness spread. Going about my business in committees and ministries, I felt that the whole atmosphere had become somehow milder and hushed in the expectation of a decisive event. The most implacable officials with sinister reputations had suddenly withdrawn into their shells. One of my colleagues, who was serving a three-year sentence as a political prisoner in Pazardzhik, told me that among the warders there was such consternation that the worst bullies had begun to ingratiate themselves with their charges. The fact that Stalin could die after all created a new concept – things could come to an end. It may seem naïve and ridiculous in retrospect, but I believe that in those years many had this feeling about Stalin's preordained immortality.

The night that the news of Stalin's death reached us I was on night duty. Towards dawn, an unforgettable tragi-comic scene took place before my eyes. Engineer Z, a former officer of the King's Army who had graduated in Germany and, I believe, been a Krupp scholar, was part of the fortified guard. He was a kind and pleasant man, but there seemed to be a blot on his political biography because the secret service often showed an interest in him. How and where he had managed to get drunk, I did not discover, but towards five o'clock in the morning I came upon my colleague lying on a camp bed and wailing tragically: 'He has gone, he is no longer, our father, our teacher.... The beloved, precious human being.... Comrade Stalin is no more...' and so on in the same spirit.

Meanwhile our Party chief Kiro, deeply moved, bent over him and in all innocence tried to soothe him: 'Calm yourself, comrade.... We all feel like you, my own heart is broken, but.... Come on, calm yourself....'

But our hero continued to wail extravagantly.

'No. No!' he shouted. 'Who will replace him now?'

'Never mind, they'll find someone ...' Kiro kept saying soothingly.

'No, no, no-o-o!' engineer Z was sobbing heart-rendingly. 'He is irreplaceable! Who dares to suggest that he can be replaced! The greatest, the wisest, the nearest, the dearest, the father, the teacher, the leader....'

A crowd of workers began to gather around us. Their good sense told them that the whole scene acted out by our engineer was a blatant mockery at the expense of the dead dictator, that poor Z's nerves had not been able to stand the triumph of this moment.... Somebody more quick-witted whispered in my ear that we should remove him from the factory before he was seen by the director, who would easily guess what stood behind the drunken tears of this unexpected mourner. We led him out, while Kiro said to me thoughtfully: 'Can you imagine such a thing! The death of Comrade Stalin shook even engineer Z!'

Within a few hours the whole of Sofia was covered in black flags. The radio played continuous funeral music. Funeral meetings were held. Armed Party activists formed guards of honour in front of the busts, statues and portraits of Stalin. There was a special guard along Vitosha Street, which was then called 'Stalin', and the newspapers described the grief of the Black Sea port of Varna, which was then also called 'Stalin'.

On the day of the funeral, it was decreed that the last honours should be paid to the dead dictator at noon. Everyone was ordered to come out of the buildings and stand motionless for three or four minutes, all traffic was to stop while the sirens of factories and locomotives, the whistles of tram-cars and the horns of cars should sound incessantly.

When we stepped out into the yard of our factory, it was a sunny but very cold day. The mood, according to how you looked at it, was either solemnly funereal or fatuously pompous. Exactly at twelve o'clock Manya sprang to attention like a soldier and the sirens of all the other factories in the area began wailing. But our own siren, which had not been used since the War, gave forth only a squeak followed by humiliating silence. Manya's face went red with anger, but she said nothing and continued to stand to attention. At that moment I saw one of our stokers, the gnarled sixty-year-old Dimiter, climbing up the iron clamps on the outside chimney wall towards the siren at the very top. It was sheer madness for a man to try to climb the chimney in this way. To our general amazement he reached the top and our siren sounded forth just as all the other sirens fell silent. I stood and thought about the limits of fanaticism. How far could it go? Perhaps there was another, more logical explanation, but it seemed to me that the same impulse which had pushed old Dimiter up the vertical chimney could have caused him to perpetrate terrible and irrational crimes. Such reckless heroics, which are a demonstration of irrational strength, have always made me shudder.

Going home through the city I saw in the window of a bookshop Bogdan Botev and Stoyan Ninov's book entitled *Always with Stalin*. Journals and newspapers were full of freshly written works by our poets and writers which declared with typical pathos a supposedly universal grief for the dead inhabitant of Lenin's mausoleum in Moscow. I remember nothing of this funeral outpouring. I did not know then that most of this literary production was inspired by nothing more than opportunism. Years later I would read Stefan Tsanev's beautiful poem about the Soviet Union whose type was destroyed by the editorial office on the order of the State Security. The poem described vividly that day in March when two men were buried in Moscow – Stalin and Prokofiev: while three million followed Stalin's coffin, only three walked behind Prokofiev's. So often since then I have reflected on this remarkable disproportion – three million against three! Three million followed the remains of the man responsible for some of the most hideous and disgusting acts ever committed on our planet. Three people walked in the funeral procession of the man who has left some of the most beautiful music of our century.

But that day I walked through the streets of Sofia reflecting on exactly what Stalin had been for us. I remembered my relatives' stories about mass executions near the town of Pernik and half-alive bodies buried in the abandoned ventilation shafts of the Pernik mines; about State Security jeeps which traversed the country at night like latter-day vampires, striking widespread terror. I remembered my friends beaten to death in the left wing of the Central Prison, the endless trials in the four court-rooms on the top floor of the Palace of Justice where death sentences were meted out, my school friends and university colleagues who froze in icy detention cells at Belene. I remembered the whole of this murderous, filthy and vile campaign against an entire nation. It was Stalin who had turned our country into a well-organized Soviet prison. It was Stalin who banished forever the optimism and freedom of action of my generation, who poisoned our future and made us the slaves of the most basic and brutal feudalism.

I am not among those who can hate and seldom have I felt deep hatred. But towards Stalin and the little Stalins I feel complete and infinite abhorrence. Perhaps nothing else on earth has seemed to me more humiliating to mankind than the record of this criminal megalomaniac. Nothing else could be more degrading than the compulsory prostration before him. His glorification was a disgusting provocation for every more or less normal person; it was the same as spitting on oneself. However, many years later I was to wonder whether Stalin was not merely a pretext for the actions of thousands upon thousands of real criminals and murderers who crushed whole nations in his

name? Was not Stalin merely the name of the sickness which – unlike
the plague and cholera – became a lasting epidemic and deprived
many millions of their lives?

There was, indeed, something sick in the Stalinists I knew, people
like Kiro, Dimiter, various officers of the militia and secret service,
Party activists. I have listened on so many occasions to the verbiage of
former Stalinists who, in their cups, would tell me with a sigh: 'You
can say whatever you like, but the man had an iron fist! If only there
were others like him today!'

And in Prague, during Dubcek's era, a Bulgarian colonel in the
secret service told me: 'Ah, how greatly we need comrade Stalin now!'

The theme of Stalin is perhaps the biggest theme of our time. It is
by no means limited to the life and works of this terribly primitive
villain, but encompasses entire human societies and penetrates deeply
into our own selves. Perhaps it is the contemporary version of the
eternal theme of evil, of the devil.

Only a few days after the dictator's death, the agitation subsided,
at least on the surface. It was clear that nothing had changed. Stalin
had gone, but Stalinism remained intact. If there was a change, it was
still very far away and very slow. Stalin continued to watch us from
every wall with narrowed eyes, to haunt us with his presence, to force
his cold breath on us. At a meeting, a comrade from my factory said
with cautious optimism: 'Comrade Stalin has gone, but now we have
comrade Lavrenti Pavlovich Beria!'

This was an ominous reminder, for soon the name of Beria began to
be mentioned along with the names of Malenkov and Molotov.

Later I was told of interesting scenes that had taken place in
Politburo and Central Committee circles, where the various comrade
leaders were at their wits' end to know which master to worship. With
the development of the struggle in the Soviet Politburo, the Bulgarian
leaders who were Moscow's appointees found themselves in awkward
and rather ridiculous situations, but their instinct for self-preservation
and their inborn servility shielded them from all imprudence.

In fact, all that concerned each big or little local dictator was that
the status quo should be preserved, that there should be no changes.
Or, if there were any, that they should be effected in a way which
would leave things essentially unchanged. For several years after
March 1953 we were still to hear that 'our Party is a Stalinist party'.

Remember that to this day not one book has been published in
Bulgaria which seriously indicts Stalin.

II

During his career as a chemical engineer, Markov wrote newspaper articles and short stories in his spare time. Even after achieving fame as a writer, he preserved a vivid sense of what life was like for ordinary Bulgarians.

THE SECRET POLICEMAN
AND THE NIGHT

My wife and I* moved to an old nationalized villa above Dragalevtsi, not far from the ski-lift station. The villa was surrounded by tall poplars and looked unusually secluded. From its terraces and balconies Sofia and the surrounding plain were clearly visible. We occupied the top floor, while the bottom floor housed an unknown family of four. A man of about thirty-five, of average build, with broad shoulders and strong muscular arms, came out to help us carry our luggage in. His face was concealed by a thick black beard. At that time, during the summer of 1964, beards were not yet the fashion in Bulgaria. But what made me slightly uneasy were his eyes – black, wide open, with an unnatural brilliance that seemed to give every one of his expressions an air of excess. I thought to myself that he was either an alcoholic, or someone mentally ill, living in permanent agitation. In contrast with his face, his voice sounded soft and concerned. This was my new neighbour, the father of two children, a girl of about ten and a boy of six. His wife was a teacher in the nearby secondary school, and the children looked nice and well behaved.

On that first day, I had no idea of my neighbour's past. I only felt that he was burdened by a powerful experience which continued to haunt him. 'Don't you think he's a little strange?' asked my wife, slightly worried. But a little later she made the acquaintance of the children and their mother, and their friendly attitude dispelled her doubts. That evening, tired out from the move, we went to bed early. But towards midnight my wife woke me. 'Listen!' she said.

Above the gentle rustling of the poplars we could hear heavy regular steps and from time to time a thick voice pronouncing unintelligible

---

*Georgi Markov was married three times; he refers here to his second wife. Dragalevtsi is a village above Sofia on the slopes of Mount Vitosha where many privileged Party officials have villas.

words. There was an almost full moon and outside it was quite light. I got up and went to the window. Downstairs, on the large bleached terrace, I saw a scene which immediately woke me completely. In the middle of the terrace stood an empty wooden chair; my new neighbour paced up and down before it, turning his head towards the chair as if someone were sitting there. His arms were crossed behind his back and his body was bent forward slightly, as if to stress his interest in the imaginary occupant of the empty chair. It struck me that the scene in front of me resembled an interrogation in an office of the secret police. In precisely such a way did a suspect sit or stand in the middle of the room, while the examining officer paced around him, waiting for him to talk. This was the classic scene which so many people in Bulgaria had experienced, and which mostly took place at midnight. The pacing of my neighbour round the empty chair was a ghostly echo of the sinister nights of the Stalin era, and of the barbaric triumph of the 'thrashers' over the bound victim.

'Silence isn't always golden!' he said to the chair in a voice which confirmed all my suspicions.

My wife and I watched this performance in stunned amazement, not realizing that there would be many more such nights when, under the influence of drink, the former First Lieutenant in the secret police would recreate with crazy persistence the scene in the interrogator's office. It was a scene in which he was transformed from a deranged alcoholic into a powerful judge, king and God, on whose unlimited power the fate of the person on the chair depended. We did not realize either that the scene on the terrace that we were watching was only the beginning of the midnight interrogator's awakening from the stupefying effects of his bottle of plum brandy.

Later we discovered that a moment came when he realized that the chair was empty and then he needed somebody of real flesh and blood to sit there. He used to rush into the bedroom, wake his wife and children (if they had not already run away) and, with a flood of the most vulgar abuse and swearing, try to provoke them into a show of resistance. His voice rose in hysterical shrieks, or dropped to low threatening tones, or burst into blood-curdling laughter. Usually it was his daughter who was the boldest. She would stand up in front of him and shout angrily, 'You are the worst, the blackest, the most horrible man in the world! And you know it and take it out on us! If your conscience gives you no rest, why don't you commit suicide instead of beating us?'

He would smile like a satisfied villain, advance towards her and start slapping her face slowly but hard as if he intended to go on beating her for hours. The mother would throw herself at him trying to save the child. So many nights the villa was rent by shrieks, the neighbours came running, while we rushed downstairs to try and hold him back! But he was so strong that sometimes, when we had called the militia, three militiamen could not overpower him.

That first terrible and unreal night, his victim was the six-year-old boy. We heard an uproar in the room below us, then the slamming of doors and quick steps. Afterwards we gathered that the mother and daughter had run away. But the little boy had been left behind. My neighbour carried the child outside, laid him on the chair face downwards and started to beat him with his belt. The child did not make a sound. It was a strange child. We rushed down the stairs and when we reached the terrace we found a totally unexpected and very different scene. My neighbour had thrown his belt away and was kneeling before the child on the chair, kissing his back and repeating with a shattered, sick and sobbing voice, 'Forgive me, my boy. Do you hear, forgive me! It doesn't hurt, does it? You will forgive me, won't you? Let my hands rot if I ever do it again. . . . Forgive me!'

His whole body was shaking and nothing seemed to remain of the imposing, frightening figure of the midnight interrogator pacing round the chair. The little boy raised himself up and we heard him say reproachfully, 'Didn't I tell you not to drink, Daddy!'

'Not another drop! Never! Never again!' exclaimed the father with the most heart-breaking sincerity.

He lifted the child up just as he had carried him out and went inside.

My wife and I were at a loss as to how to interpret what we had seen. It seemed to us a strange nightmare, very different from usual sorts of drunkenness, because at the centre of everything stood the empty chair.

At dawn, mother and daughter returned. Perfect silence reigned once more, as if nothing had happened.

The next day I observed my neighbour as he worked in the garden. His little boy was with him. Both were joking as if they were in the happiest of moods. He was explaining the life of ants to his son and I well remember what he said: 'When you walk, be careful not to squash an ant. Be careful where you tread. An ant, too, has a soul like you and me!'

Later the same day and on the following days, I discovered with surprise that my new neighbour was one of the most obliging people

I had ever met. He kept coming round, helped me move the furniture and informed me in the minutest detail about the peculiarities of my new home and surroundings. He was a little slow in his reasoning, his intelligence was clearly blunted and the whole process of thought and expression seemed to involve obstacles. I had the impression of a very confused split mind, with occasional powerful flashes of fanaticism.

Amongst other things, he told me that he did not want to start work in a government office, because it would conflict with his wish to live 'differently'. He tried to earn a little as a craftsman of wrought iron: he had a small workshop by the river where he made candlesticks, monastery lamps, chandeliers and other wrought-iron artefacts. I asked him why he had chosen this kind of work. He laughed and said in a rather odd voice, 'I don't know. ... I seem to need to strike, and when I strike the iron – it soothes me. ...'

Then he added in a most friendly way: 'If I ask you to lend me money, don't do it! I shall get drunk, and when I get drunk, things get out of hand!'

His wife told me once that when he was sober, there was no better man or husband, but when he got drunk, all hell broke loose.

Another time, when I was passing by the workshop one evening, I heard my neighbour's voice repeating words which took me back to my Scripture lessons at school. As in an unlikely and badly written story, he was reading the Bible. He had placed it on his work table and he was articulating the words slowly and solemnly, as if he savoured the sound of his own voice. I was told that quite suddenly he had become an ardent Adventist and strictly observed the sabbath on Saturdays. This strange dash into religion astonished me. Subsequently I often saw him praying for hours on end, gazing with unnaturally shining eyes into the distance. Indeed, everything in him – whether he prayed, laughed, talked or struck the iron – was odd, exaggerated, as if his character did not know any moderation.

A few days later, we had our second ghastly night. He came back drunk from the local pub, placed the chair on the terrace and managed to catch his wife before she could escape. Both children started crying for their mother and we had to run to restrain the enraged former First Lieutenant from the secret police, who was yelling at the top of his voice: 'I know you all hate me! But I hate you too! I see from your faces that you think I'm despicable! I know I'm no good! But you're a million times more contemptible than me, only you won't admit it! Leave my house!' – and he threw himself forward ready for a fight.

During yet another night, when half a dozen militiamen summoned

by phone had managed to subdue him and were carrying him to the
jeep, he shouted: 'All you militiamen are nonentities! You are servants,
slaves, vile brutes! Your brains aren't worth two leva! I'm a saint
compared with you! I'm First Lieutenant B! I'm the only first
lieutenant-saint, because ...', his voice rose even higher, '... I pay for
the sins of others!'

With time, the terrible nights became more frequent. He began
drinking every other day and was violent on the slightest pretext. In
the second year after our arrival his wife decided she could bear it no
longer. One day she took the children and some luggage and moved
to somewhere near the centre of town, at the same time instituting
proceedings for divorce. My neighbour reacted to this blow by drinking even more than before. When there was no one he could put on
the empty chair, he would rush to the village and go on a rampage.
On several occasions the local peasants gave him a drubbing, but he
was fiendishly strong. Despite all his excesses, the attitude of the
authorities towards him was unbelievably tolerant. At least a dozen
complaints addressed to the Ministry of the Interior achieved nothing.
The public procurator often summoned him to his office, but I think
that someone somewhere secretly protected him.

During all this time I tried to understand exactly what had happened to this man and what had created this insane division in his
mind between the interrogator's chair and the Bible. One evening,
when I was returning home in the car, I discovered him lying where
he had fallen in the middle of the village square. I pulled him up and
drove him home to the villa. And as I helped him into his bed, a real
fever shook him and a flood of incoherent words burst from him, which
could be interpreted as a kind of confession: 'No one is left ... they ran
away, they've all gone ... my wife, my children, they're all cowards.
... Oh, Markov, what do you know? What have you seen!' Suddenly
he started shouting, 'I didn't want it! Word of honour, I didn't....
He gives me the gun, I push his hand away, and I say "I don't want
to...." But he presses the gun into my hand again and says "Shoot,
the Party orders you to." I didn't want to, do you believe me that I
didn't want to, Markov? Have you ever shot a man at close range
when he's bound? But at really close range.... You know nothing.
Look what I've become! And he's still up there, in the Politburo!
There's nothing wrong with him! But look at me! Do you believe me?
... I didn't want to shoot!'

I never knew who the man was who had pressed the gun into his
hand, nor who the victim had been.

Many years ago my neighbour had been a simple peasant lad from the villages round Popovo. I presume that he had had a kind nature, but at the same time some ambition to better himself in life. As a member of the Communist Youth League, he was recruited into service for the secret police. As a young officer, he showed himself very willing and thorough, joined the Party and accepted its ideology as Holy Writ. As he inspired complete confidence in his superiors, he was moved to the investigation section of the Interior Ministry and in Stalin's time he took part in a series of inquests and trials. Because of his remarkable strength, he was used to beat up and torture the detainees. People who knew him at that time have told me that he was one of the worst thugs. Clearly the murder which he whined about to me had been committed at that time. And like many of his colleagues, the First Lieutenant had probably justified himself with the belief that everything he did was for the good of the Party. Therefore, one can imagine the shock he received when after 1956, without any explanation, this same Party dismissed him and for convenience's sake pensioned him off as an invalid. Later they took away his pension. I was told that amongst his victims was one of the new ministers who, as soon as he came to power, took steps to throw out his former inquisitor.

God alone knows what horrors, infernal tortures and perhaps killings had spawned the nightly activity of our First Lieutenant. Who knows how many people he had crippled forever in order to have been left with the habit of hitting. And who knows what nightmarish memories had lacerated his sick mind since, because it was obvious that those who had given him the gun had escaped unscathed, while he had been held responsible. The Party, which had turned the harmless peasant boy into a cruel 'thrasher', a brute and a common murderer, had contemptibly washed its hands of him and deprived him of the only justification for his actions. Perhaps it was because he had lost the Party's blessing that he later threw himself wholeheartedly into religion in the hope of finding deliverance from his own nightmare.

I am not among those with a profound belief in the voice of conscience and remorse. But in my neighbour's case this explanation seemed plausible, because he had started as an innocent peasant boy whose nature had not been attuned to the icy criminal spirit, the cool hypocrisy and the corrupting ideological principles of the political manipulators who had used him. With all his fanaticism he had served a regime which had turned him from a man into a beast, which had deprived him of everything and which had finally placed him on the victim's chair, without any hope of salvation. That is why instinctively and desperately he sought salvation in God.

The loss of his family broke him completely. One day the militia took him away to the lunatic asylum in Karlukovo. From there he used to send me long poems written on brown paper, begging me to offer them to publishing houses. His scribblings had little in common with poetry, but what gave them unity was the recurrence of a kind of mad declaration of love for life, nature, the flowers and the light. Almost every poem started with the assurance that now he was another man, that he was reborn, that he was beginning a new life. . . .

It was as if this poor wretch was trying to banish the fiendish darkness of his conscious mind with promises of a completely new beginning.

After six months they let him out. But nothing in him had changed. He continued to drag out his miserable existence - a living monument to the character of an epoch.

THE GREAT ROOF

May, 1959. Along the highway leading from Sofia to Pernik, exactly opposite the village known as Tsurkva, there was a large construction site. At great speed the future 'Lenin' smelting works was being built. Given conditions in Bulgaria at that time, this was one of the most important construction projects. A large labour force had been assembled and, as always, the pace was being forced in order to complete the project ahead of schedule. Most of the workers and technicians came from the surrounding villages: Tsurkva, Moshino, Studena, Dragichevo, from the regions of Pernik, Radomir and Sofia. The site itself, with its completed or half-erected huge walls, mounds of building materials, human bustle and the useful or useless presence of a mass of machinery, was an impressive spectacle. From an official standpoint the works was considered a showpiece, and every day countless journalists, feature writers, local correspondents, guests, essayists and poets milled around the scaffolding and the fitments and depicted the future steelworks as a symbol rather than as a real thing. Those sceptical experts who believed that the Soviet project was technically misconceived had long been vanquished by the passionate enthusiasm of our political leaders. The centrepiece of this works was to be the rolling mill, which for the first time would produce Bulgarian sheet iron. The rolling mill itself was an outsize monster, in both width and height. It was being built by modern methods, with big reinforced concrete pillars supporting large frames, also of reinforced concrete, which formed the ceiling substructure and which would then be filled with panels. So as not to lose time, they had started assembling the machines for the rolling and shaping of the iron at one end of the mill while they were still building at the other. The engineers in charge were making every effort to speed up the completion of this mill. And just on the day when they were fitting the last frames of the gigantic roof, when the brigade of fitters was getting ready to celebrate the completion and the management was congratulating itself, something quite unexpected happened.

Towards three o'clock in the afternoon, schoolchildren from a nearby school who were being taken round the rolling mill had stopped by the smaller crane on the inside. But either because they had tired of the inspection or because some instinct warned them, they left the mill, dispersing in the direction of the outer gates. At around four o'clock only construction workers, mainly fitters, were still inside. The end of the normal shift was 4.30 p.m., but by an irony of fate only the most conscientious workers had remained at work until the last minute, most of their comrades having already left to wash and change. Then, about a quarter of an hour before the end of the working day, the last frame of the roof which had just been fitted came away from the supporting pillars and collapsed, dragging down the next frame, which in turn dragged down the next so that, like a volley of gunshots, concrete and iron rained down on the heads of the remaining workers, shrouding everything in thick dust. A large part of the roof had collapsed in a few seconds, leaving only sinister spiky pillars surrounding a concrete cemetery. I do not remember exactly which part of the roof had fallen in but, as every frame was roughly six metres wide, no less than ten frames must have collapsed. When the roar had subsided, one remaining sloping frame could be seen, hanging limply like a wounded bird, looking as if it might fall in at any moment and bring down with it the rest of the mammoth roof. ...

But this was only the beginning of the horror. Nobody had any idea how many people were left inside the mill, nor was it possible to check. Indescribable panic and chaos ensued. Most of the workforce were peasants from the same village, relatives and friends, and so everyone from all over the huge construction site rushed to the ruins of this part of the works. A salvage operation was hardly possible in this terrible confusion, with everybody shouting out names and running like madmen to look for a brother, a father, a son. ... Only towards evening did some kind of order begin to prevail. The people wandering like lunatics amongst the rubble, straining to hear every sound or groan, were led away and the rescue teams started to look for the victims in a more organized way. But what could be done without machines? Nobody would have dared mobilize the cranes and excavators, because, at the slightest vibration, the frame which remained hanging in the middle of the roof could have crashed down dragging all the rest. ... And below the roof stood the already assembled and fitted new machines which had cost millions. After an hour or two, all the senior managers were assembled, the Deputy Minister had arrived from Sofia and army and police detachments had been commandeered.

The whole building site was surrounded. And with reason. Because, hearing of the accident, wives and children, parents and relatives of the workmen from the surrounding villages had rushed to the site to look for their own. Of course, the accident had been very much exaggerated, rumour putting the number of dead at three hundred and who knows how many injured.... The chief of the security guard told me later that towards nine-thirty in the evening the crowd in front of the main entrance of the works numbered about five thousand, mostly women, wailing hysterically and trying to push their way in. Militia reinforcements had to be brought in to hold back the people. The crowd had stopped one of the ministerial cars and the militia had had to clear a path. They had also tried to stop every ambulance to see who was inside. Finally it had come to blows and nobody believed anything they were told. Despite the protestations of the head of the construction project and other managers that the name of every victim would be announced as soon as it was known, the people did not trust them, they wanted to make sure for themselves. ... In the middle of this nightmare, amidst the cries, the curses, the tears and wails of the women, one heard sudden mad cries of joy when relatives spotted one of their men alive. ... Immediately the survivor was showered with cries and questions: 'Pesho, did you see Sando? Where's my Ivan? Pesho, tell me! Where's Spas? Pesho, is Slavcho alive?'

Subsequently one of the site managers said that the most terrible scene had occurred not at the area where the roof had collapsed, but at the gates. If I remember rightly, the official casualty figures were seven dead and about twenty injured. I think these must have been correct since the people knew each other and it would have been impossible to cover up.

Late at night management and rescue teams came to a definite and clear conclusion – that in order to effect a successful salvage operation of the fitted machinery and other equipment under the part of the roof that had remained standing, it was necessary to find a group of brave men who would climb onto the solid part of the roof, reach the sloping frame and secure it with special supports. For anyone who had an idea of the roof's construction, this was a lethally dangerous task. Later I was told that the Deputy Minister had given orders for volunteers to be found. They would be made to sign declarations that they were acting of their own accord, as no sane person could have accepted responsibility for any more victims. ... And now comes the part which is the point of my telling this tragic story. They brought in a military detachment with powerful floodlights which lit up the whole roof so that it was lighter than day. But under these lights the height of the roof appeared even more awesome and the ruins, with the bristling irons sticking out of the concrete, assumed a chilling, ghostly aspect. The workshop was still surrounded by crowds of construction workers, separate groups were sifting the rubble carefully and had already found the first victims. ...

And then, from the loudspeakers that were hung around the site, the first appeal was heard. I do not know who spoke, perhaps it was the Party organizer, perhaps someone else. The appeal was addressed to the Communists, who were asked to volunteer to climb onto the roof. Phrases were used like 'The Party and the country call on you'. This sounded preposterously pompous, yet solemn and, at the same time, somehow tragic. 'Communists, your Party and your country call on you. ...' The appeal was repeated many times and directions were given as to where the volunteers should assemble. But it seemed that there were no candidates and therefore the next series of appeals was addressed to the Komsomols [Young Communist League]. Once more the voice on the loudspeaker mentioned Party and country – and every time the announcement was repeated, the voice became more hesitant and confused. In lieu of an answer many of the bystanders silently slipped away into the surrounding darkness. It was evident that no Communists and no Komsomols had come forward and the appeal for heroism had got nowhere. I was told afterwards that one of the project managers, a fanatic, had lost his temper completely, advanced menacingly on the workers and ordered them to follow him and climb up to the roof. He even clambered up himself and, seeing that nobody was following his example, started to insult the workers, swearing at them and calling them all sorts of offensive names, until finally, maddened with fury, he collapsed. None the less, there were no volunteers – and no appeals could bring them forth. An awkward silence reigned over the whole site. Even if there had been some enthusiasm, even if someone had been impelled to answer the appeals, the sight of the leaning frame arrested in its flight was enough to cool any hot blood. The efforts of Party secretaries and shop-stewards to persuade the building workers to attempt the task were also in vain. Everyone held back, because there before them they were digging out the dead. ... But the management was in a hurry.

All the same, after an hour or more of complete Party and Komsomol humiliation, volunteers were found. Only they were neither Communists nor Komsomols. Just a group of ordinary, sturdy Bulgarians with strong nerves and a feeling that somehow the job had to be done. At their head was engineer Uzunov, a fellow-student of mine from the Polytechnic, who had been expelled for several years for refusing to vote for the expulsion of other students at the time of the purges; after being reinstated, he had graduated and was now working in the assembly shop of the future steelworks. He was one of the most honest men I knew. After the episode of the roof, his name was put forward for the highest state decoration, but after a lengthy delay, because of his past record, they gave him only 'The Red Banner of Labour'. During that hellish night, he had merely told his people that they must try. Perhaps the funny aspect of all this was the demand that they should sign, in black and white, that they were going up voluntarily. . . .

From here onwards, only films about the transport of nitro-glycerine can compare in terms of fear and tension with the progress of the group on the roof. There was ominous silence over the whole site. Many of the people down below had covered their eyes so as not to see, others turned their heads away at every creak, until the group reached the end frame and, after taking safety measures, started work. . . . The frame was supported and the rest of the roof was saved.

The commission of inquiry which looked into the collapse of the roof produced nebulous conclusions. I was told that the technical reason for the fall of the first frame that had dragged down the rest was the indoor crane which had simply caught the frame. Maybe this was the immediate cause, but given that this roof was meant to carry great weight and that on top of it they planned to instal hoisting equipment and tracks for the future production of the rolling mill, the finger pointed at the project itself which, as far as I know, was a Soviet one. Somehow or other, the question of responsibility was finally glossed over - and that made me think that the error had been fundamental.

But the collapse of the roof, for me at least, signified much more than an industrial accident. Such accidents happen everywhere. But what distinguished the caving in of this roof from other accidents was that it became a classic test of the ethics of Bulgaria's socialist society. Such tests are a kind of spontaneous popular referendum, and they occur at times of great disasters, catastrophes or wars. The image of the Communist, praised to the skies by the regime's propaganda for his Party virtues, turned into the reality of a coward out for himself, who would not risk even his little finger for his Party or his country. All those fanatical comrades who made fiery speeches at meetings, indulged in breast-beating and belched hatred against everyone who did not agree with them, were shown up as calculating opportunists, frauds and cowards. It turned out that there were no special Communist virtues, that the Communist as the incarnation of new, perfected human qualities was a figment of the imagination, while the man who ten years before this accident had dared to stand up and protest against the foul expulsions of Bulgarian students from the Polytechnic showed the same courage in climbing the roof in order to save his society from another disgrace. How I would have liked to meet the fanatical supporters of the purges of my student days the next day and to ask them how many real heroes they had kicked out and how many real talents they had destroyed!

The theme of the collapse of the roof of the rolling mill preoccupied me for a long time. Years later I gathered documents and researched material which strengthened my conviction that this accident had produced a microcosm of the morality of our society. Of course, not even the most circumspect report of this event was ever allowed to appear anywhere. But, told by the people who had taken part in it, the story became a legend. In the fall of this roof I perceived a symbol of the inevitable collapse of the roof of lies, demagogy, fallacies and deceits which the regime had constructed over our country. I wrote a novel entitled *The Great Roof*. After many trials and tribulations with various publishing houses and censorship committees, the novel was shelved for the time being. But during the thaw which followed de-Stalinization, the screening committee of the Bulgarian cinema industry showed considerable enthusiasm for a film on the subject. After all, it demonstrated the native heroism of the people! The production team was set up and Willy Tsankov was appointed as director. Together we began looking around the country for suitable locations; but when we came back we heard that the production had been shelved. A well-known chief of an equally well-known ideological department took me by the arm and said: 'Listen, brother, don't play with fire! Can you imagine the effect of these collapsing frames on the screen? This would be a film of destruction, an allegory and document of degradation, because it's not just the frames which are collapsing! Even if we filmed it, it would never be allowed to be shown to the public!'

I think he was right. The collapse of the roof of the rolling mill of the Lenin state steelworks was both an allegory and a document of moral degradation.

PASSPORT ODYSSEY

If an ordinary Englishman, German, Italian, American – or any citizen of a country that neither enjoys the benefits of some October, September or any other revolution nor calls itself socialist, popular or popular-democratic – wants to travel, all he has to worry about is the amount of money he will need and his chosen timetable. Today's Western citizens have become so used to this unassailable human right that many not only cannot understand, but refuse to understand, that their brethren in Eastern Europe have almost no possibility of free travel abroad. They do hear, of course, of problems connected with the emigration of minorities in Eastern Europe, they know that there is a Berlin Wall and Communist frontier guards who shoot people like dogs, but none the less their minds refuse to accept the truth about the fate of human beings in these countries – just as their fathers, some years ago, refused to believe in the existence of Stalinist terror. Perhaps this is a matter of naivety, or of ignorance, but perhaps also of irresponsibility. Every Bulgarian who lives in the West is frequently subjected to the following absurd dialogue:

'Do you see your parents often?'

'No. I haven't seen them for twenty years.'

'Why is that? Are you on bad terms with them?'

'No, but I can't go to see them, and they can't come here.'

'What! Why can't they?'

'Because the regime is Communist and does not allow people to travel freely.'

'But I see from the newspapers that some people from Eastern Europe do travel. . . . In fact, once I even saw a Soviet group here on the main street. . . .'

'True, there are some who are allowed to travel, but not my parents.'

'But why? Forgive me, but perhaps they have been deprived of their civil rights . . .?'

'They have never had them.'

'How is this possible! Bulgaria is a member of the United Nations, a signatory of the UN Charter of Human Rights, and of the Helsinki agreement. . . .'

'My parents cannot travel simply because they are my parents. The regime considers that in this way it punishes both me and them.'

'But why should it punish them?'

Here the patience of the Bulgarian runs out. How can he explain to these Western children? Meanwhile the Western citizen shakes his head and says helplessly:

'I'm afraid I really don't understand!' Then he suddenly asks the final question:

'So, then, it's possible that you won't ever see your parents again?'

'Yes,' agrees our countryman and continues on his way.

It is precisely for these citizens of the West that I wish to tell the story of how a Bulgarian goes about obtaining permission to travel abroad. To make it easier for them, I shall choose a case free of political and economic complications.

My imaginary Bulgarian citizen is called Pencho Danchev. He is a fifty-two-year-old senior carpenter in a tram-car depot in Krasno Selo. He manages to make ends meet because his eldest son has just returned from military service and has started earning, while his wife, who is an assistant cook in the depot, is frugal with her wages. Politically, Pencho has always been on the side of the authorities. At meetings, when everyone else raises their hands, he raises his – sometimes without even knowing what is being decided. People think of him as a kind and gentle man. As a workman, he is considered one of the best: he has won seven competitions for shock-workers and has been awarded the People's Medal for Labour (bronze). He has never had any links with abroad . . . with one exception. His grandfather came from Vrabcha, a village in the Trun district which borders with Yugoslavia, and one of his cousins, Tosho, who used to live in the Yugoslav half of the village, later moved to Belgrade. This Tosho is also a carpenter, but has his own workshop and builds wardrobes. During the last few years, Tosho has visited his cousin in Sofia three or four times, and, of course, each time he invites Pencho and his wife to visit him in Belgrade. At first Pencho is not very keen on the idea, because the journey will cost money and they are not that well off. But one day, suddenly and inexplicably, Pencho is filled with a strong desire to see Belgrade, to stay a week or two with Tosho's family, to buy something for his wife (they say Belgrade is cheaper) and, so to speak, to add to his biography the fact that once in his life he has been abroad. He tells his wife about this, but she says:

'Fine – but what if they don't let you go? I hear that it's very difficult to obtain a passport.'

'Why shouldn't they let me go?' replies Pencho. 'Am I a thief or a murderer? All my life I have toiled like a beast. Why shouldn't they let me go? Why should Tosho be able to come here when I'm not allowed to go there?'

'There's no harm in trying,' says his wife.

The next day Pencho joins the long queue in the large room on the first floor of the Directorate of the Militia by the Lions' Bridge. Pencho is impressed by the tense silence of the slowly moving crowd, the serious quasi-churchgoing air of the waiting people, their polite, almost obsequious, expressions when they reach the counter and the contrasting harsh voices of the female officials who seem to have been deliberately chosen to look like prison warders.

'I want to visit my cousin in Belgrade, so I've come to find out what documents are needed ...', says Pencho in his politest tone.

'Can't you read? It's all written there on the wall! What are you doing in this queue!' bellows a virago.

'I only came to ask ... if one can visit a cousin....'

'A cousin? Impossible! Only direct relatives – father, mother, son, daughter, brother, sister!' the comrade behind the counter reels off, and she turns impatiently towards the next in the queue.

Pencho Danchev backs away, ashamed to have asked something which he was supposed to know. As his eyes peruse the poster on the wall which lists all of the documents required for foreign travel, a funny old man approaches him and says in a friendly way:

'Don't you listen to them! Fill in an application! If they refuse, try again. And again! And again! Until they're tired of it!'

The man pats him encouragingly on the shoulder and moves on. And Pencho decides to fight. He fetches forms and instructions on how to fill them in. That is how he learns that he needs an invitation and a maintenance guarantee from Tosho, certified by the Bulgarian embassy in Belgrade. Pencho immediately writes to Tosho asking him to send such a declaration. He does not know that this declaration costs money, that it is issued at the consul's discretion, or that it is often used as bait for intelligence activity amongst Bulgarian emigrés. Anyhow, he soon receives the declaration along with a joyful letter from Tosho who is looking forward to his visit. Then it is the turn of the other documents: from the Inspector of Taxes certifying that he has paid his taxes, from the military authorities certifying that he can leave the country, from his office certifying that there is no objection to his travelling abroad. Some years later, these documents will become more complicated and, in order to exonerate the passport authorities from blame for refusals, individual enterprises and institutions will themselves deny the applicant permission to travel. Pencho goes to his head of personnel and explains that he wants to go to Belgrade. The first reaction of the man is disagreeable, as if Pencho were asking for a loan. Afterwards Pencho will tell his wife sadly:

'If you want the authorities to take against you, tell them you want to go abroad. You should have seen his face when I told him – as if I had shoved my finger up his . . .'

'I'll speak to the director,' says the head of personnel and suddenly changes the conversation to other things. He asks Pencho about work in the carpentry shop, what the people there talk about, and especially what he thinks about Simo who has been shooting his mouth off rather a lot lately. . . . Thinking about getting permission to travel, Pencho talks volubly about the state of affairs in the carpentry shop. Having sensed that the head of personnel hates Simo, he is not ashamed to admit that he, too, dislikes him and so on. The head of personnel dismisses him approvingly. A few days later he receives a document certifying that the enterprise sees no objection to Pencho Danchev travelling abroad.

Having obtained all the necessary documents, he takes a day off work and returns to the Passport Office, waits in the queue and has to pay the equivalent of a day and a half's wages, just for the pleasure of having his application accepted by the ministry. He is told that he should have a reply in anything up to two months.

'I really wanted to go in the autumn but the spring won't be too bad either,' Pencho says to himself.

After about a month Pencho's neighbours, who are also his colleagues at the depot, call him mysteriously to their home one evening and tell him in secret that the local stool-pigeon, a certain Mako Takov, had come to gather information about him and had questioned them at great length, but Pencho need not worry as they knew what to say. Takov had shown a particular interest in the people with whom Pencho's son, Gosho, consorts.

'It's probably something to do with that beating,' Pencho remembers. Five years earlier, Gosho had given a good thrashing to the son of an important official in a row over a girl and had nearly been expelled from school.

Mako Takov had also asked in great detail about Tosho's visits from Belgrade and had wanted to know what sort of a man he was. Finally, he had shown an interest in Pencho's elder brother who had served in the gendarmerie in bourgeois times.

'Why do they need to dig up these old things?' mutters Pencho, feeling that his five levas for the application may have been in vain.

'Didn't I tell you, brother,' his neighbour says, 'when you want to travel, they start raking up everything and no good can come of it'.

All the same, no obvious calamity ensues. Instead, after two months precisely, a brief communication from the Passport Office: *Travel permission has been refused.*

Pencho reads the note once, twice, five times and his hands are trembling. Perhaps for the first time in his life he feels the sharp pain of injustice intensely. He has met and experienced many injustices, but this one seems to him the most cruel because, for the first time, he is told directly that he is *nobody*, that he has no rights, that all his years of conscientious work count for nothing, that even the medal they have given him is not worth a pumpkin.

'Why shouldn't I travel? Why? Why?' he repeats as if his whole life depended on this journey, on this passport. [...]

All his life a gentle and compliant man, Pencho Danchev has never hated anyone. But now he feels that he hates them – the people who have spat in his face and told him in so many words: 'How does a nonentity like you dare to think himself our equal?' And it is this hatred which makes him want to continue the struggle.

'Let them be: damn them,' says his wife. But here his son Gosho chips in and says:

'Father, you must fight to the bitter end! If necessary, you must go to the Pope.' [...]

And so he finds himself once more in the gloomy building by the Lions' Bridge whose stark atmosphere reminds him of visiting days at the Central Prison. All his life Pencho has feared the authorities; but now he feels driven on by the force of his own question:

'Why shouldn't I be able to travel? Why shouldn't I indeed? I'm no criminal – I've worked like an ox all my life for the good of this country – I've never ever been against socialism or Communism.... I've never had the slightest intention of running away, or smuggling, or stealing....' [After waiting a long time in the queue, he demands to see the head of department but is told that he will be away for three months.]

The next three months in the life of Pencho Danchev have a new direction. Hitherto his life has had only two dimensions: work and home. Now there is a third: the passport. Slowly and powerfully, the passport theme invades the nights and days of the carpenter. In his family, with friends and acquaintances, it dogs him like an illness, leaving him no peace. Unable to stop himself, he confides his bitterness to his friends. And, to his great surprise, he meets with the warmest response. The first thing he now learns is that almost half the people around him have been through the same experience, have attempted to travel and have met with similar refusals. Only now does he understand that the passport is not his problem alone.

Now not a day passes, or an hour, in which he does not talk or listen to stories about passports and foreign travel. His poor brain is inundated by an amazing amount of information. All the others seem to know more than he does, to be more experienced and no doubt more intelligent and ingenious. And they tell him that his meeting with the head of department will get him nowhere. [They are proved right. The head of department confirms that cousins are not accepted as a reason for travel.]

A surprise awaits him at home. His wife opens the door and at one glance understands everything. But instead of saying: 'To hell with this trip, we can live without it', she suddenly smiles and says: 'Listen, cheer up! We're not going to lie down and give up just like that!'

And while Pencho gets out of his best suit, she tells him excitedly that she has been able to find a very important 'connection'. It is Ivan, nicknamed 'the lamb', the stranger from another village who married her cousin Kina after his first wife died.

'And do you know what he is now?' Pencho's wife asks triumphantly. 'He's the manager of the garage used by the Council of Ministers.'

'So what if he's the manager of the garage!' Pencho Danchev says gloomily.

'You're stupid and you'll die stupid! How do you think you get to be the manager of the ministers' garage? Who can they trust with the cars which they ride in? If something happens to the car - and the minister inside comes to grief - who will conduct the enquiry, who will control everything? Only the most trusted person! Don't you realise that "the lamb" was an officer in the militia for five years? Do you see now?'

'All right, all right,' Pencho agrees. 'Do you think he can help?'

'If he doesn't help, Kina will!' his wife says. 'I'm going to visit them tomorrow.' [...]

In the evening, his wife returns in triumph. She has been received very well at the Shilevs, who have a brand new apartment and have just built a villa in Simeonovo near Sofia. Pencho's wife is full of superlatives about their carpets and the various gadgets she has seen in the kitchen, and Pencho makes sad comparisons with his own poverty. He has never regarded himself as a failure, but this unattainable and inexplicable success irritates him. His wife says that Shilev listened carefully to her, laughed and said that he would expedite matters. He took a note of Pencho's full name and everything.... Here his wife pauses: 'But he needs you too!' she says.

For, as she was leaving, Shilev had told her, without beating about the bush, that he needed a carpenter for his villa – so could Pencho, when convenient ... at weekends, or perhaps he would rather take a day or two off? It was a matter of some shelves and fitted cupboards and, of course, some floor-boards....

She looks beseechingly at her husband. There is nothing insulting in this. Just a favour for a favour. And if he can start work this Sunday, the other will be in his debt and will *have* to ring the ministry.... Pencho can see that what his wife proposes is very reasonable, but he thinks to himself: 'So that's how you get a passport.'

On Sunday he finds himself in Simeonovo and starts work. Somehow the carpenter has taken a liking to the manager of the state garage. He is cordial, self-confident and generous. For the first time in his life Pencho smokes a cigar and tastes French wine. He is already convinced that a man like Shilev can get him a passport. He gets on well with his work and the floor does him credit. Shilev is happy. He jumps on the floor-boards, laughs and says:

'Fellow countryman, I promise you that you will see Belgrade. I'll make a bet with you! Only, take my advice: never hand in documents without fixing matters at the top. Do you get it? Because now it'll be a hell of a sweat to cancel the Commission's decision! It's much easier when no decision has been taken.'

Pencho nods and now looks at Shilev almost dotingly. Here is the man who will get the better of that repulsive head of department.

'Fellow countryman,' Shilev repeats, 'what would happen if we didn't help each other? It may not be proper, or even honest, but it's life. You for me and me for you!'

For nearly a month Pencho works every weekend in Shilev's villa. Shilev comes and goes in a large black Mercedes, and usually drives the carpenter home at night. One evening he says to him: 'And now, let's go and see Dodov!' Pencho has no idea who this Dodov is, but clearly he is a comrade who knows about passports. The black Mercedes takes them to the Sofia suburb of Banki where Dodov has his villa. The man who receives them is a short, fat, fifty-year-old with a sour face, but Shilev's laughter and good humour melt the ice.

'And now Pencho,' he says, 'tell your story to comrade Dodov from beginning to end!' [...]

'I'll see what I can do,' mutters Dodov, who takes down Pencho's particulars. It is obvious that he does not want to disappoint Shilev to whom he seems indebted.

On the way back, the talkative Shilev explains:

'This is how it works, brother. Dodov has to do me this favour because I've saved his skin. He is a Colonel [in the secret police] and has power in these matters. What haven't we done together! Once we even stole some files belonging to the head of the Passport Office and destroyed the memos with the final decisions on the applications! So, another time before you apply, remember to come to me! Well now, congratulations!'

Pencho Danchev still does not believe that he will travel. Oddly, Shilev and Dodov seem to him representatives of the same absurdity that is personified by the head of the Passport Office. He remains sceptical the next day and the next – until the day when the letter arrives announcing that he has been granted permission to travel. His wife jumps for joy and even embraces him – something she has not done for a long time. But strangely Pencho feels no happiness; there is no trace of that fervent desire to go abroad for the first time and no enticing vision of Belgrade station, Terazije Square and the Danube. Everything seems lame, forced, meaningless.

Nevertheless, he follows the Passport Office's instructions. He pays the fee which is the equivalent of one month's salary; he waits for hours in the queue in the building by Lions' Bridge and looks closely at the crowds around him. At the entrance, he meets a pleasant old lady whose daughter lives in Belgium and who has been refused permission to see her grand-daughter more than twenty times.

'No luck this time either,' says the old lady. 'But when the six months are up, I shall apply again! I shall go on applying until I die!'

And Pencho thinks to himself: 'You can go on applying if you have nothing better to do, but if you don't know comrade Shilev or comrade Dodov, if you can't lay a floor or make a cupboard without payment ... you'll never see your grand-daughter.'

And now he hits on the only plausible explanation for the whole barbarian nonsense: the only people who need this system – a system fit only for prisoners – who exist through it and benefit from it, are the Shilevs and the Dodovs, because this system enables them to obtain services without payment, to rob and exploit all ordinary, defenceless people. He remembers once more all the stories about young women and girls who have been forced to share the beds of lustful secret service colonels, about all the unpaid workers who have had to render services to some big boss. (Kiro, the tailor, for instance, makes suits for nothing for a Party official.) He remembers the commissions from abroad, the obligatory presents that the traveller has to bring back for those who have helped him get a passport, the undisguised bribes, the selling of passports, the whole of this socialist-Communist passport mafia.

'I wonder,' muses Pencho Danchev, 'if there is a single person in this country who has ever obtained a passport straightaway, in accordance with the law! Without connections, without friends, without floor-boards, without cupboards....'

THE STING AND THE
HONEY OF TOURISM

We decided to go with friends on a family holiday, without taking advantage of our privileges as writers and journalists. Even before the start of the season we had organized everything. We bought railway tickets to Vidin [on the Danube], then we booked cabins on the boat *Georgi Dimitrov* to Ruse, where we reserved rooms in hotel *Balkantourist* [run by the official state tourism organization of that name]. From there, via Varna [on the Black Sea], we planned to go for twenty days to the holiday resort called *Slunchev Bryag* ['Sunny Beach'].

The journey to Vidin passed off normally. However, when we arrived at the quayside in the evening to claim our cabins, in which we hoped to get some sleep as the ship was due to leave early next morning, we received our first surprise.

'No cabins for Bulgarians!' declared the officer on duty roughly.

It transpired that a group of Western tourists, Frenchmen I think, were occupying the cabins reserved for Bulgarians.

'You must understand, comrades', explained another official, 'that we can't leave the Western tourists stranded; they pay in hard currency. This is a case of helping our economy.'

We were not impressed by this patriotic appeal and we reacted sharply. We pulled out various cards, because as usual in contemporary Bulgaria when there is a similar row, what matters most is who can shout loudest: 'Do you know who I am?' Everyone who fails to make use of this phrase is doomed to lose out. Perhaps because my friend was an important citizen, the Captain made a gesture and installed us all in his own cabin and that of another naval officer. As we were settling in we heard an elderly woman crying in the passage because she had been forced to abandon her cabin to these wretched foreigners. It was all so disagreeable that our mood was spoilt, as if we had a premonition that the incident on the ship was only the beginning. All the same, the next day the beautiful weather, the charm of the voyage down the Danube and above all the excellent restaurant on the boat helped us to forget the unpleasant evening.

I have often travelled down the Danube and I think this is one of the most beautiful trips that the Bulgarian countryside can offer. On our left was the boundless Romanian plain, on our right the imposing Bulgarian shore. The boat glided elegantly along with the current of the river, we sunbathed on the upper deck and cooled off under the showers, the radio played pleasant light music, when suddenly somebody – on every journey, this ghostly voice speaks up – said: 'Belene'.*

All the Bulgarians on the boat turned and stared for a long time at the green island until it was left far behind. It was as if the music on the wireless had suddenly become the hooting of an owl, the whole innocent enchantment of the river had disappeared and the sun had faded, darkened by frightening memories of so many tales and rumours about this island, Bulgaria's Calvary. There is hardly a Bulgarian living who has not known some inhabitant of this socialist showcase. Close friends from our school or university days had undergone hellish ordeals only a short distance from our pleasure-boat: Vassil, who was kept bound with chains for two whole weeks in a boat stuck in the ice of the river during the coldest February; Stamen, confined for several days and nights in a solitary cell with water up to his neck; boys from the Polytechnic who were shot on the spot without reason or sentence.... I remembered how, feet dangling over the edge of the boat, a youth with a guitar once sang a strange song:

Danube, white river, how quiet you flow
Danube, black river, what anguish you know....

Of course, the Bulgarian tour guide did not say a word about the island to the Frenchmen. What point was there in the foreigners knowing? Moreover, this was Stalin's work, and now Stalin was no longer and things were different....

In the evening we reached Ruse and quickly made for the new *Balkantourist* hotel, where we were to engage in the second round of our tourist fight. As we had foreseen, our rooms had been given away, this time not to Frenchmen but to Soviet guests attending some music festival. The contract for our holiday, the receipts and the prepaid money meant nothing to the officials of *Balkantourist*.

---

* Belene on the Danube estuary is known as one of the most notorious labour camps for political prisoners run by the Communists.

'The Bulgarians must manage as best they can,' declared the manager, pronouncing the word 'Bulgarians' without any embarrassment as if he himself belonged to another nation. He reminded me of a Soviet official of *Intourist* in Leningrad who gruffly explained to me that we Bulgarians were third-class tourists according to Soviet classifications. The first category included only Americans, West Germans and – surprise – Hungarians. That was in 1959. The second included all the other non-Communist countries and some countries of special interest; and the third, tourists of no interest to them. Indeed, I know of no other society where people are more strictly divided into categories than the classless socialist world.

But towards midnight, while we were dozing in the hotel lounge wondering what to do, our luck changed. A group expected from Bucharest failed to arrive, so we were going to be able to sleep after all. So far everything had discouraged us from staying in Varna, and the next day the four of us headed for the south, to 'Sunny Beach'.

I must have heard hundreds of tales of disgraceful behaviour in the hotels and restaurants along the entire Black Sea coast. But I never expected to experience such human and national humiliation.

In 'Sunny Beach', too, the contract with *Balkantourist* turned out to be a useless bit of paper. Again we were told that because of an influx of tourists from the West, the Bulgarians had to go. Finally, after much pleading and expostulating, we were accommodated for one night in a brand new hotel, but warned that the next day we must leave. In the evening we discovered that in the restaurant, a few uncomfortable tables at the edges of the room were earmarked for Bulgarians – there one could die, if not of hunger, of waiting. The next morning, well before lunch, we were ejected from the hotel with the familiar phrase: 'There's no room for Bulgarians!' But we resisted. We frantically tried all the hotels, hoping to find accommodation for the following night. Late in the afternoon, when it had become clear that in the whole resort we would not be able to find room for 'Bulgarians', I spent three hours at the Post Office trying to phone a friend in Sofia, who happened to be a friend of the head of *Balkantourist*. It was my misfortune that the chief was then away from the capital but my friend pledged his co-operation for the following day, advising us that we should borrow blankets and sleep on benches or on the beach. In the evening we started out again on our hotel round, desperately begging for rooms. Meanwhile we noticed that we were not alone in our tourist predicament. At least a hundred other Bulgarian wretches were going round helplessly just like us. There is nothing more dispiriting in Bulgaria than when you happen to want something but the man on the other side of the counter thinks you are nobody. In many places the various hotel managers and people in charge did not even listen to us; they turned their backs and not only did they fail to express any sympathy, but they retorted with a kind of vindictive pleasure: 'Well, who asked you to go on holiday!'

In another place, I heard a manager with a moustache tell a weeping woman: 'I am not interested, comrade, in whether you will sleep or not!'

In these circumstances, I found it particularly difficult to accept the usual form of address: 'comrade'. Despite the influx of foreigners, I had the feeling that the hotels were not really so overcrowded, and that everything was more likely to be the result of bad organization. But nothing could excuse the war that the officials of tourism had declared on their countrymen. Subsequently every day would bring reminders that the worst thing a visitor to 'Sunny Beach' could be was Bulgarian. A few days later we spotted a piece of cardboard hanging in the alley behind the casino on which some vengeful wit had written 'Out of bounds – for Bulgarians and dogs'. My friend, who in the past had spent years of hardship abroad, observed sadly: 'Nowhere has anyone ever humiliated me more as a Bulgarian than these people here, in Bulgaria'.

The Bulgarian press often commented on the unforgivable humiliation of Bulgarian citizens at the hands of *Balkantourist*. In my view, in Bulgaria there are two constant and most disagreeable sources of national humiliation; the first is the Passport Office at the Ministry of the Interior, the second – *Balkantourist*.

And so, once again, we faced an impossible night. Exhausted from running around, faint with hunger, disgusted by everything, we had to choose between sleeping on the sand or on the benches. It was August, and cold. But then we had a stroke of luck. At about midnight, while we were seeking consolation in one of the bars, my friend was accosted by a little man in shirt and trousers under which the outline of a large automatic pistol could be seen. It turned out that this comrade was one of the most important people in the district. The barmaid called him 'the little prince'.

Years ago my friend had rendered an invaluable service to 'the little prince' and got him out of trouble. He looked to me a nimble, spontaneous man whose rough, imperious manners were in inverse proportion to his slight build. Hearing about our hotel Odyssey, he lost his temper and angrily went to the telephone. I heard his voice booming in a tone that would not be disobeyed.

Only a few minutes later a car arrived in front of the bar and out of it jumped the most important resort officials who picked up our luggage and then offered us a long list of hotels from which to choose.

'Would you like to go to the Primrose? No, no, it's rather noisy, too near the motorway.... You'd be better off in the Globe, or why not the Seagull. ..?'

I listened to this music and did not believe it. 'The little prince' sent us off with a triumphant smile and, as if he had understood my feelings, he said: 'Well, we are Bulgarians, but we still live in Turkish times!' [i.e. in servitude]

And to demonstrate the full extent of his power, he invited us to dinner the following day in a restaurant called the 'Neptune'. Previously we had not realized that, after hotels, the next worst torture chambers for Bulgarians were the restaurants. On the day of our arrival we had tried to go into 'Neptune', but the waiters had refused to serve us because they were busy looking after foreigners. I felt a certain primitive satisfaction in observing the servile bowing of waiters and managers as they tried with unctuous smiles to ingratiate themselves with 'the little prince'. Everything they served was of the best quality, and I was sure that the bill at the end would be pleasantly reduced.

We were to remember this dinner for the rest of our stay in the resort. Not only because it was not repeated, but because to a large extent it exactly reflected the character of socialist man.

Gradually we were beginning to learn the rules of the game. We ceased to be inexperienced fools and instead adjusted to the spirit of the times. Now we regularly had a table reserved for us in one of the best restaurants – thanks to the ancient law of tipping. Right from the start we simply slipped a large note into the pocket of the senior waiter, and from this moment on all went smoothly. The tip opened every door. It was not necessary to stand in a queue, to wait for hours and drink cold soup or eat yesterday's dish. All this reminded me of a barber in Moscow, not far from the University, who hung a big slogan over the mirror in his shop: 'The tip is a humiliation of Soviet man', but had written under it: 'Do please humiliate me, comrades!'

Subsequently we met friends and acquaintances who told us of unfortunate Bulgarian citizens thrown out of their rooms in the middle of the night, the surly attitude of officials, the brazen overcharging on restaurant bills, the rude manners of the staff and many more regrettable things. I walked on the beautiful sands and I thought about what this stretch of beach had represented only ten years before. This was the six-kilometre-long beach of Nessebur, a long desert expanse with undulating dunes, hot sun and translucently clear sea. As students, we used to wander here, lie down in the folds of the dunes and enjoy the freedom of sun and air. One could do as one liked because nobody was looking and holiday-makers were few and far between. In Nessebur itself, in Sozopol, Akhtopol and Primorsko, the inhabitants lived a simple unspoilt life. The fishermen were real fishermen, the vine-growers were real vine-growers and the people were real people. Anyone who has lived in or visited Koprivshtitsa before the development of tourism always has remarked on the real old Bulgarians to be found there. They would remember with profound nostalgia how in Koprivshtitsa or in Kalofer or Karlovo strangers would say 'Good day' and friendly smiles would transform their faces. Can anyone forget the wonderful hospitality, moral rectitude or eager inquiring minds of these real, good Bulgarians of old! Far from the plastic civilization of tourism, far from modern commercialism, and far from the new morality of the regime, one could meet pure and honest people. God forbid that someone should ask for more in rent than the reasonable cheap price. Often landlords in all these places even refused to accept payment, saying: 'We are all people. Today you were my guest, tomorrow I shall be yours, and that is how it should be!'

So many of us remember, and will continue to remember, those warm evenings spent in someone's house or a merry gathering at an inn, when generosity flowed from the emptiest pockets and a great, undeclared human understanding reigned.

This old world was to die on that day in 1956 when Nikita Khrushchev saw the beauty of the Black Sea shore and advised the Bulgarian government to exploit it through tourism. Probably few would object in principle to this idea. In the end, international tourism really does help different peoples learn to know each other. But the trouble starts with those who promote such exchanges, who reduce their own people to the status of a third-class nation and who turn encounters with tourists into encounters of national humiliation.

Cascading reflections of neon lights dance on the shiny asphalt of the avenues. They come from the flamboyant advertisements of hotels, restaurants and shops. Where ten years ago only the sea spoke in the desert silence of the dunes, now one hears thousands of voices, drowned in the music of the orchestras and the noise of the cars. On the main avenue in front of us, where the neon lights change human flesh tones to blue, orange, green or red, there stroll Germans, Czechs, Poles, Swedes, Frenchmen, all sorts. The crowd swarms from every entrance and alley, moves in all directions, speaks all kinds of languages, so that the four of us feel somewhat alien and lost amidst this invasion of our Black Sea coast by the world.

Every place in every restaurant has long since been filled. We look in from the street and see white shirts with ties, multicoloured dresses in all fashions, faces reddened or tanned by the sea, a parade of hair-styles, of smiles, of glances, and we hear the rhythm of the orchestras booming like massed anti-aircraft guns.... But there is no room. It seems the whole world has gathered here tonight. And because it is Saturday, everywhere is swarming with 'herring-gulls'. I do not mean those innocent ungainly seabirds. These are young (and not so young) people from the district or further afield, who have arrived to offer their fleeting sexual services to every solitary lady amongst the holiday-makers.

The 'herring-gulls', as they are called by everyone, are a new social class that has arisen in Bulgaria in response to the needs of tourism. The emergence of these peddlars of love – another amenity offered by the tourist industry – has been partly provoked by visiting foreign girls who hunger after entertainment, pleasure and mysterious adventures. Many of them expect from their holidays not merely strong sunshine, lovely beaches, delicious salads and muscatel wine from Karlovo, but also the more tangible company of some lithe Thracian youth. These foreign girls are the main attraction on the beaches, a tempting invitation to open adventures and secret pleasures.

The first 'herring-gulls' were workers from the surrounding countryside, Turkish boys from Deliorman and gipsies from Bourgas. Gradually they were joined by people of a better class, clerks, officers, engineers, sportsmen, artists, journalists. Perhaps the most appealing amongst them are still the innocent, sexually not very experienced peasant boys who move dazedly through this unknown, brilliant world of women and shyly try to start a conversation with a foreign girl, using the five foreign words that they have managed to learn with Herculean efforts. For months or years they have lived with legendary stories of the successes of Bulgarian Don Juans; they have entered into the tales of male conquests of enticing beauties from foreign lands, they have dreamt of these mysterious moments as if they could change them into something bigger and more significant, lift them out of the grey drudgery of their everyday life in field or factory, and place them on an imaginary pedestal. All this is a crazy mixture of adolescent urges and sentimental day-dreams, *machismo*, liberated sexual fantasy, plus the nebulous hope of a stroke of luck and another kind of life. Most of the 'herring-gulls', like true natives of the Balkans, believe that there are no real men in the West and that all these foreign girls are desperately searching for any man. It is with a mixture of sadness and cynicism that one watches their efforts (mostly clumsy and uncouth) to achieve their objective. Those coming from afar have planned their holidays a long way ahead so that they coincide with the season when the greatest number of foreign girls will be visiting the coast. They cannot afford to stay at a hotel and most of them live in tents pitched at some distance or in lodgings in the surrounding villages, having to walk miles before they reach the resort complex. Those from the district and nearby villages embark on their Don Juan campaigns only on rest days. In the beginning, one became accustomed to the spectacle of some 'herring-gulls' making desperate efforts at conversation with foreign girls whom they had stopped by using all the eloquence of their hands. With time, their outward appearance improved. The shy, red-faced, stammering youths disappeared, giving way to self-confident, sometimes unpleasantly arrogant bucks, who had mastered the necessary minimum of foreign words. Sometimes the interests of the 'herring-gulls' conflicted – then there were fights and whole battles between the various groups. At other times, they acted collectively. Gangs, usually composed of youths coming from the same parts or friends from the same factories, would include one or two representative good-lookers, who were used as bait so that more bored foreign girls would be hooked to provide enough amusement for all.

But behind the original aim of the 'herring-gulls', to chalk up as many male conquests as possible (or as they dubbed them – 'items'), there stood something else which subsequently would turn out to be more important. They were meeting a world as brilliant and attractive as it was foreign and distant, which cruelly emphasized the difference between the spectacular colourful life in the West (of course, seen from outside) and their own grey, miserable days. Their imaginations transmuted this difference into a painful feeling, made up of hunger, aspirations, ambition and sometimes a desire for action. This inferiority complex, born of the gulf between the two worlds, charged them with tremendous energy and the unquenchable desire to alter their world or exchange it for another. That is why eventually the sexual adventures of the 'herring-gulls' gave way to rather more long-term plans. Many began to look not for a girl for one evening, but for a steady girl-friend, a mistress, who would agree to something bigger – for instance, an invitation for a visit abroad or marriage (fictitious or real), or, at worst, a decent present from the special hard-currency 'Corecom' shops. How often have I seen these youths standing in front of Corecom's show windows gazing longingly at the shining goods. I remember how overjoyed an acquaintance of mine, a young carpenter, was when his Swedish girl-friend bought him Western swimming trunks. He jogged around the resort all day so that the whole world could see his brightly coloured trunks. Another acquaintance received an electric razor, which made him feel almost like the owner of a Rolls-Royce. Even the older 'herring-gulls' reaped similar successes. There was one Uncle Pesho, who at fifty-six enjoyed an enviable reputation amongst the visiting ladies of middle age. Once he appeared on the beach in a scarlet bathrobe, his head wrapped in a gorgeous turban which made him look not like the tinsmith he was but like an authentic maharajah. When I asked him why he set so much store by the present of a bathrobe, he replied:

'Because nobody in this country has a bathrobe like mine! Do you understand, little comrade? Some take pleasure in power, some in money, others in connections, while I take pleasure in a bathrobe. What's wrong with that?'

With the development of tourism, more and more foreigners visited the different resorts. The wealthier Western citizens came with magnificent cars, even with yachts. Some made a flamboyant show, others had no less extravagant intentions. People wanted to have a good time, to have their fling in a country which in those years still had the reputation of being untravelled territory. For many of them the local population might have been aborigines. Others immediately surrounded themselves with a circle of native friends and admirers in which one could pick out the calculating glances of a Bulgarian beauty.

At the same time as the 'herring-gulls', a huge number of girls from all over the country made for the coast to hunt for all kinds of Western lovers or husbands. The stories of a few successful marriages of such girls had become famous legends, and considerably increased the number of Bulgaria's daughters on the Black Sea coast. I know mothers from Sofia who sent their daughters on intensive courses for foreign languages and then, on some pretext, tried to find them a place in one of the sea resorts. I know quite decent and serious-minded girls who spent whole months every year hoping to be discovered by some

Prince Charming who would lift them onto his white steed and take them to his crystal palace. Funny or sad, but the holiday resort was like a window on the world, yet also a window of sighs. A lovely girl from Sofia found herself an Austrian lover (I think she married him later) and every day made him buy her another swimsuit so as to make her girl friends jealous. I know another absurd story which I wanted to make into a play. Four of my acquaintances, very attractive and intelligent Sofia girls, jointly hired a house in Nessebur, with the distant hope, naturally, of finding the foreigner of their dreams. Gradually, keeping things from each other, every one became involved in a mysterious love afair. The ghastly dénouement arrived when, in the course of a conversation, they discovered that they had all been meeting the same man, who presented himself as a Finn, spoke Russian, but in the end turned out to be an art student from Pleven [a northern Bulgarian town]. . . .

So, finally, here we are at the end of the avenue along which we have been walking. In the last restaurant, too, there is no room for us. We get angry because we are hungry and to console ourselves we make for one of the nearby bars. I know the barman, Dancho, from Varna. He is dark-skinned, about thirty years old, with a noble face and unfaithful eyes. He serves the drinks with the manner and assurance of a circus magician and presents them with assorted compliments to every client. He speaks the abbreviated waiter variation of seven or eight languages with total self-confidence, and artistically offers his speciality – 'cocktails à la Dancho'. Women find him very attractive and he is rather busy in his free time. Apart from serving in the bar, he does a number of other things which only regular clients know about. He is an informer to the secret police which, in turn, allows him to deal on the black market in currency transactions and to offer shy and lonely foreigners relations with a beautiful girl. Few would believe that the elegant, charming Dancho is a pander, a black-marketeer and an informer. Two years on, he will appear either to go too far with his profits or to make some other imprudent move, because the secret service will dispense with his services and he will find himself in prison with a heavy sentence.

While Dancho enthusiastically prepares his cocktail for my friends, I spot another familiar face on the other side of the bar. It is Lyubka from Burgas. She is here again this year, like last year and the year before. This is the Lyubka known to all local people, whose life is lived during the evenings and nights of the resort. She is perhaps the first swallow of the flights of girls avid for an easy life and adventure, which socialist reality produced in the 1960s. Lyubka is an intelligent girl; she speaks two or three languages, she could find work in some holiday resort office, but she does not want to, she prefers the uncertainties of new meetings and being caught by the dawn in night clubs. She has dark hair, blue-green eyes and a deep alto voice. Although no longer so very young, she is still attractive. The nicest thing about her is her smile. There is something very warm-hearted and kind in that gradual brightening of her face, in the way her smile travels from her lips to her eyes.

For me, she is an enigma. I have seen her many times on the beaches, sitting alone, gazing ahead, in a kind of trance. I have the feeling that she is fully conscious of what she is doing, as if she is punishing herself for something. Sometimes she finds herself in the company of extremely rough and uncouth males, Bulgarians or foreigners, and then one can sense the huge difference between her inner life and the existence she has chosen. Once I provoked her into a frank conversation:

'I don't want to justify myself', she said, 'because in this particular country nobody has a right to reproach me. Have you ever lived in a room where the ceiling is lower than you? And every time you want to stand up you hit your head? Well, I got bored with it, I'm fed up with hitting my head on that low ceiling and that's why I choose to be here in the open. It can rain on me, paving-stones can fall on my head, but the important thing is that there's no ceiling. ...' [...]

This particular evening in the bar, Lyubka is with a middle-aged Bulgarian with a thick neck and half-closed unfriendly eyes glazed by alcohol. He is one of the local bigwigs, either a factory manager or a head of department. There is no doubt that he is a middle-ranking Party boss who has escaped this evening from the cosy embrace of wife and children to look for secret pleasures on the coast. Clearly, Dancho has been the procurer. I imagine the man's armoury of petty dodges and mean stratagems born of lust and male vanity. Almost certainly he is on some state business, has visited a plant or a civil service department, and then has sneaked away to hurry here. His car, too, belongs to the state. And his bill at the bar will be part of his travel and daily expenses. For this Communist, a member of who knows how many bureaux and committees, Lyubka has no other value than that of a forbidden, sweet, mysterious fruit. He has one strong conviction: that this fruit is owed him like everything else he can lay his hands on. But he is not experienced at this game. He appears clumsy and ungainly because he follows the most banal strategy. Everything he is saying can be reduced to one question – 'Do you know who I am?' Lyubka doesn't know, nor does she want to know. She is not keen to differentiate between all these men, who follow each other with deadly monotony. She has often met this kind of provincial Party upstart, whose lustfulness mingles with an instinctive fear – that he will be seen, that someone might recognize him and tell his family. That is why he has taken her deep into the bar and sits with his back to the window; that is why he bends his head over the table and says half-jokingly: 'I have so many friends here that I cannot get rid of them'.

Together with the 'herring-gulls', the hunters of Western wives or mistresses, the members of the secret police and girls like Lyubka, such comrades are the next most important element on the Black Sea coast. Lyubka calls them 'mayflies'. For a day or two, they are the coura-geous heroes who have escaped from family bonds, the nuptial bed and the narrow circle of responsible comrades. They arrive with plenty of money compared with the impecunious 'herring-gulls', pay for expensive evenings and find ways of insinuating themselves into places of entertainment reserved for foreigners. Having had a few drinks they throw their weight about, let themselves go, play at being noble. And when they have drunk more, they soften up. The stentorian Party voice and the affected airs disappear, and long suppressed complexes escape from between the covers of the Party card. Then one can hear protracted sentimental confessions poisoned by the bitter conscious-ness of personal and general degradation. This is perhaps the only time when such citizens tell the truth about themselves.

Time is flying. Dancho invites us to dine at the fishermen's hut, which is nearby. We venture out into the night. As we are passing their table, I hear the podgy comrade embarking on the usual, half-drunken monologue. Lyubka listens to him, but probably does not hear. Her smiling eyes look somewhere far beyond him, out into the night, where at least there are no ceilings. . . .

NATIONALIST SERENADE
FOR VULKO CHERVENKOV

August 1964, Arkutino. By the Black Sea, at the mouth of the River
Ropotamo with its tropical water-lilies and trailing creepers, there
stands a newish hotel complex with a restaurant, a large parking area
and about three hundred bungalows and huts. The beach in front of
the hotel is of golden sand – perhaps the most beautiful stretch of sand
on the whole coast because it feels like velvet against the skin. And the
sea is crystalline and clean. Here by the river there is always a slight
breeze which makes even the hottest days bearable. The tourist industry is still in its infancy and the whole environment conveys a
feeling of unspoilt beauty and uncharted nature. The hotel is full of
tourist parties from West and East Germany, but there are also rooms
for Bulgarians. Meanwhile the bungalows, the huts and the tents are
occupied by us – a large group of people from Sofia who know each
other slightly and have come here for the second year running. These
are the holiday-makers who will create the legend of the enchantment
of Arkutino. But apart from the natural beauty of the resort, many
are attracted by the flamboyant manager of the hotel, the famous
'Uncle' Ivan. Despite his greying hair, he does not deserve this epithet;
his attitude to the girls alone lifts him right out of the category of
'uncles'. He is probably the ideal type of hotel manager and restaur-
ateur, who knows all the tricks to please his clients. He is a personal
friend to everyone, but in reality – no one's friend. Unlike most of his
colleagues up and down the coast, who are usually gloomy people
with square faces and predictable manners, Uncle Ivan is elegant,
smooth, the possessor of an arsenal of expressions which he can vary
constantly, according to the occasion – in three seconds he can switch
from being happy to see you to being stonily indifferent towards
someone he does not want to recognize; or from being toadyingly
submissive to people whose power he has assessed faultlessly to being

unscrupulously rude towards those who have no power. He constantly fosters the impression that he is the keeper of many secrets. But one of these secrets is known to everyone. For, after all, the militia does not give guns to just anybody. Moreover, Uncle Ivan has the unpleasant habit of questioning people about everything, affecting a kind of absurdly naive interest.

To quote my friend Goran, 'when somebody asks too many questions, alarm bells start ringing inside me!'

Uncle Ivan plays his cards recklessly in front of those whom he judges to be loyal to the regime, or simply more perceptive. He tells them candidly that he is a stool-pigeon and has been told to find out this or that. Whether sincerely or as part of the game, I don't know, but he tries to 'save' customers who have caused trouble from unpleasantness with the authorities.

'Listen, my boy!' he will say smilingly to someone who still smells strongly of alcohol. 'Last night you said a lot of silly things, and if I hadn't taken you away, I don't know where you would have found yourself today.... Look here – we all need to let off steam from time to time ... only it's important to know where! It can't be done everywhere!'

After this patronizing speech, the culprit is bought for life. Moreover, Uncle Ivan knows how to flatter us. He never fails to congratulate his customers on their successes, about which he makes it his business to be informed. And when there are no successes, he compliments them on their companions, whether men or women. You might have gone to Arkutino with the ugliest woman on earth, but on your next visit Uncle Ivan will greet you with the words: 'But where is that lovely creature? She was quite something! I ask myself, where do you find these godesses!' and he licks his lips like a tom-cat.

Anything that is done for you within Uncle Ivan's dominion is done 'especially for you', so that a person gradually gets used to the feeling that Uncle Ivan and the hotel exist exclusively for him.

He puts his nose into everything. He appears where you least expect him and at the most unlikely times; he confides his personal and official problems to you, he introduces you to countless people and, altogether, never rests for a minute. Sometimes I wonder when he sleeps. In this very rough and ready epoch of ours, Uncle Ivan is the angel of favours.

'Ask and Uncle Ivan will give it to you!' is his slogan.

This explains his great popularity amongst the Sofia intelligentsia. When he comes to the capital in wintertime, we give special 'dinners for Uncle Ivan'. People are not stupid. They know exactly what Uncle Ivan represents, but he is one of the few who knows how to flatter long frustrated ambitions, how to show respect (even if only outwardly) to people who have ceased to respect themselves. This is perhaps his most important gift.

Besides, Uncle Ivan's Arkutino offers a marvellous cuisine, perhaps the best along the coast, and a bar where one can drink and dance until dawn. Unlike the managers in the other hotels along the Black Sea, Uncle Ivan prefers Bulgarians and does not much like foreigners. As far as morals are concerned, he is a true democrat – it does not matter in the least to him whether you share your bedroom with your wife or your mistress. In the bar, they play the latest records and you can dance to your heart's content. The manager uses his imagination to plan constant entertainments – special evenings to celebrate the catch of some huge fish, or to honour Neptune, feasts for name days or birthdays, or for the arrival or departure of some special guest.

That is why we are at Arkutino. Heavy drinking and sleepless nights do not leave us much time for the beauties of nature. In fact, it is quite usual for the beach to be deserted until midday.

Most of the guests belong to what is described in Sofia as 'the scientific-technical intelligentsia'. The majority are engineers, architects, doctors or people with technical qualifications, and only a few are painters and writers. And it is precisely this scientific-technical intelligentsia which is responsible for the human and informal atmosphere. Here no one feels obliged to hold forth on books or pictures, or to pretend to be more intellectual than he really is. The talk is about food, drink and fun, for these are the pleasures with which people wish to fill that eagerly awaited holiday fortnight, a fortnight which must compensate them for the other eleven and a half months. Here, passions are released with dangerous speed; the sea, the weather and the alcohol are a heady mixture and each feels the urge to shed his old self. The silent ones suddenly become talkative, the shy ones suddenly become bold, the repressed overcome their inhibitions and discover freedom and blissful irresponsibility. All this is accompanied by music, shouts, songs, noise and constant movement.

There is one essential difference between the past lives of the members of the technical intelligentsia assembled in Arkutino and the artists holidaying in Sozopol. While writers, actors, painters, composers and musicians are people who have mostly enjoyed harmonious relations with the authorities, here in Arkutino almost everyone is burdened with a past in which, to use the Party expression, there is 'a big black spot'. But this black spot has been temporarily forgotten by the regime *only* because of the exceptional qualities of the engineer, the architect or the doctor in question. In the final analysis, these are the men who are shouldering the most responsible economic and technological jobs.

In the bungalow next to mine lives Vanyo, a doctor in chemical sciences and a university lecturer, one of Bulgaria's brightest hopes in chemistry. The prisons destroyed his father. His mother spent the best years of her life in one concentration camp or another.

Next to him is the tent of architect K, a remarkable planner, whose past record includes three years in gaol for a student conspiracy. Next to him lives his friend, engineer G, a 6ft 10 inch giant, who was expelled from the Polytechnic in Stalin's time and subsequently spent more than three years serving in a hard labour unit. Behind him is their inseparable companion D, sentenced to eight years in prison for having been a pupil of the American College [on the outskirts of Sofia] and having had relations with foreigners. In front of me are housed the University dean R and his girl-friend, whose family was exiled to the provinces for over ten years, and so on.

More than a dozen know all about the mosquitoes in Belene. Others harbour memories of their prison careers near Pazardzhik; still others can spend hours telling you about their experiences in the Central Prison in Sofia or about the misery of those exiled to the Omortag district, or about their police examiners. . . .

Now, in 1964, all this is over. As the Party says, it belongs to the period of the 'cult of personality' and it is best for the victims to forget it, though the Party remembers it all and can remind them of it when the occasion arises.

On this particular Sunday, we are holding a carnival. Uncle Ivan has dreamt up the traditional 'Arkutino Carnival'. While the East Germans lie huddled together on the beach, and the West Germans promenade pompously around them in the anticipation of some kind of East-West German dialogue, we are engaged in feverish activity. Rags, old T-shirts, paper and torn sheets serve to make up our fancy dress for the carnival: turbans, all sorts of female head-gear, cassocks, medieval armour and vestments, all kinds of masks and half-masks. However, as the material runs out, Zdravko Mavrodiev, who has just returned from Paris, decides to paint clothes onto our naked bodies. He produces his colours and soon we are transformed into Hindu fakirs or tatooed Red Indians. Many of the men wear women's clothes of all periods, while the women have turned themselves into an assortment of men. We also have an orchestra, which Ivan has conjured up especially. By the time that the carnival procession begins, in the late afternoon, an audience of many thousands has gathered around the hotel and applauds us enthusiastically. So as to encourage the carnival atmosphere, Uncle Ivan has already managed to sell each of us a big litre bottle of cognac. The procession ends with everyone dancing on the large dance-floor outside the restaurant. But this is only the beginning. As night falls, and particularly after the dinner which is liberally washed down with wine, feelings begin to rise. One of our architects makes a funny speech in which he tries to explain why we have chosen to dress up as this or that. 'In the end,' he says, 'each one disguises himself as he really is!'

While the restaurant resounds with our laughter, I notice that Uncle Ivan has slipped out on some urgent business. Five minutes later he returns, but his face has acquired a pompous solemnity, as if he has swallowed his revolver. He comes to our table and says in a funereal tone: 'Vulko Chervenkov† is here! He wants to stay the night! Where shall I put him?'

On such weighty matters of state, Uncle Ivan always solicits advice while looking searchingly into our eyes. My neighbour Goran makes a rude reply. But Uncle Ivan does not seem to mind and tries to convince us that we matter much more to him than Vulko Chervenkov, and that the latter's presence, though flattering to his vanity, is really tiresome.

'I have only one free room! The one over the bar! But how can a normal person sleep there, with all this noise?'

'But is he a normal person?' drawls D, who was sentenced under Chervenkov's dictatorship.

'Listen', Uncle Ivan says confidentially. 'You've got to help me! When you go to the bar later, please don't make a noise. Drink and dance quietly. You see, he may no longer be in power, but his friends are! Don't get me into trouble!'

We nod noncommittally while Uncle Ivan goes to minister to the needs of the former 'beloved leader and teacher' of the Bulgarian people.

However, two hours later, in the bar, something evolves which I have never seen either in real life or in the cinema, a kind of orgy or Bacchanalia. About a hundred masked and unmasked holiday-makers are crammed into the tiny bar; someone has brought his own record-player and plugs it into the loudspeaker. Then the penetrating voice of Bill Hailey gives the signal for the attack and the sounds of rock and roll engulf everything. Around me a forest of bodies, which gradually shed their garments, begins to sway irresistibly. I see frantically jumping legs and waving arms, faces in a trance and lips uttering savage cries. This is the most deafening barrage of sound I have experienced. Abundant sweat flows and everyone seems possessed by furious energy, determined to dance on until the end of the world. The rock and roll is followed by a Twist called 'the end of civilization'. Now I spot a well-known couple who have jumped onto a table which is slowly collapsing under the weight of their bodies. Towards midnight, when the drunken revelry reaches its zenith, I manage to slip out through the wide open door to breathe some fresh air. And then in the light cast by the bar I see a tall, exhausted-looking elderly man walking up and down, the skin of his double chin hanging loose like that of a turkey. He has clasped his hands behind his back and walks slowly but tensely, looking repeatedly towards the doors, perhaps in the hope of being noticed.

I turn round to my friends and, in the pause between two dances, I manage to shout: 'Look who's here! Chervenkov!'

Within seconds, the gaping doorway is filled with heads. Somebody switches off the music and a deadly silence ensues. At least twenty people are watching. Chervenkov understands that he is the focus of this unexpected attention and draws himself up facing the bar - a veritable monument to himself. The thought occurs to me that this is the first meeting between the former victims and their former inquisitor. There they are at the door - the people who have suffered sleepless nights under interrogation, beatings and tortures, their comrades murdered or broken, years of forced labour behind them; people whose early youth was poisoned by a terrible injustice. And there, facing them, stands Lucifer himself, who personally unleashed the black force of pain and suffering against them. I read nothing on their faces except the cool thought: 'Here he is! So that's him!'

Opposite, Chervenkov's face expresses indignation and ill-concealed fear. Although he has been demoted from all his former posts and expelled from the Party, he tries to suggest that he still has a certain power. Perhaps this is just a habit.

It occurs to me that in this electric silence, a bomb could explode, anything could happen. I see in the faces of my friends the shadow of confused intentions. The heads at the door continue to stare at the living monument of their black past, the silence drags on menacingly and just as I expect something terrible to happen, I hear a clear voice shouting an order: 'For Comrade Chervenkov, *Shumi Maritsa!*'*

Several voices immediately begin to intone the old national anthem....

'*Shumi Maritsa, okurvavena, plache vdovitsa lyuto ranenà....*'

At once all the others join in. About a hundred voices, strained to the limit, shatter the silence of the Arkutino night with the national anthem of *their* Bulgaria, which they sing in bitter honour of the man who once tried to obliterate it with blood. Never before have I known this anthem to sound so powerful and moving.

'March! March! Forward with our General!' resounds the cry from the bar, while anxious East German faces and knowing West German smiles appear at the windows of the hotel....

'Let's fly into battle to vanquish our enemy....'

The enemy can hold out no longer. He wheels round abruptly, like a soldier, hangs his head and disappears into the darkness.

A little later, the black limousine which had brought him drives away towards the high road....

I have just managed to get to sleep when loud knocking on the door of my room wakes me up. Uncle Ivan is there with two policemen in plain clothes. They ask me to come out.

'There you are!' says the oily voice of Uncle Ivan, 'comrade Markov will tell you; he was there.... Nothing at all happened. ... Someone may have been joking, but these are serious people – doctors, engineers, architects....' I have the strange feeling that he might have added: 'Generals, admirals.'

One of the men in civilian clothes apologizes for having woken me and asks if I have heard any singing of *Shumi Maritsa*.

'No!' I say. 'I was there all the time....'

'Only one person sang *Shumi Maritsa*', says Goran suddenly, emerging from the darkness.

'Who? Do you know him?' ask both men who have come all the way from Burgas in their jeep.

'Vulko Chervenkov!' replies Goran with the utmost conviction. 'He stood there in front of the bar and bawled out the whole anthem!'

---

*Shumi Maritsa is the title of the old proscribed national anthem of pre-Communist Bulgaria. It tells of the river Maritsa flowing with the blood of slain Bulgarian soldiers, mourned by their cruelly stricken widows, and exhorts their comrades to march on to victory behind their general.

Goran's audacity is so great that the others are at a loss as to how to react.

'Why don't you go to bed and sleep it off!' says Uncle Ivan, extremely cautiously.

Goran walks away. The others leave too. It is clear that they have no idea how to handle this one.

THE SAVING GRACE
OF LAUGHTER

Of all the attributes that one could admire in the character of one's countrymen, I am proudest of the Bulgarians' incredible sense of humour. How often have I marvelled at the natural way this feeling bubbles up, and remarked how closely it is linked to public judgements, the expression of political views and profound popular wisdom. I think that this sense of humour has something in common with the striking absence of blind fanaticism in the Bulgarian people. In our country, only the stupid are fanatics. However passionately and convincingly you may defend some true and attractive cause, you will notice in your interlocutors a slight smile, as if to say: 'Is it really all that important?'

This feeling for humour always goes hand in hand with self-irony and self-mockery, which is its greatest value. Everyone knows how to laugh at others, but it needs character to laugh at yourself. It is even more remarkable that in the darkest periods, in the most cruel and gloomy situations, a sense of humour not only did not desert our Bulgarians, but seemed to become the main safety-valve for pain and grief. Nowhere and never have I laughed more than in Bulgaria, where life so often plays simultaneously on the strings of tears and laughter.

I think the modern theatre of the absurd, particularly the plays of Ionesco, is but a natural continuation of the Bulgarian story about Gyuro from Trun, who went on a bear hunt and entered the beast's lair but had his head torn off by the bear. When his friends got him out, they began to wonder whether he had ever had a head before. So they carried him to the village to ask his wife. She thought and thought and finally she said: 'Well, I don't really know if Gyuro had a head or not. But I think that he must have had one, because last year he bought himself a cap!'

I shall not easily forget the visit of Enver Hoxha [the Albanian Party leader] to Bulgaria. People were herded along the Volyak-Pernik railway line to cheer him. When the train passed us, not far from Divotino village, various activist groups started chanting his name rhythmically. But Enver was holding on with both hands to the open window and did not even lift a hand in salute. Then I heard two local peasants talking to each other: 'Why didn't he even wave once?', asked one of them.

'Can't you see that he's afraid to let go of the window!', replied the other.

'But why should he be afraid?'

'Well, all his life he has been used to riding donkeys and holding on to the saddle! Where would he see a train in Albania?'

At the time of enforced collectivization when the peasants were herded into co-operative farms, secret police agents used taxis in which they held their victims prisoner until they signed the necessary documents. In the Pernik region I witnessed such a taxi, spewing out an elderly peasant whose face was stained with blood. But he picked himself up, laughed and said: 'All my life I have wanted to ride in a taxi and now, with God's help, I have had my fill of it!'

Nor can I forget uncle Vesso, the cabby of the sanatorium at Vladaya, who fetched me from the bus stop. It was a period when the bookshops were inundated by the most unreadable Party literature and almost no decent books were being published. Noticing that I carried a suitcase full of books, Uncle Vesso, who had once been a grave-digger, turned round and said to me:

'I like books very much. ...

'I used to read a lot when I worked in the cemetery. And what books! Give me *Pod Igoto** any time – but it must be by Ivan Vazov!'

This simple man did not want an adulterated *Pod Igoto* and he feared that his favourite book might have been rewritten. His remark 'but it must be by Ivan Vazov' summed up all the popular wisdom about the rubbish published by the Party.

Political jokes flourished like a national genre. During the last thirty years, I must have heard several thousand political anecdotes. Who does not remember what a figure of fun Dobri Terpeshev† became or the later stories about militiamen, Nikita Khrushchev and Todor

---

* *Pod Igoto* (*Under the Yoke*) is one of the best-loved Bulgarian historical novels by Ivan Vazov (1850-1921),† describing life in Bulgaria on the eve of the liberation from the Turks.

Zhivkov?† One of my colleagues in the Writers' Union attempted to write down all the stories he had heard. If this collection could only be published, I am sure that everyone would admire the incredible ingenuity and wit of the nameless inventors of these anecdotes. How marvellously rich in content is the story about Vute, which was particularly popular at that time. I cannot resist telling it. At a meeting, after the official report, the Party representative invites the audience to ask questions. All are silent as usual. He insists: 'Ask, comrades! Ask freely, comrades!' Silence. Finally Vute gets up and asks: 'What has become of our grain?' At the next meeting, the Party representative again urges the audience to express themselves. And again, they remain silent. He repeats his request. Finally, a peasant raises his hand and asks: 'What has become of Vute?' . . .

In the factory where I worked, there was hardly a day when one of the workers did not ask me conspiratorially: 'Have you heard the latest story?' The wave of anecdotes was the constant accompaniment of our working days. Some people became master-tellers with whom nobody could compete. But the telling of anecdotes and the listening to them was considered by everybody as a show of great civic courage, an expression of secret dignity. Of course, not a few people paid for this courage. I need only mention the fate of the well-known jazz violinist, Sasho Sladura ('the charmer'), who paid with his life to remain in the nation's memory as an unequalled raconteur.

In their essence, the jokes made fun either of the lack of morals in the Party leaders, or of their unbelievable obtuseness. Subsequently there came the wonderful series of jokes about the Armenian Radio Erevan, many of which were very witty. The following question is addressed to Radio Erevan: 'What is a labyrinth?' Answer: 'The straight path of the Party.' 'What is Soviet-Bulgarian friendship?' 'A cow which grazes in Bulgaria, but is milked in the Soviet Union.' 'Can Switzerland become a Communist country?' 'It can, but what a pity for a nice country!' I am not able to remember even a hundredth of the anecdotes I have heard, but I repeat that they mirror best the attitude of the masses towards the regime. For instance, there are many variations on the joke about the Party leader who travels in a plane with other statesmen and is regularly shown up as a nincompoop.

In the years before I left Bulgaria, the most popular jokes were about militiamen. All the stories had one common denominator – they underlined their narrow-mindedness and ignorance. Some of the stories were peculiarly Bulgarian variations on Irish jokes. And here I should pay tribute to the former Minister of the Interior, Diko Dikov, whom I have heard tell the best stories against his own militiamen.

Yet the jokes are only a small part of the vast riches of popular humour. The distortion of slogans, the parodying of declarations by prominent leaders or propaganda verse, made us laugh every day. During one September, I saw at Pazardzhik station a huge poster saying: 'Long live 10 September, day of the people's militia - the only support of the People's Government!' Another time, when I went to write a reportage from a village in north Bulgaria in connection with the Party's drive for the intensive breeding and raising of pigs on private plots, I saw that the village houses were plastered with large slogans which said: 'Every co-operator - a pig! Every Communist - two!'

Thus a comic ambiguity was imparted to the idea that the Communists should double the private production of ordinary co-operative farmers. In the factory where I worked, the most popular slogan was: 'Let's build socialism and Communism, so that afterwards we can live again like before 9 September.' When the Party wanted to fulfil the Five-Year Plan in four, somebody hung up the slogan 'With all our force - five for four!' Party and administration functionaries were universally despised because they did no useful work, but only walked about with attaché cases - so they were nick-named 'baggers'. Quite often the workers would say to us managers: 'It's easy for you baggers!' The agents of the secret police and their stool-pigeons had many popular nicknames, but the most widely accepted was 'hook'. One can still hear in Bulgaria today: 'What was I to do? I went to our "hook" and I appealed to him.' Or: 'How was I to know that he was a "hook", and what's more one of those that can't be unhooked?'

The workers and peasants were particularly sarcastic towards the pen wielders - journalists and writers. Immediately one said to an ordinary citizen that one was a journalist or a writer, there was the inevitable dividing wall. I do not exaggerate if I say that the reputation of my writing colleagues was that of professional liars. One of my workers never read newspapers until suddenly one day he took out a subscription for *Rabotnichesko Delo*. 'I've got the hang of it', he explained to me, 'whatever it says, take it to mean the opposite. When it says that in France the workers are starving, it means they are

THE SAVING GRACE OF LAUGHTER

enjoying life, and when it says that in Romania they are happy, it means that they are at the end of their tether! Quite simple!' I relish the following true episode which happened in Dragalevtsi. The eminent writer Georgi Karaslavov was among the first to build himself a large villa in Dragalevtsi. One day a journalist arrived in the village square and asked a group of peasants: 'Do you know where Karaslavov lives?' They shrugged their shoulders in silence.

'The writer Karaslavov, the one who writes books.'

'Now everyone writes', one of them answered.

'But he has a new villa ...', continued the journalist, when a peasant exclaimed: 'Ah! You must mean the one who built himself a palace!'

In everyday life the *double entendres* and the mocking insinuations never ceased. Words, newspaper headings, film and book titles were distorted, official pronouncements were parodied, important Party officials were imitated. I knew an ordinary worker with a remarkable gift for imitating Vulko Chervenkov, Todor Zhivkov and others. His imitations were amazingly accurate and we made him deliver whole speeches. Local folk epigrammatists spawned like mushrooms and had fun rhyming the name of our leaders.

There was something very healthy as well as profound in this folk humour. I think people used it as a means of self-preservation. The Communist Party and its members, the mass of whom seemed to have no sense of humour whatsoever, reacted sharply and intolerantly against this popular laughter. They knew, and know, that it was aimed at them, but they were too narrow-minded to be able to show generosity. Not a few folk humourists were arrested, beaten up, imprisoned for having told jokes. In the files of many Bulgarian citizens it is solemnly stated that they told or repeated anecdotes. The persecution of laughter was particularly virulent in Stalin's time. Shortly before his death, the notorious Stalinist ideologue Andrei Zhdanov (the old Pirotska Street in Sofia still bears his name) published an article on laughter, in which Soviet citizens were instructed when to laugh and at whom. This article, which was clearly written at Stalin's bidding, provided the occasion in Bulgaria for a veritable wave of punitive measures against laughter. Sometimes even mere smiles brought the representatives of the regime to the verge of hysteria. At the funeral of Georgi Damyanov [a Politburo member] in Sofia, I actually saw a militia commander try to arrest a girl student from the Academy of Art because she had had the effrontery to smile. A former secret service investigator once confessed to me when drunk: 'What I really couldn't stand was their smiles! When I saw them smiling, it was as if they were spitting in my face. Then I would jump up and shout: "How dare you laugh at me, you bastards!"'

After 1956 the Party's persecution of laughter became much milder. But, anyhow, who could stop a nation laughing!

THE ENDLESS PARADE

My friend Kolyo and I have retired to the Number Three Reading room of the National Library where we are scanning the pages of newspapers and magazines dating from the spring. We want to see what current problems have been preoccupying readers sending in letters and what has worried them most. We are fully aware that the letters published in the newspapers offer us only carefully selected and heavily edited material, but we hope that something unexpected and interesting might turn up all the same. In other words, we are looking for 'a slice of life' to flesh out an already completed plot for a film. The turning of thousands of pages proves to be a very quick and easy task. For on every page, cover, supplement, in every article, notice, sketch, review, comment, poem, short story, in all these editions, whether central or local, the same name crops up: Georgi Dimitrov.† This name is repeated more than ten times in one column, and often several times in the same sentence, together with a veritable deluge of a newly coined protean adjective: Dimitrov-like fatherland; Dimitrov-like justice; Dimitrov-like Party; Dimitrov-like loyalty; Dimitrov-like heroism; Dimitrov-like wisdom; Dimitrov-like dynamism; Dimitrov-like policy; Dimitrov-like approach; Dimitrov-like concern; Dimitrov-like youth; Dimitrov-like army; Dimitrov-like achievements; Dimitrov-like consciousness; Dimitrov-like duty; Dimitrov-like perception . . . as if in the whole world there could be nothing positive that was not 'Dimitrov-like'. Thousands of slogans proclaim: let us live in a Dimitrov-like way, study in a Dimitrov-like manner, struggle in a Dimitrov-like way, orientate ourselves in a Dimitrov-like manner, and so on, and so forth. And all this is accompanied by thousands of portraits, drawings and photographs, which, in various forms, bring to life the 'beloved leader and teacher of the Bulgarian people'.

'As if the whole of Bulgaria is drowned in a Dimitrov-like flood', says Kolyo.

The habitual pomposity of such propaganda has here reached the climax of a mighty crescendo. Eye-witnesses give their reminiscences of Dimitrov, philosophers and public relations men give long lectures about Dimitrov, six authors are engaged in writing novels about Dimitrov, the theatres offer several plays about the Leipzig trial, symphony orchestras play Dimitrov-like works at Dimitrov-like concerts and art galleries are swamped by the features of the leader in different forms. There are sports tournaments in his honour and every office or factory strives to celebrate his birthday. The co-operative farms and the machine tractor stations promise to produce so much wheat in honour of Dimitrov – as if otherwise they couldn't produce at all. The Journalists' Union, the Writers' Union and the Academy of Sciences hold national conferences to discuss bulky reports starting with the adjective 'Dimitrov-like'. Even the army hold Dimitrov-like manoeuvres and the Sofia trams run Dimitrov-like. And my friend Vassyo, who went back to his profession of grave-digger and had to dig a mass grave for women from an old people's home whom an influenza epidemic had suddenly despatched to the other world, said to me: 'I dug the grave in a Dimitrov-like way!'

An Italian who is studying Bulgarian language and literature and who also comes to the Number Three Reading room peers at our work and shakes his head in bewilderment: 'Every second word is "Dimitrov-like". Don't they use Dimitrov also as a verb?'

'No', says Kolyo, 'we use it as a word-bullet.'

'How do you mean?' the Italian blinks with puzzlement.

'Well, with it we kill the content of all other words', explains Kolyo.

'But doesn't it give you a headache?' asks the amazed Italian who seems to have mastered Bulgarian well.

'We are immunized', we reply. 'Every year, they vaccinate us with a similar word so that our digestive system remains unaffected!'

And we show him the newspapers of 1949, when we celebrated the seventieth birthday of the even greater father, leader and teacher of 'all progressive mankind', our beloved Joseph Stalin. The Italian's face gets longer and longer as we read him the first page of *Rabotnichesko Delo* and he says quite seriously: 'Impossible! This must be the house magazine of some madhouse! Don't you know that sometimes they allow the inmates to publish their own paper?'

We warn him to be careful what he says, because all these campaigns are conducted by more or less the same people who believe in their great public importance.

'And how often do you have such campaigns?' he asks.

'Non-stop!' we say and we show him how the whole of 1960 passed submerged under the even more terrible verbal flood caused by the celebration of the ninetieth anniversary of Lenin, which in turn was merely a preparation for the fantastic celebrations of his hundredth anniversary in 1970.

In the 1960 'Lenin year', the lips of all Bulgarian citizens seemed to be ordered to pronounce, converse, rejoice, suffer, exclaim with one single word - 'Lenin'. In the vocabulary of the year, this word became the synonym for bread, water, wine, vegetables, hamburgers, everything. All was 'Lenin'. And once more, the well trained army of journalists, writers, painters, composers, artists, circus clowns, radio and television announcers marched into battle firing millions of such Lenin-bullets, which had the same lethal effect as the Stalin or Dimitrov-bullets.

'But doesn't all this make these celebrations quite meaningless?' asks the Italian who patently remains Italian to the last.

Kolyo and I exchange a look pregnant with the silent question: 'How can we be sure that this Italian is what he seems?' Nevertheless, we reply:

'Not at all! On the contrary, in this way the celebrations acquire a special meaning. That is precisely why we cannot find the material we are looking for - for everything else has to stop so that the celebrations can be given their proper place. For instance, if there is some protest in Pazardzhik because of appalling supplies of vegetables, this protest is engulfed in the wave of publicity about the celebrations and remains unanswered. If some Bulgarian author has written a slightly controversial novel, priority will be given to works on a more "topical theme" because of the celebrations and his novel will have to wait until they have ended.'

'But do they end?' Decidedly the Italian is beginning to be tiresome.

'Very rarely. They just follow each other. It is all planned beforehand. The moment one lot of celebrations are over, the next lot start. It's like an unending Venetian carnival!' explains Kolyo.

'But the Venetian carnival is rather amusing!' the Italian remarks and leaves.

And we too go home, because it is quite senseless to look for real everyday life in newspapers and journals which have been thrown into the vortex of the prevailing celebration. Which one is it this time?

'Do you know, Kolyo', I say, 'I think that every campaign, every parade, celebration and anniversary has a precise task - to mask reality.'

Kolyo smiles and takes down from the shelf a long forgotten boys' novel, *The Headless Horseman* by Mayne Reid. In the opening pages, where the author describes the public feasts in ancient Spain, he writes more or less the following: 'The richer the fireworks and celebrations in a country, the more miserable is the condition of its people.'

And so the two of us were unable to find true-life material owing to the barrage of fireworks, rallies, celebrations and endless propaganda festivals.

After the most festive celebrations for the twentieth anniversary of 9 September 1944, the Party and Government decided that special attention should be paid to the twenty-fifth, because the expression 'quarter of a century of socialism' sounded very imposing to the ears of some comrades. Preparations began as early as 1966-7, gathered momentum in 1968 (when the campaign against Czechoslovakia was also unleashed) and reached their climax in the spring and summer of 1969. Almost the entire country was enlisted in all sorts of committees, drives, movements, initiatives, which began and ended with the number twenty-five. I personally took part in God knows how many ventures which were suddenly given priority over regular work. Cinemas, theatres, television, publishing houses, editorial offices, operas, symphony orchestras, amateur groups, and so on, were all harnessed to extol the glories of this 'quarter century'. In offices and factories, special competitions were 'in full swing'; in the world of the arts, national surveys were being 'conducted'; countless initiatives were 'deployed' from the shop-floor; the State and Party authorities 'framed' new measures; sports tournaments were being 'launched' ... and it seemed as if the Church was alone in not holding a thanksgiving service for this 'quarter century'. Tremendous energy and huge resources were thrown into these celebrations and it must be said that many people made a handsome profit.

I don't know of any festivals on a similar scale in any Western country. English, American, Italian or West German celebrations and anniversaries take place much more modestly and much less noisily. They are also comparatively rare. Even the celebrations for the two-hundredth anniversary of the independence of the United States was much less ambitious than any Bulgarian or Soviet parade.

'It's terrible that we live only for parades!' exclaimed an acquaintance of mine who had been 'entrusted' with the task of mobilizing the neighbourhood for a rally.

Going back to the time when the Communists first seized power, we cannot find one year without a big national campaign for some celebration or other. The anniversary of the Buzludzha congress,* the jubilee of the Communist Manifesto, the anniversaries of Dimiter Blagoev† and Karl Marx, plus those I have already mentioned, plus the anniversary of the October Revolution, plus the solemn annual parades and rallies for 9 September Day and May Day, plus two months each before every election for the National Assembly or a Party congress, plus many other Bulgarian and Soviet dates. These are only the national campaigns. If you add to them the local celebrations, you might conclude that life in Bulgaria is a constant festival.

Any elderly Bulgarian citizen will remember that such phenomena were unknown in Bulgaria before 9 September 1944. The military parade on St George's Day and the religious service for the feast of the Epiphany were far more modest affairs than the ostentatious celebrations for May Day, for instance. Somehow, it isn't in the character of Bulgarians to participate in such noisy public spectacles. An innate scepticism and wisdom have always kept the people at a decent distance from such alien outpourings of an even more alien fanaticism.

I well remember how surprised we were by the manner in which the first May Day under Communism was celebrated in 1945. This was a spectacle such as we had never seen before, lasting several hours, which grew even more imposing during the following years when the procession through Sofia's Ninth September Square became the centre of life. They started preparing us for May Day months ahead. How strange and un-Bulgarian it sounded: 'in honour of 1 May'. Everything had to happen in honour of 1 May. The city was buried in slogans, pledges, appeals. In all offices and factories, they organized (and still do) 1 May competitions and people went to bed at night and got up in the morning with the idea of 1 May. The radio broadcast 'reports' on the fulfilment and over-fulfilment of labour norms in honour of 1 May. Every citizen earning a living somewhere was enrolled in some sort of 1 May activity. A few days before the rally we were warned and sometimes even forced to sign an undertaking to come to the assembly point dressed in our best clothes, with bunches of flowers and appropriate slogans, at 7 a.m., because trams and buses were going to stop at 8 a.m. Later on the orders became more lenient. But in the beginning, whole networks of fanatical watchdogs and over-zealous activists tormented us with a multitude of demands.

---

* This congress, held in July 1891 at Mount Buzludzha, near Sofia, marked the foundation of the Bulgarian Social Democratic Party, in which the Communists were first organized.

Somehow or other, on the day itself we found ourselves at the appointed place and death alone could be a reason for absence. I still remember this interminable hanging about of the multitudes, waiting sometimes five to six hours for their turn to pass in front of the official rostrums. It was tiring, but when it rained it was awful. Leaving the line was considered a great offence and one had to give the most convincing explanations. There can be no question but that the main factor which had assembled so many people in the streets of Sofia was compulsion. Without compulsion, without the constant looming threat to their liberty and livelihood, I doubt whether the organizers would have been able to muster even one-tenth of the people. In the Polytechnic and at work, these threats were often delivered quite openly: 'Mind you come, or else!'

'You can choose to stay away from wherever you like but *not* from the rally!'

There was something very depressing and humiliating in this waiting about in the streets for hours on end. Later, the irony and contempt in the faces of many people at the time of the first rallies turned into lasting bitterness.

From time to time those in charge of us who wore arm-bands ran up and down, herding us together like cattle and making us advance a hundred paces towards the main square. Every section of Sofia had its own route, but in the square the columns usually passed with three districts abreast; otherwise the rally would have lasted two days.

Around midday or early afternoon, our turn would come at last. Suddenly we would surge forward and quick-march past the National Bank through a double line of militiamen until we found ourselves in the big square and merged with the moving masses. The most unfortunate amongst us carried either outsize portraits of the great leaders of the proletariat or huge slogans and banners. Over-zealous firms marched with large-scale models mounted on lorry platforms which illustrated labour feats or significant political events. Thus, for instance, on one platform women dressed in white demonstrated how chocolate was being produced in the Malchik chocolate factory, while the next float displayed Tito in a cage, followed in turn by the model of a locomotive, after which came a few scarecrows mounted on long poles. The faces of these scarecrows changed with the years – Nikola Petkov† was replaced by Traicho Kostov,† who was replaced by Tito or General Franco, or Adenauer or Eisenhower.... On other floats women were gathering roses or spinning or weaving, or partisans with sub-machine guns attacked an invisible enemy, or the dragon or crocodile of international reaction belched forth smoke. . . .

In my view, the most unbearable part of each demonstration was the relentless noise that poured forth from thousands of loudspeakers. One particular form of anti-music called 'Party song' or 'mass song' dominated, with powerful choruses bellowing meaningless words in a welter of senseless sound. But the climax came when the actors at the microphones of radio Sofia, their voices swollen with unbearably artificial pathos, declaimed 'poems' of pure doggerel. Even to this day I can hear these voices bawling pathetically: 'Oh Fatherland mine, oh red fatherland, your people rejoice today!' or 'Rejoice, oh people, for Dimitrov leads you!' Or the verse by Pantelei Matev: 'Rise up, you native expanses!'

When this poetic material ran out, because the Party poets had failed to meet their production targets, a stream of words would be substituted in which the most frequently employed and favourite verb was 'rejoice'. Everything rejoiced. The people rejoiced, the Party rejoiced, the trees rejoiced, the little birds rejoiced, the poets rejoiced. The Soviet Union rejoiced, the forests and the rivers rejoiced, the army rejoiced and *Rabotnichesko Delo* rejoiced on its first page.

And then would come the solemn moment when we, a mass of human bodies, passed the raised platform of the leader, who also rejoiced. . . .

The sublime moment of all rallies has arrived. Our column turns the corner by the National Bank but, owing to the bend itself, the ranks break up, with the left flank lagging far behind so that the huge slogan carried by Pesho and Nasko inclines dangerously backwards and hits the women on the head, spoiling the elaborate hair-style of the tall Vera.

'Silly clots!' cries Vera, who has spent three hours grooming her hair.

'Come on! Come on! Don't lag behind!' shouts our eternal watchdog Moncho, giving us a mighty push before he rushes to the rescue of the sloping slogan which proclaims: 'Let us live and work after the manner of Dimitrov!' We belong to the Fourth Blagoev District, but in parallel with us marches the First Lenin District – women workers from a printing works, whose slogan no less earnestly declares 'Let us live and work after the manner of Lenin!' It is one o'clock, the sun is baking hot and the blouses of the printing workers shine like snow. They look pleasant and attractive girls and the heads in our male column turn leftwards towards them rather than to the dais which is on the right. At this Kiro, marching proudly in front of our column, goes mad with rage. Red in the face with fury and sweating profusely from the heat, he turns round to face us and, while continuing to walk backwards, shouts: 'Don't gawp at the girls! Heads right! Do you hear what I'm saying?'

'And the whole of Bulgaria rejoices before your gaze/Free from any yoke and all disgrace ...!' booms the voice of my friend Dantcho Matev from the nearby loudspeaker.

'Right! Heads right, I said!' Saliva flies from Kiro's mouth. 'Moncho', he shouts, 'give a shove to those laggards!'

Moncho dashes back again to try to separate our contingent from the next one belonging to some leather factory. Their advance-guard and our rear-guard, where I find myself, have merged.

'Go back!' shouts Moncho. 'Don't queer our pitch, you sharks!' he yells venomously.

'Leave them in peace, it's all the same!' I say to Moncho while we all surge onwards.

'No way!' bellows Moncho against the loudspeakers. 'They're not going to pass under our percentages!'

What Moncho means is that we have fulfilled the State plan, but they have not and must not receive the congratulations which have been earned by us. And while he is engaged in warfare aimed at separating us from the leather factory workers, something unforeseen happens to our column. A hole has opened up in its very middle and our ranks are thrown into confusion.

> Just as the sun shines and the peaks glow,
> So you, our Party ...!

This time the voice over the loudspeaker clearly belongs to Miroslav Mindov.

'You good-for-nothings, are you at a rally or in the market-place!' Kiro can be heard shouting amidst the general confusion.

'Kiro, it's my shoe! It was new!' explains old Dikran and tries to push us all back. While we advance towards the dais, Dikran walks backwards forging a path for himself. Kiro runs after him and yells: 'Leave it, I tell you! You can march barefoot! You'll disgrace us all!'

It transpires that poor Dikran, who had borrowed a good pair of shoes from his brother, has now lost his brother's shoe.

'If it had been mine, I wouldn't look for it! But it belongs to my brother, don't you see, Kiro?' he counter-attacks, succeeding in putting more distance between them. Meanwhile we have reached the dais and Kiro cannot risk more delay. While Dikran at our rear disappears into the human waves which have engulfed his brother's shoe, Kiro's voice rises again: 'Agitgroup – your turn!' This propaganda group consists of a dozen boys and girls who have been practising various slogans for the last month.

'Eternal glory, oh working people!' recites a female voice, which I cannot identify, over the loudspeaker.

'Eternal glory!' screams Kiro.

'Eter-nal glo-ry! Eter-nal glo-ry! Eter-nal glo-ry! Hurrah!' – the high-pitched shouts of our chanting propaganda group are accompanied by the raising of arms waving bunches of flowers which are by now quite dead.

Now we are exactly opposite the dais, where about a dozen fat people are standing, statue-like. Some of them, probably tired out by the long rally, are leaning on the railings, some have crossed their arms, and one even scratches his head.

'A-head with B-K-P!* A-head with B-K-P!' chants our Agitgroup.

Meanwhile I hear behind us the powerful roar of the leatherworkers articulating their quite incredible slogan: '*More* and mo-re skins for the Pa-a-rty!'

The pretty typographers also have their Agitgroup, but it is not so vociferous and literally nothing they chant can be understood amidst the general fusillade of sounds. Discouraged, they take up Kiro's next slogan: 'Hail, belo-ved Party lea-ders!'

Our procession in front of the dais lasts no more than half a minute, but this is probably the moment of greatest ordeal for my ears. It is a kind of universal competition – among groups and individuals – as to who can shout loudest, plus the military band opposite which continuously blares 'Long live, long live, noble labour!' plus the salvoes fired by the loudspeakers, which once more spew out with newly manufactured unction:

> One country – one people
> Praise you, oh marvellous Party ...!

I wonder whether Dikran has found his shoe and try to guess if it is the left or the right one. I also imagine the scene his brother, a terrible miser, will make. And then it occurs to me suddenly that this whole

---

* BKP: Bulgarian Communist Party.

incident with the shoe is deliberate, that our carpenter probably took a bet that he would lose his shoe just in front of the dais, and I grin.

'That's the spirit!' shouts Kiro, who imperceptibly has found himself next to me. 'Smile like comrade Markov! Don't drag your feet as if you're at a funeral! Smile! Eyes to the right!'

I look to the right. The view between me and the dais is obscured by Vera's beehive. When she has passed, I see the soldiers of the National Army who have formed a thick cordon between the leaders on the dais and the rejoicing masses. I peer closely at the faces of the young recruits. Probably on orders they seem frozen into inanimate objects, each one concentrating on some invisible point in front of him, to all intents and purposes deaf and dumb.

'Long live the People's Army!' shout the girl typographers, but the recruits do not move even an eyelid.

But instead, high up on the platform, a tired hand begins to wave in response.

'Hurrah!' yell the leather-workers who have not fulfilled their plan and the typographers who have over-fulfilled it.

And so we pass. We turn to the right towards the Ministry of Defence, while the girl printers march triumphantly in their white blouses along Russian Boulevard towards Hotel Bulgaria. Some of our young men look wistfully after them and clearly would change column if it were not for Kiro's threatening voice: 'No diversions! The rally isn't over yet!'

'Kiro,' Nasko pleads with him, 'tell somebody else to take the slogan, my arms are quite stiff!'

'And let somebody else take Georgi Dimitrov!' scream the bearers of the huge portrait of the leader and teacher.

'What about us?' pipe up two workers who are carrying a giant portrait of Lenin.

'Just a little longer, comrades!' says Kiro encouragingly because he knows full well that nobody will volunteer for the task of carrying such weights.

In front of the National Theatre, we stop for a while, because streets in front of us are congested. Kiro does not hide his rapture.

'Did you see?' he says. 'Comrade ———— waved specially to us when he saw a hundred and ten per cent marked on our poster! Specially to us!'

'Perhaps they were waving to the girl printers too!' someone says. 'With those white blouses and so young...!'

'What are you trying to say?' Kiro rebukes him. 'The comrades on the dais haven't got girls on the brain! You might get besotted by white blouses; others look at these things from on high!'

'True!' agrees Moncho, of whom the workers used to say that he was certifiably stupid.

At my side, Marin and Christo are having a conversation of remarkable fatuity.

'I thought Comrade Ivan Mihailov† had aged a bit, and he also seems to have put on some weight!' says Christo.

'No, I don't agree, he was the same as last year and the year before that!' replies Marin.

'But this year he didn't seem quite at ease. The other times he smiled, but today he just stood looking at the sky!'

'Comrade Encho Staikov† wasn't in a good mood either!' Marin adds significantly.

'It must be terribly tiring standing for several hours on the dais!' Georgi joins in. 'I couldn't do it, not if I were paid in gold!'

'Well, probably they rest from time to time – there must be chairs at the back – perhaps even cups of coffee.'

'Never!' says Kiro categorically, having overheard the exchange. 'There are no chairs and no cups of coffee! These are our leaders! They stand there and will go on standing to the bitter end! Chairs and coffee have nothing to do with it!'

He walks on indignantly. It is only now that the bedraggled figure of Dikran appears from somewhere, but he is unable to make his way to us through the crowd. Everyone looks at him and shouts: 'The shoe! Did you find it?'

Dikran suddenly bends down and then lifts his arms above his head to show us both his shoes.

'Hurrah!' shout the members of the Agitgroup, but this time gaily and sincerely.

Our column moves towards the Post Office, where Kiro and Moncho tell us that we can go home. We disperse amongst the milling crowds. The rally continues, however, and the loudspeakers pursue us insistently from every tree. Miroslav, Spas, Dancho and a dozen other 'poets' tirelessly keep up their production of pathos, using the same clichés which we heard in previous years and will no doubt continue to hear in the future. As always, the rally will end with a parade of gymnasts followed by the inevitable groups performing various folk dances.

Then the loudspeakers will cease, and at last the most longed-for silence in the world will descend.

The tramcar for Knyazhevo starts from Macedonia Square, now renamed Dimiter Blagoev. But it is impossible to take a tram because huge crowds are filling the space by the stop. Somewhere there I spot my fellow-student and friend Sasho. He is a strange youth, always shut up in himself and lost in his books. We walk together towards the Russian Monument and from there into the long alley lined by poplars. Perhaps we shall manage to board the tram at the Krasno Selo stop. Around us the human stream is still flowing. Sasho seems to me rather nervous; his eyes are shiny.

'At the next rally, I shall burn myself,' he says to me. 'There on the square, exactly in front of the dais, I'll strike a match and set myself alight!'

'Nonsense!' I reply. 'Why do you take these things so seriously? What normal person can take them seriously?'

'But they humiliate me!' he cries. 'They humiliate me and they provoke me!'

And now there follows a tirade, which Sasho spits out like a madman: 'They make you line up and take your place in the herd, then pass in front of the high dais, turn towards it, doff your hat, smile ingratiatingly and bellow some nonsense! Addressed to whom? To people who are in no way superior to me except in the power which they hold!'

'That is quite something,' I say.

'And you have to bow to them, as you don't even bow to your mother and father! Where's my dignity? I think of myself as a human being with equal rights and of equal worth, not as some kind of ape! That's what's driven me mad, that moment of humiliation! Because they deny my human essence, they deny my personality, my character, everything I really am! Every year, twice a year!'

'Well, can't you get used to it?' I say, without any sympathy.

'No!' he says. 'And I'll never get used to it!'

'Then, set fire to yourself!' I say to him. 'I shall give you the matches next time!'

He will not set himself alight, nor will any of those I know. After all, it is much easier to suffer humiliation than to incinerate yourself.

This is May Day. In only four months, on 9 September, there would be the same kind of rally, with the same people, the same music, the same gestures, the same slogans, the same everything. The preparations for 9 September would start in a week or two, with hardly a break. Everywhere the May Day competitions, initiatives, actions, measures and general upsurge would be replaced with 9 September equivalents, and that is how it would go on. Celebration after cele, bration, parade after parade. Twenth-fifth anniversary, thirtieth anniversary of 9 September, fiftieth anniversary, sixtieth anniversary of the October Revolution, Marx, Georgi Dimitrov, all round figure anniversaries, thirteen centuries of Bulgarian statehood, a century since the liberation ... all these would be pretexts for saturating the atmosphere in Bulgaria with the same unctuous cacophony, the only aim of which seemed to be to prevent people from thinking for themselves, to deny them a tranquil and quiet environment in which man can feel human and concentrate on his proper destiny.

The painful themes in life, the awkward questions of fairness, freedom, independence, dignity, the daily heartaches and protests, the thousand examples of 'small-scale justice', and the calm and harmony within each human being – are drowned and carried away by the muddy waters of the endless parades.

EASTER OUTSIDE
ALEXANDER NEVSKI

It is the Saturday evening before Easter Day. Friends drop in and
suggest that we should go to Alexander Nevsky Square [in Sofia] to
see if anything will happen. Not one of us looks like a believer and we
are motivated merely by curiosity, along with, perhaps, a secret desire
to irritate the authorities.

'I bet there'll be a lot of people there this year!' says Tsvetan,
adding: 'Their silly blunder last year is bound to bring five times as
many!'

We all know about the incident that occurred inside the Alexander
Nevski Cathedral during last year's Easter service. The initiative was
taken by a newly promoted Party or militia chief who had been
alarmed at the rising number of young people attending church.
According to other rumours, though, the idea of the attack on the
Easter service had come from the Soviet Embassy, from whose windows the mass gathering of believers looked like an open anti-Soviet
demonstration. Under the auspices of the security service a shock
detachment of Komsomol activists, mainly students, had been formed
and instructed in hooligan behaviour. On entering the cathedral,
shouting, laughing, jeering, pushing and offending members of the
congregation, they had aimed at disrupting the service itself. The
climax of their outrage had been to pelt the officiating priests with
eggs and other missiles so as to provoke the churchgoers. In any event,
their objective was achieved. The Patriarch had to call in the militia,
who were already deployed in readiness in the adjoining streets.
Needless to say, the militiamen seized this opportunity and rushed in,
arresting numerous people and bundling them into police vans. An
hour later the Komsomol hooligans went peacefully home, while
completely innocent young people were subjected to strong pressure
to ensure that they would not dare attend another Easter service.

This gross provocation, organized by the regime against the Church, had consequences which unequivocally showed how carefully these events had been staged. Subsequently the authorities announced that the Church needed their protection and that at important church services, such as the Easter one, believers would be admitted only if they possessed permits issued exclusively to adults and *bona fide* Christians. No permits at all were to be issued to young people, as if the Christian religion was the exclusive preserve of the over-seventies. It was strange indeed to hear that the militia had classified the attackers at the Easter service as politically indeterminate 'hooligan youths', when they were its own *agents-provocateurs*. Later students at Sofia University confessed to me in confidence that they had been carefully trained to participate in the action at Alexander Nevski Square.

There can be no doubt that this action boomeranged, and later it was admitted in Party circles that it had been an example of the militia's consummate stupidity. The very next day people started to flock *en masse* to all the churches in Sofia. The rumour of what had happened in the Cathedral roused general indignation and even awoke long extinguished religious feelings. From the point of view of religion, it seems to me that there could have been no more effective way of directing people's attention back to the Church. Until this provocation, the overwhelming majority of Bulgarian citizens looked on the Christian religion more as an ingrained tradition than as a source of faith. Too many terrible and cruel things had befallen them for their faith not to have been shaken. I think too that religious fanaticism, or fanaticism in general, has never been part of the Bulgarian character. The Church's struggles in Bulgaria's past can be seen not so much as the aspiration towards closer communion with God but as an expression of the national struggle for independence.

I believe that the same holds true of Bulgaria a century later. More and more people began to go to church, not so much to express their Christian faith as to demonstrate their desire to show themselves independent of the regime's atheist dogmas. But, once within a church, people suddenly discovered the mystical attraction of a world which offered refuge from the ugly noise of everyday life. The atmosphere of the churches, with their semi-darkness, the flickering light of the candles and the noble worn faces of the saints, the mellifluous choirs and the chanting of the priest, invited meekness and introspection. People discovered that the simian shrieks of life outside had robbed them of that quiet beauty of contemplation which enables man to seek the truth about himself and his life. I remember how impressed an eminent Communist comrade (a woman) was when one day out of curiosity we entered a church together while a service was in progress. The priest was reading from the Gospel of St Matthew, Chapter 18:

'Then came Peter to him, and said, Lord, how oft shall my brother sin against me, and I forgive him? Till seven times? Jesus saith unto him, I say not unto thee, Until seven times: but, Until seventy times seven.'

These words affected my companion profoundly. She came out of the church in a state of great excitement and kept repeating: 'And why is it that I cannot forgive even once?'

Later on, this comrade became a regular visitor to the church, which her family put down to an intellectual whim.

Thus, examined in more depth, the provocation on Easter Day was not without its reasons. After the merciless Stalinist winter, when the whole of Bulgaria had become a silent graveyard, interest in the Church had begun to revive. By the beginning of the 1960s more and more young people started going to church. My grandmother and her contemporaries in the neighbourhood complained one Sunday that, because of the young people, they had not been able to find comfortable seats in church, but that was their way of expressing satisfaction that the young were becoming churchgoers. I personally know of several cases of convinced Communists who quite unexpectedly turned towards religion, as if they were hoping to find a vital answer there. One night, when I was strolling along Lenin Boulevard with one such comrade, he suddenly asked me what exactly Pascal had meant when he wrote that without God, man is utterly alone. If this citizen had invited me to take part in a conspiracy to topple the regime I would have been less surprised. I was even more amazed when he went on to speak at great length about the link between God and the meaning of life.

It stands to reason that if a convinced and well-read Marxist could turn his attention towards the Church, then the attitude of the mass of people not handicapped by ideological dogmas would be easy to predict. More and more people began to look to the Church at the most solemn and important moments in their lives – baptisms, marriages, funerals. Perhaps this coincided with the officially sanctioned Party line on fostering national consciousness – a line whose aim, of course, was quite the reverse. It even became the fashion to go to church and to seek the ministrations of the clergy. One of the proofs of this process was the developing cult for ikons, not merely as a material asset, but also as an expression of fatalistic religious feeling. During a whole decade the Sofia intelligentsia plundered and bought up the ikons of every little local church or chapel. There are few intellectuals in our capital today whose homes are not adorned by expensive or rare ikons. Recordings of Russian or Bulgarian liturgies and church songs were in greater demand than the latest records of pop music. Subsequently the church music of the Alexander Nevski choir and especially the performances of the old Slavonic chants by the Ivan Kukuzel* choir were in vogue throughout the country. We used to gather at special evenings to listen to church music; and I have known my comrades, moved by the sound of the Slavonic liturgy, to whisper: 'This is Bulgaria! The real Bulgaria! The eternal one!'

And this was the spirit and the atmosphere that were to be disrupted by the Easter provocation of the well-trained Komsomol hooligans.

It is eleven o'clock when we park our cars on Aksakov Street and the whole group moves along Shishman Street to the square in front of the monument of Tsar Alexander II, the Liberator. The late evening is very pleasant, warm, almost like summer. The crowds are milling all around us and moving in the direction of the Cathedral, their mood clearly a happy and festive one. But no sooner have we approached the square in front of the National Assembly than we see a militia cordon which bars the route to the Cathedral, letting through only very few people who wave white passes. We understand that the Easter service can be attended by invitation only.

'What on earth are these invitations for? How can one go to church by invitation?' grumbles an angry woman standing nearby.

The militia lieutenant in charge of the cordon smiles and says: 'The Patriarch is obviously afraid of the believers!'

In the large crowd that gathers in front of the cordon I recognize two well-known Bulgarian film directors with their wives, a few journalists and some theatre producers including Willy Tsankov, whose familiar French beret stands out. The great majority of the people around us are young – between twenty and thirty years old. More than half, perhaps, are women. With the swelling of the crowd near the cordon the noise rises in a crescendo. Another high-ranking militia chief, a lieutenant-colonel or a colonel, passes by and says in a loud voice: 'Citizens, why don't you go home? The religious festival is not for young people! Those who should attend have been invited!'

'We want to watch!', someone shouts.

---

* Ivan Kukuzel, nicknamed *Angeloglassny* (the angel-voiced), a fourteenth-century monk who was the greatest Bulgarian medieval musician.

'Do you believe in God?' asks the officer and supplies the answer himself: 'You don't. So what have you come for? Just to add to the traffic jam. Citizens, let us leave religion to the religious!'

'I am religious, comrade!' shouts an elderly man from the middle of the pushing crowd.

'Where's your invitation then?' demands the officer.

'I have no invitation. I didn't know that one needed invitations ...', and the old man painfully makes his way towards the militia chief. He must be about eighty years old and he walks with great difficulty. Everyone around him suddenly falls silent.

'Please, let me through!' says the old man, looking imploringly round, as if it was up to us to let him pass.

And now the crowd intervenes. From all sides can be heard voices saying: 'Why don't you let him pass, comrade chief! Look how weak he is! Let him go!'

The militia chief hesitates, but at the same time seems to consider the possibility of bargaining with the whole crowd: 'All right! I'll let him through, but on one condition – that you withdraw behind the monument. If you want to stand around, stand on the pavement! Agreed?'

'Agreed, of course, comrade!' someone shouts. 'Just let the old man go to church!'

Willingly and with lifted spirits several hundred of us retreat, while the militia commander admits the old man, who limps away in the direction of Alexander Nevski. Although there is no hope whatsoever that we shall be able to get there, nobody goes home. People remain standing and their numbers seem to swell all the time. Somebody suggests that we should cross over to the other side, by the Academy of Arts, and that we should use the Academy's door to gain access to the basketball field which is situated exactly opposite the church. Alas, this plan too falls through because the militia has cunningly blocked the door of the Academy. And, while we are shifting aimlessly, together with another huge crowd, between the buildings of the Polytechnic and the Academy, real pandemonium breaks out. The militiamen standing in front of us suddenly surge to the right in the direction of the area outside the gardens facing the university office. In the distance I can see a skirmish going on. And then – I can hardly believe what I see! More than twenty militiamen run panic-stricken across the square pursued by a group of enraged boys, one of whom is wielding a piece of wood. We hear the piercing sound of militia whistles. Behind the church, from Eleventh August Street, a whole militia company bursts out and tries to bar the way of its fleeing comrades. Then a few big militia vans roar to a halt. At the other end of the church something is happening which I am unable to see. It transpires that about a dozen young men were involved in an argument with the cordon, and when a militiaman tried to arrest one of them the others surged forward and a fight started. In the ensuing tumult the boys showered blows on the militiamen, who appeared to be either cowards or inexperienced in such boxing matches. Later, a friend told me how the whole surrounding crowd roared its approval when it saw the militia's caps flying into the air. After that, the numerically superior militia forces had been routed, and this is what I and all others around me had witnessed. I shall never be able to forget this scene of the frightened policemen in panic-stricken flight.

Yells, screams and shouts suddenly pierce the air round the Cathedral. One of my friends tugs his wife by the arm and says anxiously: 'Let's run. Something big is about to happen!'

But nothing happens. The numerous militiamen who invade the square quickly bring the incident to an end. We see how they drag the poor youths, kicking and hitting them, and load them into trucks. Then they drive them away, God knows where. But, as a result of the whole commotion, the cordons encircling the square have vanished and from all sides the crowds rush towards the Cathedral. Everything all around gets completely blocked and no militia force has a hope of reversing this movement.

'The poor boys!', say people around me. 'Not much of a Resurrection festival for them!'

When the bells start ringing, I manage to climb on a bench and I see around me an ocean of people. And now something quite incredible happens! Thousands produce candles from nowhere and start lighting them. Somebody pushes a candle into my hands. In a second I see a miraculous sea of candles which illuminate the human faces from below, giving them an extraordinary appearance. Everywhere people embrace, around me they engage in the age-old custom of knocking painted hard-boiled eggs together, and from all sides one hears the never-ending: 'Christ is risen!' and the answer: 'Christ is risen indeed!'

Perhaps because of the earlier trouble, which has shaken us all, perhaps because of the measured, solemn tolling of the bells, the whole atmosphere seems to me infinitely heightened, stormy and yet triumphant. As if at this moment the crowd is ready for a new and much bigger explosion.

But no one provokes it. The militia has quietly withdrawn and we let ourselves drift slowly towards Rakovski Street. On the benches facing the monument of Ivan Vasov† I see the two writers Yordan Radichkov† and Diko Fuchedjiev with their wives. Diko tries jokingly to extinguish my candle and mutters that they have merely come as onlookers and have been surprised to find so many friends and acquaintances in the Cathedral square.

'I wonder what they have come for?', he says.

'Well, just to look!' I say.

Then someone mentions that between ten and midnight, purely out of interest, he had driven round a dozen churches in the district and everywhere they had been filled to capacity by local people.

'I have the feeling', Tsvetan says, 'that people look to the churches for what they cannot find outside them!'

III

On 9 September 1944 life for Markov and for every other Bulgarian citizen changed drastically with the advent of Communism. (See Historical Note on p. 247)

A BIOGRAPHY OF
THE REGIME

Few would doubt that the life of every Bulgarian citizen depends completely on the power of the regime ruling the country. This is as true of the right to live as of the way of life. Precisely as George Orwell described in his novel *Nineteen Eighty-Four*, the thoughts and acts of everyone in our country are constantly watched and controlled by the regime and its organs. In its unlimited power, this control exceeds all dictatorships known to history. Moreover, the career of each of my countrymen, quite apart from their abilities and shortcomings, is determined by the regime's attitude towards them. Our regime, a perfect copy of the Soviet system, has deprived society, social groups and individuals of the right to have a decisive say, a personal criterion for right or wrong, or their own model of behaviour. Instead they are ruled by the regime's criterion, which is determined by the political needs of the day and follows a limited but rather flexible doctrine.

It is, therefore, quite natural for everyone to want to know who is behind this power, who represents it and identifies himself with it. Who are the people who control the workings of the social apparatus, give the orders and enforce them? Whom can history hold responsible? The first, strictly official, answer is that the power belongs to the Bulgarian Communist Party and its subdivisions. This is a fact. Personally I consider the rump of the Agrarian Union* and its leaders to be no more than a flower shop which helps to decorate the Party mansion for ceremonial occasions; the real source of power in Bulgaria is its Communist party, which rules the country on behalf of the Soviet Union. Thus the power at the disposal of our comrade leaders has been delegated to them by a foreign state, a world power – the USSR.

---

*The largest of the former political parties, which were subsumed in the Communist-dominated Fatherland Front.

I want to make myself absolutely clear: I reject utterly the assertion of any disagreement with the Soviet Union. Such a claim diminishes up to a point the direct responsibility of those who rule our country and who, without a doubt, meekly carry out the orders they receive. I stress these basic and self-evident truths because they explain the great inner conflict of the Bulgarian Communist Party, which has shaped the careers of all living or dead Party figures. In this context I fully agree with the Party claim: that the determining factor in the life of every Bulgarian Communist is his loyalty to the Soviet Union.

But what did these people who ruled us represent? Where did they come from, how did they rise, what were their personal lives, their interests, their characters? Even in the 1950s I was very curious about our top leaders. For me, as for all other Bulgarians then, the enigmatic Politburo lived on a distant inaccessible Olympus and we were allowed to see the gods and make our obeisance to them twice yearly – on the 1 May and 9 September celebrations. How often did I peer at their portraits, in which their faces, as if intentionally, looked all the same, and ask myself: what were they? One could not divine anything from their speeches, because they all seemed to be written by the same man and delivered as if by one voice. This was the period of the almost mythological status of the Politburo. Slightly less baffling were the figures of some of the ministers, district secretaries and more junior army officers. Thus we saw the regime's face mainly through our direct superiors, most of whom were Party members. Through them and their behaviour we had to build up a picture of the regime's leading figures *in absentia*. Usually they were people whose life was ruled by a basic and simple principle – to hold on to their positions and, if possible, to rise higher. Normally, in the application of that principle, no scruples were observed. They all seemed to follow exactly the same pattern in their choice of means for their advancement. And yet, in the performance of the standardized Party career song, one could detect different voices and sometimes strident dissonances.

Subsequently, in Khrushchev's time, the vast icy expanse between the peak and the lowlands was much reduced. Especially in Bulgaria, the Politburo members, headed by the Party's First Secretary, began to widen their circle of acquaintance and to surround themselves with other rather different people. That was also the period when my literary career enabled me to meet, see and observe at close quarters many of the main performers on our socio-political stage. My observations were helped by the fact that almost all former and present Party figures suddenly seemed to feel the urge to talk and write about themselves. It was as if each of them, inexplicably, needed to justify himself, while the lesser characters blatantly laid claim to heroic immortality. For the last fifteen years or so our country has been flooded by a whole literature of memoirs devoted mainly to the pre-War period. All sorts of noble deeds are narrated at length and in great detail in hundreds of books; as if by mutual agreement, various authors have been busily pouring concrete into the rickety frameworks of their political biographies. I have very good grounds for disbelieving the major part of this essentially boastful literature. Indeed I do not attach great credence to many of these heroic legends, for according to them there was nothing in Bulgaria prior to the War save Communist heroes and Fascist policemen. These memoirs and their 'artistic' imitations fabricated by professional writers should be seen as part of the deliberate rewriting of our recent history, a conscious distortion of characters and events. The history of the Bulgarian Communist Party itself is a collection of brazen lies and of suppressed or fudged truths.

But to return to my question: 'Who were the people who ruled us?' I was able to give a full and convincing answer only in 1968. Then my own impressions of many leaders were either confirmed or contradicted by documentary evidence about the reality I had not known personally. Rummaging through the archives, I perceived that, by the time of the so-called 'anti-Fascist resistance', four different groups of Party figures had emerged, which later – indeed, to this day – would play an important role in our people's life. Forgive me if I digress, but I wish to uncover the roots of many of the things which happened in Bulgaria in the 1950s and 1960s and thereby help to reveal the real face of the regime.

In 1968, the Party launched a big campaign in Bulgaria in preparation for the solemn celebration of the twenty-fifth anniversary of 9 September, which fell in 1969. On an initiative from the top, the Committee for Art and Culture decided to entrust three playwrights with the task of writing a play in three acts about the history and struggles of the Bulgarian Communist Party from its foundation until 9 September 1944. I was one of the three authors and the period assigned to me was the so-called anti-Fascist period, that is, the time of the War. Subsequently, my two colleagues Nikolai Khaitov† and Nikola Russev declared that they could not meet the deadlines and withdrew from the commission, so that I remained the only author of the documentary play *Communists*, which dealt solely with the War period. I don't know whose idea it was that the approach should be 'strictly documentary'. As far as I can remember, one of our leaders had seen Peter Weiss's play *The Representative* – hence the insistence on a documentary play. And so I received special permission to look through two hundred police files, carefully stored in the archives of the Ministry of the Interior. These were the personal dossiers and court records of almost all the well-known Communist heroes of the resistance, who had perished, been shot or hanged. In the course of nearly six months, I used to go every two days to the building of the Ministry of the Interior on the corner of 6 September and Gurko Streets, where a clerk would lead me to a little room in the basement. There the archives were brought to me, while another official remained all the time at my side to watch me reading. I gathered that this precaution had been taken because of the sudden disappearance of important pages from the archives. Once one of the employees told me with undisguised irony that on 9 September 1944 a few Party comrades with considerable foresight had made straight for the Police Directorate to look for their dossiers. He presumed that important information had been destroyed. Many others were reputed to have been searching frantically for Nikola Geshev, the man known to have held the whole illegal Communist Party organization in his hand, whose name cropped up regularly in the archives I consulted. This is how I came to visualize the character of this exceptional policeman, the head of Section A at the Police Directorate, whom I made the hero of my play and whose role at the dress rehearsal (the only performance) was played by the distinguished actor Ivan Kondov. The television version was also written by me and in it this character was acted by Georgi Cherkelov. Nikola Geshev had shown a remarkable ingenuity in unravelling the Communist organizations and conspiracies, and I thought that his network of agents had worked most efficiently. The information contained in the records of investigations personally conducted by him without doubt reflected the truth. In conjunction with my work on the archives, I met and talked to people who had been investigated by Geshev or had had other dealings with him.

You can imagine my feelings as I turned the pages of judicial proceedings and police interrogations: thousands of pages of evidence including the names of many still living acquaintances whose paths had crossed those of executed Communists. I looked up the records of well-known Communist heroes like Yordanka Chankova, Liliana Dimitrova, Malchika, Yordan Lyutibrodski, from the whole group of Central Committee members put on trial during the War headed by Anton Ivanov† and including Traicho Kostov† (the pages relating to him were missing) and the poet Nikola Vaptsarov,† down to little known names of rank-and-file Communists and their followers. I handled statements and notes made by special agents under a pseudonym or a number, reports by ordinary policemen or their chiefs in which certain facts were established with chilling precision. Some of the dossiers enabled me to follow the whole process of breaking down a prisoner or a witness. From the handwriting in which the testimony was written, it was possible to deduce the inexorable reality.

But my first and most immediate impression was of the immense difference between the content of these documents and the picture offered to us by the official literature of memoirs as a whole. The difference principally concerned the character of these heroes and the nature of their participation in the struggle. Following the Party prescriptions for facile pathos and high-flown heroics, our writers of memoirs consciously omit the human behaviour and the human face of the heroes they describe. A reality which is eloquent and powerful in itself is replaced by painfully sentimental and unsophisticated bombast. The inner drama of these people facing death, the tragic division between the demands of life and the demands of the Party, the acute conflict between real experience and Party fanaticism - all this is translated into sugary epic folk legends. The simple substance of real life is replaced by dutiful slogans.

The wealth of the documentary material at my disposal revealed to me the tragic, doomed characters of this harsh Bulgarian drama, figures who quite naturally seemed to fall into four national categories: Communists who were idealists; Communists who were Soviet agents; Communists who were opportunists; and chance Communists. In fact it was quite usual for Communists to change categories or to hesitate painfully between them - which had fatal consequences for the idealists. [...]

The wartime archives had truthfully preserved the characters of these Communist heroes, with all their human frailties as well as their greatness, who carried within themselves the seeds of Bulgaria's future Communist tragedy. With my own hands I turned pages sated with physical pain, testimonies exuding the premonition of early death, records resounding with the merciless voices of examiners and public prosecutors and, finally, those heart-rending last letters and notes written minutes before the execution by the trembling hands of the condemned. Most of these notes, letters and last messages made an indelible impression on me with – I stress – their human tragedy. These people were ordinary beings who had endured their trials in a very human way – bearing no resemblance to the portraits of Party fanatics which the ideological industry was to draw a few years later. I don't know how many descriptions I have read of the heroic death of Malchika and the slogans he is said to have shouted. In fact, when I came upon the rather pedantic report of the police officer who was present at his execution, I was overwhelmed by the simple human truth. To the prosecutor's question as to whether he has a last wish, Malchika replies: 'A glass of water please!' They give him a glass of water. Then the prosecutor asks him again: 'Is that your final wish?' Malchika replies: 'Another glass of water, please!' They give him the second glass of water. Then they shoot him. There is no 'Long live the Red Army'; nothing of the kind. Or let us take the answer which Nikola Markov, a secondary-school boy sentenced to death for the murder of a policeman, gives the prosecutor when asked why he became a Communist. Markov replies: 'I was very lonely ... and because of my loneliness I became a Communist.' The most moving thing was that almost all those who were executed had reserved their last words for their mothers, and not for their Party. 'Dear Mother', 'Dear Parents', 'My dears' ... and always there followed some excuse. Many apologized to their parents for not being able to live out the life they had been given, for causing them grief and pain, for dying. ... I shall never forget the short message of the student, Boyan Chonos, who wrote: 'Dear Mother, soon I shall be hanged.... I am cold Mother, very cold. ...'

And there is something even more significant: despite their bitter regret at parting with life, many declare that they are doing this for the sake of another world. In scores of letters, declarations and notes they painted the world for which they thought they were dying. Almost all of those who can be described as idealists were dying for a world of 'real freedom, genuine brotherhood, uncompromising justice, the abolition of all organs and institutions of oppression, the destruction of frontiers, the right to work and a decent life....' In short: they were dying for all the things which would not exist in the country that was to build their monuments.

These were people, the majority of whom had no conception of Marxist-Leninism, who had no notion of what the Soviet Union really represented: like children, they had believed in some abstract Communist ideal. They did not know exactly how it would be under Communism, but they believed and insisted that it would be a decent, noble, human world. Many of them were dreamers who, in the desolation of their lives, had embraced the Communist idea as their banner which pointed in the direction of happiness and beauty. More than 90 per cent of them were older schoolchildren or university students.

But behind the idealists was ranged a whole network of Communists – Soviet agents, including most of the members of the underground Central Committee, and the parachutists and submarine crews sent from the USSR during the War. The subversive activity of the Soviet Embassy in Sofia is well documented. Thousands of dollars were handed over by various Soviet attachés to the military section of the Bulgarian underground Central Committee. In the archives of the Ministry of the Interior I remember finding information about the seizure of $5,000 just handed over by the Soviet military attaché, then of another $2,000 ... and so on. People like Anton Ivanov were professional revolutionaries who knew what they were doing. Not a few Communists of that period, like the future head of the investigations section at the Ministry of the Interior, Stefan Bogdanov, were Soviet spies masterminding spy networks. They recognized only one fatherland – the Soviet Union. But the fact that they were Soviet agents did not preclude idealistic motivation. They believed in the triumph of world revolution, in the victory of Communism. People like Traicho Kostov and Yonko Panov† harboured their own illusions about the meaning of their struggle. We shall see later how quickly many idealists became unsrupulous careerists and expected payment for their heroism. But at that time, when Bulgaria was too dangerous for them, the careerists were safely abroad. In the maelstrom of the War years and the underground struggle, quite a few were indirectly drawn into the movement through their humanity, compassion and charity without having any ideological links with Communism. They are the people I call chance Communists, although many of them later claimed to have been born Communists. When the outcome of the War was clear, we experienced the first wave of time-serving Communists who, in the few days preceding 9 September 1944, prudently took to the hills and staked their claims for the jobs of future officials. After that wave, came the large powerful waves of citizens quickly adapting to the new situation, swelling the numbers in the Party by tens of thousands to over half a million. Many pseudo-heroes were to emerge from their ranks. They were to be the most devoted servants of Bulgaria's new master – the Soviet Union.

According to the rules of this struggle, few of the Communist idealists lived to see 9 September 1944. It is easy to see why the best, the most honest and the most steadfast perished. This is how it has always been throughout history. It was frequently rumoured in Bulgaria that many of the partisans and political prisoners who survived had no reason to boast of their behaviour, and even that they were not entitled to claim active participation in the struggle. This is particularly strongly suggested in the memoirs of Slavcho Trunski,† who talks about those who stayed away for a time in the mountains avoiding all danger.

In one of the archive dossiers I came upon the case of a young partisan captured somewhere near Makotsevo. The police commander who interrogated him had offered him two ways out. If he betrayed the hiding place of his comrades, he would be formally sentenced to death; but the sentence would not be carried out and he would live to see freedom. In this case, the police promised to plant false documents proving that the information had been received from other sources so that the partisan in question would remain untarnished and, in the event of a Communist victory, would be awarded all honours due to a hero. On the other hand, if he refused to give up his comrades, the police were confident that in a few days they would manage to find the rebels by their own devices; but as a punishment the prisoner would not only be shot – they would also leave 'proof' that he had betrayed his friends, so that everybody would forever look on him as a traitor and spit on his grave. The young partisan went mad.

This is a remarkable case, which explains why many of today's Party officials tremble in their boots at the thought that the police chief Nikola Geshev may still be alive and stage a reappearance to expose those who did not go mad, but turned informer, yet today live happily, honoured as heroes by their regime. And at the same time there is the question of those who were declared traitors but may not have been traitors at all. In this horrifying story I see a large question-mark concerning the accepted truth and the suppressed truth. It also raises the question of the betrayal not only of a group of partisans but of the ideals in whose name the struggle was waged. It forces the ceremonial gates of many alleged heroic feats and insists that the only true record is in the life of the living.

Today we know that some underground Communist activists, like Yonko Panov, opposed the senseless sacrifice of Party cadres and that their misgivings were justified. The Party lost the flower of its membership. On the other hand, there are those who believe that it was the objective of Georgi Dimitrov to sacrifice all that was young and talented in the Party ranks because these were the people who would defend their ideals and refuse to take part in turning their country into a Soviet prison. My own impression, after reading the archive material, was that I could not picture the many Communist heroes who had lost their lives playing either obedient puppets or greedy feudal lords who wanted to have their fill while the going was good.

A few days before the coup of 9 September, the number of Communist idealists had already diminished considerably. To compensate, numerous time-servers began to emerge from all sides; they had unerringly divined the direction of the prevailing wind and were ready, at the first sign of change, to abandon the sinking ship. Thus the opportunists and the Soviet agents came to play the major roles, while the idealists dimly perceived that the great trial and the real struggles were only beginning. Loyalty to Communist ideals and personal qualities were put to the test only after the Party came to power. Clearly it is much easier to fight an external enemy, however powerful, than to struggle internally in order to remain true to oneself. Only a few days after 9 September, the fate of the idealists was already sealed. An impressive number of them merged with the mass of opportunists and official Soviet agents, while a predictable small group withdrew silently. The tragedy of the Communist idealists is an important and powerful theme which life in Bulgaria has produced, but in the sugar-coated official Communist literature it is never mentioned.

The play I wrote was entitled *Communists*. To a large extent, it was a literal transcription of the documentary archive material I had researched, with extensive footnotes in which I gave precise references for my sources. Thus, in the strictest sense of the word, this was a documentary play. The text of the play was personally vetted by the Minister of the Interior – Angel Solakov. A second check established that the quotations were accurate, and that the only character subject to a certain amount of guesswork on my part was that of the policeman, Nikola Geshev. Production was entrusted to the very gifted theatre producer Assen Shopov and the cast was really first-class. I shall never forget the amazing performance of Ivan Kondov. The play was staged in Sofia's 'Tears and Laughter' theatre and included in the repertoire of almost all theatres throughout the country. Posters, promotion letters and publicity material had been widely circulated. When the rehearsals were over, a special preview took place at which I was not present. It was a few days before 9 September 1969. Perhaps I was the only one who knew that there were people at the top who would not be able to bear this confrontation with documents from their past. The play ended with the parting words of the Communists going to their executions. They spoke of the world for which they were dying: a world which had nothing in common with that of the people in the audience who were going to watch the performance. Friends told me later that, precisely because of its documentary nature, the play had a most harrowing effect. I had written into the programmes a request that the audience should refrain from clapping and walk out silently.

My misgivings proved justified. The play was stopped and banned by the very people who had commissioned it. The reason for the ban, as communicated to me, was the play's 'depressing effect'. The naked documentary truth had affronted the commercial needs of a shallow celebration. Or, more likely, the comrades had no wish to celebrate in memory of dead Communists; they wanted to celebrate in honour of themselves.

Thus it was that the twenty-fifth anniversary of 9 September had no special commemorative play on its programme.

However, all this story is but a small detail in the biography of the regime.

But what options did the Communist idealist in Bulgaria have?

If I dwell on the fate of our Communist idealists, it is because I believe that it conveys the truest picture of contemporary Bulgaria and reveals the real nature of the regime. From bourgeois, capitalist or nationalist positions, we judge the situation from outside, while from a purely Communist position we get an inside perspective on things. Besides, I am deeply convinced that, under present conditions, radical internal change can come about only through the Communist Party itself. It is, after all, the main power in the land. We have seen the result of the highly romantic attempt of the Czechoslovak Communist idealists to break loose from the Soviet-Stalinist corruption of their regime and to return to pure, honest, and human principles.

And so what roads were open to the Bulgarian Communist idealists at the beginning of the 1950s when the regime's new order was being stabilized?

The first road was to continue to believe blindly in the Soviet-appointed Party leadership, to accept all shortcomings, mistakes and distortions as a necessity of the moment, to justify one's own participation in all kinds of murky deeds knowing that others did it too, to try to secure a better place for oneself and to believe in remuneration for services rendered in the past and for suffering. The whitewashing of one's conscience, the justifications, were left to the Party; there was no more expedient slogan than that enshrined in Christo Radevski's† poem: 'Lead me, oh Party'.

The second road was to see and understand that the cause had been betrayed and the ideals mocked, but, evaluating the situation, to pretend to believe in the Party and its leadership, while trying to follow the voice of one's own conscience, avoiding complicity in the misdeeds of the regime and fighting quietly and consistently to change things from the inside. This was a very dangerous road, because on either side there was an abyss. Not to fall out with the Party and yet to stay true to oneself seems to me infinitely difficult, particularly as the Party leadership slavishly copied the Soviet way of life, which, in its essence, had been constructed and established by Stalin. 'Soviet norms are our norms! Soviet morality is our morality!' proclaimed the slogans which the Politburo foisted on the lower Party echelons.

And, following the example of the Soviet Union, the majority of the former idealists took the obvious road, a kind of Soviet motorway to socialism. This was the widest and most comfortable road and it led furthest. Moreover, nobody had to walk along it. Every deserving comrade could use a car – from a Moskvich to a Chaika according to his rank. The natural preference for this road showed that the idealism and selflessness of many of the Party members in question were little more than a youthful romantic impulse, a shortlived outburst of restless adolescence. The struggle for the 'happiness of the people' ultimately turned out to have been a convenient prelude to personal prosperity. The Soviet model of Communism, founded on the theory of the dictatorship of the proletariat, provided the necessary soap to launder one's conscience (where it existed). It was of no importance that there had never been a proletariat in Bulgaria, and that not one of the Bulgarian 'proletarian' dictators came from it. As far as class was concerned, the great majority of Bulgarian Communists came from a middle, agrarian stratum. But why shouldn't they claim to be proletarians and affect a cloth cap – especially since the formula 'the dictatorship of the proletariat' justified everything: oppression and terror, inequality, injustice, corruption and privileges. Put simply, its meaning was: 'Now our chance has come, we'll do exactly as we please.'

I think nothing deprives this type of Communism so completely of humanity and degrades people to the level of a pack of wolves or a herd of sheep as 'the dictatorship of the proletariat'. If the devil wanted to impose his own regime on our planet, it would be called 'the dictatorship of the proletariat'. It is a dictatorship of spiritual cripples who believe that the world owes them something, is guilty of not having given them enough, and must go on repaying them for a lifetime.

In Bulgaria, too, the time came when people began to be paid for past services. Ninety-nine per cent of the Party members demanded material rewards for their real or imaginary past records. Even people who had a genuine claim to recognition as heroes joined the queue for the reward of past services. They forgot the ancient truth that heroism ceases to exist as soon as it has been paid for. The payment was not only in money, of course, it came in the form of power and privileges.

Many of our former idealists now discovered the intoxicating sweetness of power. Suddenly they understood that their important posts had lifted them above the level of ordinary people and moved them to the centre of the world. This fanned their primitive ambitions and transformed their innate inferiority complexes into coarse shows of superiority. The vulgar demonstration of power became one of the most characteristic traits of the regime. I know people in whom the exercise of power became a kind of mental disorder, a mad search for any means of demonstrating superiority. But the time came when the taste for power was no longer expressed only in epaulettes, medals and titles, but also in the gross indulgence of material pleasures. The overwhelming majority of these former 'fighters for universal justice' decided that the time had come to live it up. Ingenuously, they convinced themselves that they had 'struggled' and 'suffered' enough, that it was time to start enjoying the delights of life. This was the period of the modern apartments, the country villas, the new furniture and the lovers and mistresses. A logical sequel was the rising number of divorces. The ruling Party bosses now turned their backs on their not very attractive (though loyal) comrade wives. Young girls, and especially the graceful and well-bred daughters of the defeated bourgeoisie, were in particular demand....

After just a few years spent within the corrupting influence of their own power, there was no trace left of the idealism of the idealists.

'I want to live! This is my chance!' a former Minister of the Interior and Politburo member declared with drunken frankness, lying on the carpet before me. I kept thinking that this same man had once been sentenced to death and that, if he had been shot, there would have been a street named after him in Varna.

'How did we change so much?' exclaimed another former idealist.

But I think that there was no real change. A simple analysis of the motives which pushed the great majority of these former youths into the resistance (I deliberately leave out the word Communism) would show that they had little in common with a conscious desire to serve the people, the poor, the cause of justice or the happiness of others. At best, their motives were instinctive or linked to an unsophisticated vanity, a desire to swagger, to impress the world, an adolescent longing for heroism and exploits, and, at the same time, an instinctive hatred for everything superior or unattainable. So, in effect, the greed, sycophancy, toadying, baseness and cruelty of the comrades in question had always been an integral part of them, though we did not recognize it. The lobbing of a bomb into a police station was an act which gave a misleading impression of the real character of a partisan. We accepted the man as a brave bomb-thrower but overlooked his nature, which would stay with him all his life. A short-lived heroic gesture could act as a convenient disguise for a twisted or criminal character. That is why, in later years, we got used to the spectacle of former heroes behaving like villains and cowards. It was precisely these people, with their base instincts, who were to become the prime force of the regime, its nucleus, and the core of the Party.

Matters were thus very far removed from Karl Marx, who was only a name and a pretext. Very few of these men, including the leaders, had ever bothered to understand in depth the ideology and philosophy under whose banner they marched. I know hardly any who had seriously read even twenty pages of Marx. I doubt if anyone had ever laid hands on *Das Kapital*, while their knowledge of Engels did not go further than familarity with his photograph. Even knowledge of Lenin was limited to the parroting of selected quotations. It is doubtful whether Marx, with his lack of experience of life, could have foreseen the nature of his followers. Quite seriously, if tomorrow a new Stalin decreed that the ideological justification of the regime and the joys of power were grounded in Islam, all these travellers on the motorway to Communism would switch effortlessly from Marx to Mahomet. Indeed, the only things which are important to them are their comfort, security and personal happiness. People will say that this is also what motivates any Italian or English grocer. But the difference is that our own Party heroes deceive themselves that they are doing everything for the future happiness of others, while ordinary grocers in the West declare openly that they work for their own interests.

And so: 'Lead me, oh Party!' Lead me to promotion, to better pay, to greater privileges, to more power, while I shall find more glittering amusements for myself. In exchange, you can count on me. I am yours. I realize that I am nothing without you. I offer you my principles, my mind, my morality .... If you, oh Party, veer to the left, I too will turn leftwards, if you veer to the right, I too will turn right; if you stop in the middle; so shall I and I will not move until you start again! If you order me to honour Stalin, I shall praise him to the skies; if you tell me to spit on him, I will cover his face with filth; if you want me to call myself a Bulgarian, I shall beat my chest and I will shout until I faint: 'I am a Bulgar'; if you want me to renounce Bulgaria, I shall forget even the letter 'B' .... It is as you say, oh Party! *As long as I can keep what I have!*

Such, more or less, was the credo of those who had chosen this glorious road.

I have often thought of the folk wisdom contained in Christo Smirnensky's famous short story 'The staircase'.* I know of no other literary work where the process of the betrayal of ideals and the alienation from people and reality is described with such graphic simplicity. If I had been the First Party Secretary in Bulgaria and if I loved my country, I would have ordered all ministers and responsible officials to read this story every day, while I would read it three times daily. Unfortunately, the First Secretary merely says sententiously:

'That's how it is in the Soviet Union, that's how it will be in our country!'

*For a translation of this story, see the Appendix.

THE RAVAGES OF
THE PERSONALITY CULT

One Bulgarian characteristic which I particularly respect is the cool, critical attitude towards every kind of idol. Looking at our entire history, we can claim that the worship of people and events is definitely not a Bulgarian weakness. In this respect Bulgarians have shown more wisdom, intelligence and realism than many other peoples, in particular the Russians who seem to have idolatry in their blood. It would be difficult to imagine a genuine Bulgarian kneeling outside the Kremlin walls, banging his head on the paving stones and shouting hysterically with outstretched arms: 'Little Brother Tsar', 'Little Brother Stalin, you are all, I am nothing!' The deification of another human being, no matter who he might be and no matter what his achievements, has always provoked a sceptical and rather condescending smile from my countrymen. Probably every one of them has felt that this is somehow humiliating, a denial of oneself, a mockery of mind and intelligence. On the other hand, though, perhaps it can be a source of strength and hope for those weak people who lack the necessary self-confidence and faith in their own qualities.

Thus, when we speak of the deification of people or, as it is now called in our part of the world, 'the personality cult', we must put it down decisively as an achievement of the Communist regime, which artificially created a phenomenon that had no roots in our history. A people who have always doubted everything – from God to the gamekeeper, as the saying goes – who have instinctively considered themselves as estimable and deserving as all other beings, who have bowed their heads only out of self-preservation, would hardly kneel voluntarily or sincerely before the plaster bust of a human megalomaniac.

The cult of personality arrived in Bulgaria with the aeroplane which brought Georgi Dimitrov.† Never before had our country witnessed such a vulgar pageant of human abasement. The introduction and establishment of the cult should be seen entirely as part of the general movement, both spiritual and physical, which was aimed at undermining and destroying the independence, human dignity and self-respect of every individual Bulgarian. For the overwhelming majority of our people (with the exception of a handful of Party fanatics), the cult was an expression not of bigoted worship, passionate faith or boundless devotion, but of fear. For many, the mouthing of phrases like 'our beloved teacher and leader, father of all progressive humanity, Comrade Stalin' was a kind of vaccine against terror.

I remember how stunned I was by the first signs of the invasion of this Soviet-made cult. It began with the propaganda groups' incessant chanting of 'Stalin-Tito-Dimitrov'. Later Tito was dropped from circulation. I can testify to the ceaseless bellow: 'Stalin-Stalin-Stalin!' Such parades of human voices were always organized, never spontaneous. Usually, the signal was given by a group of Party agitators and security agents. Years later, the feeling of mockery would anticipate the signal. One of my colleagues in the Polytechnic was always the first to jump up and start chanting the relevant name, forcing the Party masses to yell every two minutes. I remember a particular end-of-season performance at the National Theatre. The play was called *The Exploit*. Shortly before the curtain rose, Vulko Chervenkov,† who at that time was King and God, entered the Royal box. The whole audience immediately jumped to its feet, incessantly shouting: 'Cher-ven-kov, Cher-ven-kov. ...' I looked at the people around me. Most were regular theatre-goers; they looked intelligent, with none of the grey uniformity of typical Party faces. And that is when I suddenly sensed that they triumphed in their effort to worship the man whom they deeply hated in reality, that their voices were really shouting the most degrading and hostile insults, that the incantation of the dictator's name had a quite contrary meaning. Life had forced them to participate in this circus and they did so with the exaggeration of clowns. All the while, the man above them accepted all this with imperial condescension. Afterwards, a friend said to me: 'I gave him such a "Cher-ven-kov" that his hat flew off!'

The other ritual of the cult of personality was the quotation mania. We quoted until we were blue in the face. I cannot remember a meeting or a conference where, every minute, someone would not volunteer the priceless cliché: 'As Comrade Stalin says. ... As Dimitrov says. ... As Chervenkov says. ...' Later the name of Lenin began to crop up; and now, when I read the Bulgarian newspapers, I see that things haven't changed much, for they say 'as Comrade Zhivkov teaches us'.

The mania for quoting also serves as a proof of loyalty. I know so many people who, in order to remain at the university or get a job, would be ready to repeat for the rest of their lives 'as comrade ____ teaches us'. But during that time there was also a flood of mockery. It was particularly in evidence in the examination papers of aspiring students, each of whom either cited non-existent quotations, or quoted in such an ambiguous way that everything plainly became ridiculous. Often what the 'comrade' had said was - judged by normal thought processes - pure rubbish. Sometimes I am tempted to draw up a catalogue of the utter nonsenses, the megalomaniac phrases and the stupid pronouncements of all these former and present deities. On the other hand, I consider that the regime deliberately forced us to repeat these inanities in order to kill off the last resistance of our personal dignity.

One of the most banal manifestations of the personality cult was the so-called 'red corners'. In every institution, office or business establishment, and even in the homes of the more zealous Party members, there was the inevitable corner covered in red material in front of which stood a small bust of Stalin, Dimitrov or Lenin, as the case may be. Sometimes all the saints were grouped together. When there were no busts, plaques were used or just photographs. Over the 'red corner' there always hung a slogan. These special Communist altars to the cult of personality were subsequently left to gather dust. But I know a lot of pseudo-artists who made considerable fortunes by producing busts or plaques for this purpose. There were also the usual funny stories about offices which laid on a reserve of different busts. Today the 'red corner' continues to exist in many places, with Lenin occupying pride of place.

Perhaps the most humiliating and inhuman expressions of the cult of personality were the political rallies, which continue to this day - albeit in a less ostentatious way. They, too, are exclusive products of the regime. Every older Bulgarian citizen remembers that parades on such a scale were quite unknown in our country before 1944. The traditional military parade on St George's Day or the religious procession and service for the Epiphany were a thousand times more modest events than the Communist celebrations of 1 May. I have often questioned the point of these pompous Party carnivals. Are they not well-organized rituals, aimed at suppressing, defacing and destroying the natural instinct of every person to be himself? Perhaps there is some similarity with religious rituals. But whereas in a religion man is expected to pay homage to the spiritual image of good, to the love of his neighbour, to the aspiration towards a just and lofty life, things are quite different in the case of the Communist religion. You have to stand in line, to take up your place in the herd, then with hundreds of thousands of others you must pass in front of an elevated and distant rostrum, turn towards it, take off your hat and wave your hand in greeting while your face produces the most pleasing possible smile. Like a well-trained monkey, you are expected to bow to other human beings, who are not superior to you in any way except in the power they hold, which they have assumed without asking your consent. The leader of your group will make you shout the name of the creature standing in the centre of the rostrum, while this creature, tired and bored by the four or five-hour procession of the human herd, does not even notice you. On all sides you are hemmed in by portraits of people, who may be like you biologically but whom you do not know person-ally; though you are in no way convinced of their worth, you must bow to them as reverently as to your mother and father. And this very bow is the death blow to your dignity, to the consciousness that you are a being of equal worth and with equal rights, and not an animal or a slave. To recognize and value the qualities of this or that man is normal in human relations, but to fall on your knees before somebody whimpering his name negates everything you are. I stress this moment of humiliation which is a kind of death. It is the main blow which the cult of personality has dealt and continues to deal to the spirit of our people. The basic principle of the personality cult has always been 'I am everything, you are nothing'.

One of the most tragi-comical expressions of the personality cult was the renaming of streets, towns, villages, factories, hospitals, schools and even mountain peaks. The ridiculous thing was that they were awarded the names of living Party figures. There was no Bulgarian town without its 'Stalin' street or 'Georgi Dimitrov' street. Foreign Communist parties provided material for immortalization with the names of Molotov, Tito, Gheorghiu-Dej, Tolbukhin, Clement Gott-wald and Kalinin, while the members of our own Politburo competed amongst themselves in proffering their names everywhere. I recall that I trained in a railway plant at Kostenets called Anton Yugov,† that I visited a factory named Tsola Dragoycheva, that I walked along a street called Vulko Chervenkov. Numerous sites and projects bore the names of many other still living Party bosses, such as Georgi Damy-anov, Dimiter Ganev, Vassil Kolarov and so on. Subsequently it transpired that some of the comrades were not so distinguished, while others (like Tito) passed out of the Communist camp, which led to all sorts of comical rechristenings until it was finally decided that only the names of dead Party leaders could be used for this purpose.

Of course, the personality cult had its hierarchy which was decreed by the Party and strictly observed. Nevertheless, while Marx was inevitably accepted as the first and the greatest, there were disagreements as to whether Stalin's image should precede that of Lenin. But even more amusing was the struggle about the distribution of the secondary positions of these self-appointed Party Olympians. Veritable wars were waged over the order of precedence in the Politburo's portrait gallery until, finally, the alphabetical order prevailed.

The Communist cult mania has always been the expression of a two-way lack of intelligence. If a handful of crippled human beings with Party tickets fanatically look up to a leader whom they identify with the Party and who fills their limited empty lives with faith and devotion, satisfying their instinct for servility, what is to be said of those whom they look up to? Often, observing these self-appointed saints at close quarters, I have asked myself if they take all this comedy seriously. Do they really believe that they are exceptional representatives of the human species to whom others should pay obeisance, as if they were gods? Unfortunately the answer is *yes*.

In character, these Party counts, marquesses and barons were and are mediocre people, often possessing a below average intelligence. An ironic play of chance and circumstance had enabled them to occupy such elevated positions; but they lacked the necessary intelligence to perceive this and so ascribed their good fortune to their own exceptional qualities. They believed that they were worth more than the common people and insisted on being treated accordingly. This explained their inaccessibility, their unbearable pretensions, the fact that they surrounded themselves with fawning servants, their encouragement of every kind of worship of themselves and the constant demonstration that all depended on their power. Add to this the fact that they published an official Bulgarian calendar, which they had stuffed with the dates of their births and all the more important events in their lives, thus convincing themselves that they had displaced St Iliya, St Nicholas and St Dimiter.

That they forced on people the cult of their own personalities was in itself a proof of their repulsive mediocrity. Not one of them was a real personality. And when they fell from power and mingled with the people, everyone was amazed by their ordinariness.

THE SOVIET FEUDAL SYSTEM

I find it very difficult to imagine the kind of Communist development Bulgaria might have had if we had not followed the Soviet model. Would we have ended up like today's Yugoslavia or Albania? Or would we have found the way to a Bulgarian socialism most suited to our circumstances? Today's Bulgarian theorists skate over the fact that Bulgarian pre-War society was characterized by two salient factors: first, the absence of powerful capitalism and exploitation; and, second, the inherent socialism of our strongly developed co-operative movement. So, looked at in a historical perspective, Bulgaria, without any Communist help, was already successfully practising its own form of democratic socialism. Against this background, any Bulgarian government with a claim to be socialist would have built upon the natural development of these native tendencies and striven to strengthen them. To this day I fail to understand why our peasants had to be beaten up in order to join the co-operative farms, when before the war there had been massive support for the idea of village co-operatives, the expression of a most democratic and meaningful form of socialism. I only mention this to show that the Soviet regime in Bulgaria had no interest whatsoever in furthering these native socialist traditions of our people, just as it had no interest in their well-being and prosperity. Like real invaders and faithful servants of foreign masters, the Bulgarian dictators undertook to apply an utterly alien and completely unsuitable social scheme to their own country. The history, the life and the character of the various Soviet peoples are totally different from those of our people. Even if we accept that some elements of the Soviet system were an indirect continuation of features of Tsarist Russia, or that Soviet violence was, in a sense, a response to a previous historical violence, these elements and this violence had nothing to do with the history and character of the Bulgarians. The literal application of the Soviet model, whether it be good or bad, made no more sense than trying to mate a bear with a dove, or to graft a pumpkin onto a vine. There can be no justification whatsoever for the forcible and irrational imposition of the Soviet model in Bulgaria; one concludes that the aim was to crush the people and eradicate their best qualities and traditions. 'According to the Soviet example' became the incessant ritual cry of Bulgaria's rulers. I still don't know exactly to what extent things were ordered by Moscow, and to what degree the spirit of imitation was an expression of blind loyalty. Volumes could be written on the subject of the Soviet example and experience as applied in Bulgaria, with often absurd results and huge material and spiritual losses. Years had to pass before, under the pressure of real conditions in Bulgaria, it became at last permissible to criticize the aping of Soviet experience and to give silent preference to some Bulgarian ways. Even these concessions to common sense were, of course, very limited and cautious.

The description which, in my view, fits the Soviet regime best is 'socialist feudalism', an expression coined in anger by one of our best poets. Indeed, the social structure of the new society is amazing in its resemblance to the feudal order – a resemblance even more astonishing if we compare the rights and obligations of the various social groups involved. I am sure that a historian could draw an illuminating parallel between the kingdom of Boril* and contemporary Bulgaria. The difference is that the *boyars* of the thirteenth century did not imitate the Byzantine feudal lords as slavishly as their modern successors.

But let us look at the social order in Bulgaria after the invasion of the Soviet army. At the head stood the first Bulgarian feudal lord, appointed by the Soviet Union in order to rule the country in its name. The Bulgarian origin of the feudal overlord was and is merely a matter of courtesy. Usually he is chosen after an arranged contest with other feudal lords who all aspire to the highest position. Their ambitions are periodically nourished by the USSR in order to keep the first feudal lord in a state of insecurity, and, at the same time, to facilitate the control of the various forces engaged in the country. The main criterion for the selection of the first feudal lord is obviously his loyalty to the Soviet Union, regardless of whether Stalin, Malenkov, Khrushchev or Brezhnev is at the helm. In essence, the feudal overlord is a high Soviet state official, loyal to the Soviet Union. He has the

---

* During the Second Bulgarian Kingdom (1186-1389), the rule of King Boril (1207-1218) was marked by anarchy and the increasing defection of the feudal lords who conspired with the Byzantine Court.

power of an absolute monarch with regard to everything which does not touch on Soviet interests. He is not obliged to give an account of his actions to anyone else except to those who have appointed him. After him in the pecking order come the feudal lords, who are Politburo members. Almost all are appointed by the Soviet Union, often against the wishes and despite the protests of the feudal overlord. They have strong but limited power, which is mainly concentrated in their own fiefs. But, like the feudal overlord, they too cannot take a decision or act independently in any matter which touches the interests of their employer. They are insecure because ambitious barons below them are constantly striving to displace them. Special care is taken that no one amongst them should grow into an autonomous powerful ruler. As history shows, the monarch at the apex has always favoured weak, unintelligent, faceless feudal lords. If by chance a strong independent personality arises amongst them, the USSR takes good care to liquidate him. The group that constitutes the highest caste lives in a Soviet way – a shut off, isolated and very privileged life. To be a member of this caste is like being a duke at the time of the Sun King. The highest ranking feudal lord, the members of the feudal Politburo and their equals stand, in principle, above the law of the land. The laws, in so far as they exist, are reserved entirely for the ordinary people or, to use the terminology of feudalism, the serfs. Not one member of the high caste or the members of his family can be judged by the laws of the serfs. They can commit all sorts of crimes, make deliberate or accidental mistakes, perpetrate abuses and waste public funds, they can break oaths and promises, lie publicly, use their official positions for private gain and so on, but as long as they keep the benevolence of the absolute monarch – in this case, the USSR – they are not under any threat. If the laws of a normal democratic country like Britain, the United States or Sweden could be applied to them, they would all, without exception, find themselves imprisoned for crimes far exceeding any scandals in the West. They are not responsible to the serfs nor to the puppet National Assembly, composed of a selected group of dependent minor barons plus a few troubadours and fanatically hard-working serfs. The social behaviour of the ruling caste is dedicated exclusively to the service of its own interests, which by definition coincide with the interests of the absolute monarch. To justify its anachronistic existence, it employs a powerful propaganda machine, which dictates that truth is everything that is to the advantage of the feudal lords, and lies are everything that does not suit them. The caste has guaranteed its security by surrounding itself with a strong guard.

Chervenkov, for instance, travelled throughout the country with a dozen limousines, it being decided only at the last moment which car he would occupy. For their personal entertainment, individual Politburo members have their own secret services in miniature, which spy on each other, but all their reports end up in the same place – with the Soviet ambassador. Officially, the Politburo is supposed to oversee state and Party activities, with each member responsible for one public area. But they have mainly nominal control functions, while the real work is done by the respective ministers and their deputies. At times of parades and political rallies, this caste takes its place on the dais by the mausoleum in strict hierarchical order. Their personal lives are secretive, their children and wives meet in high but isolated circles, they live in former royal residences and palaces or newly built luxury villas, have their own private film performances at home (mostly of choice Western films imported specially for them) and often play at being patrons of the arts by making some painter, musician, poet or actor their protégé. The more energetic barons have their great love affairs, or less romantic purely sexual escapades. They and their children live ever-conscious of their blue blood, which places them above all others, and secure in the knowledge that what they own is theirs by the law of the new aristocracy – 'the dictatorship of the proletariat'. But if someone should slip up and call them proletarians, they would be mortally offended; they would feel much more flattered by being compared with Marie-Antoinette than with Rosa Luxemburg.

After this small but exceptionally powerful group of the highest in the land comes the considerably larger caste of the leading central and local feudal lords, which includes the members of the government, the central feudal committee, the county feudal committees, the presidents of local districts, the generals, the higher apparatus of the State security service and, for good measure, a few of the feudal troubadours. The estimated number of this second caste is a few hundred and, in effect, these are the people who directly govern the country. They can be divided into two main groups – rightful barons and necessary barons. The rightful barons occupy their positions on the strength of their special links with the mightier barons and the absolute monarch. Usually they have representative functions or direct activities of secondary importance. The necessary barons are mostly organizers or experts, promoted on the strength of their own abilities, whom the feudal order most needs in order to function. This whole caste answers individually to the Politburo, although some of its more important members have direct links to the absolute monarch and set their watches by the Kremlin clock. The life and actions of this caste are also above the law. So long as they are loyal to their monarch, they need not fear punishment for any sins or crimes. Their privileges are also considerable, though more limited than those of the most powerful barons. Their private lives, too, are relatively shut off though not as inaccessible as those of their superiors. The relationships between them are very complex and subject to constant alliances and feuds. This is mainly because of the different camps which have formed round individual Politburo members and which are often regrouped according to the needs of the moment. In their own district and department fiefs, the barons of this caste are absolute masters. Like the Politburo, they cannot be criticized by the press or the public, nor are they responsible to the National Assembly or any other democratic forum: they answer only to the Politburo and, above all, to the first feudal lord. Often they are obliged to sacrifice the interests of their jobs because of the complicated power network and, in all their actions, they are very dependent on those above them. The main aim of their lives is to hang on to their positions and, if possible, to move higher. They wade in the muddy waters of gossip, scandal, careerist stratagems and intrigues behind the scenes. Almost every one of them has tried to surround himself with relatives and faithful childhood friends. They, too, live in exceptional comfort with their families and try to inter-marry, keeping at a safe distance from the serfs.

Then comes the third, or feudal middle caste, which includes most of the managing directors, managers, deputy ministers, department heads, editors-in-chief, the more eminent representatives of feudal art and culture, the middle Party apparatus, members of various committees and councils. I should put the number of this large caste at several thousands. This is, so to speak, the motor and chassis of the feudal vehicle, in which the two higher castes ride. Membership of the third caste is a necessary springboard for greater heights, because to serve in it is a proof of loyalty towards the absolute monarch and the first feudal lord. It enjoys its own high standard of living, many privileges and is also not answerable to the laws of the country. By virtue of its middle position, it is in closer contact with the serfs, although it is conscious of its superiority and tries to keep itself apart. The lords of the middle caste are particularly powerful in the provinces, where the serfs attached to them are at their mercy. Woe to any serf who incurs the enmity of the local Party boss! The power of the middle feudal caste can be said to be so great that no decision can be taken and no work can be done without the assent of its representatives. Sometimes the members of the middle caste interpret ideas and instructions from above in such a way as to change their substance. They are the ones who come in for criticism, and when policies dictated from above end in failure the senior barons wash their hands of guilt by punishing the middle barons. Frequent reshuffles are regarded as another good way of keeping up discipline.

The last group in the Soviet feudal system imposed on Bulgaria consists of the feudal small-fry, including the Party secretaries of local organizations and Party activists, the lower military and militia ranks, the lower state and Party management, a large part of the propaganda and ideology machine and other small functionaries. All these carry out the orders of the caste above them. In exchange, they have a certain power over the surrounding serfs. They, too, enjoy minor privileges and can escape from the law when they commit petty abuses. More often they are the ultimate scapegoats for the failure of the policies handed down to them from above. In the life of the serfs, however, they play the greatest role because they are the direct representatives of the feudal powers: the life of a person who finds himself at war with his immediate feudal lord is black indeed. The members of this group interfere not only in the work but also in the private lives of their serfs and their families, and even impose their vetoes on divorces, marriages, changes of address, holidays and so on. From an ethical point of view, the feudal small-fry are an assorted mob of intellectually limited fanatics, born lackeys for whom the master's will counts above all else, unsuccessful ambitious careerists, petty schemers for whom the most important thing is to assure their place at the table of power, and young climbers determined to fight their way up. Nevertheless, because of their direct contact with the serfs, the feudal small-fry are more flexible, more inclined to compromise, and sometimes they act as a buffer between the hammer bearing down from above and the anvil of the serfs' world. They are proud that at least something and somebody in the country depends on them.

At the bottom of this typical Soviet ladder are the serfs. These are people who, according to the laws of feudalism, must always be tied to a certain place and a certain job, and who have not got the following rights:

to displease the regime,
to doubt the feudal ideology,
to have their own opinions and express them,

to criticize the barons,
to organize freely,
to hold free elections,
to travel freely,
to change their jobs freely,
to enjoy the fruits of their labour,
to have a fair system of justice,
to have their own religion,
to be treated humanely by the militia,
to listen to foreign broadcasts,
to read books not approved by the barons,
not to serve in the feudal army and, finally,
to be what they want to be.

The only right which the serfs have is to produce diligently and unprotestingly the goods required by the feudal castes, and to hope that something will be left over for them. In his capacity of production unit, the serf enjoys certain medical and social services which keep him fit for work.

This is the structure of the Soviet feudal system, which is the backbone of the Bulgarian regime.

LOVE FOR 'BIG BROTHER'

In the village square outside the Dragalevtsi pub a monster of a car makes its appearance. It is the latest Ferrari, its snout almost touching the ground and four shining exhaust pipes bristling at the back. The car is painted a vivid green with a lemon-green band for contrast. Inside, a middle-aged man with a Levantine face is reclining on the back seat smoking a pipe and gazing with a superior air at the mountains. The monster stops for a short time in the square while continuing to growl impressively. The people in the pub rush out to watch. Meanwhile, I am trying to help a friend from the film world to turn his stranded Moskvich so that it will face downhill, in the hope that it will start by itself. But seeing the foreign car behind us we shamefacedly abandon our efforts to make the wretched Moskvich move and join the crowd in front of the pub. Nearly everyone has come out with their glasses and they observe the Ferrari thoughtfully.

'Well, well, look what cars the Russians have started making!' says my neighbour meaningfully.

A strange light appears in the faces of most of the drinkers.

'When you look at it, you can see straightaway that it could have been made only in Moscow!' a short co-operative farmer with a large moustache continues in the same tone.

'The driver is a Russian too!' adds another one. 'Look at the gold buttons on his sleeves, the pipe, the watch ... a typical Russian....'

'I tell you that neither the Germans, nor the French... nor the Americans ... nobody can make such a thing! Only Big Brother!'

And now one of them turns to my friend, whose Moskvich has starting trouble, and says: 'Well, Kolyo, how many times have I told you not to buy an Italian car!'

Then the foreign car disappears round the bend on the main road to Aleko and the drinkers return to the pub, while Kolyo and I resume our efforts to start the Moskvich.

This and many similar scenes come to my mind every time I read in various Bulgarian or Western newspapers of the great traditional love which the Bulgarians supposedly feel for the USSR.

But while such claims are quite understandable when they come from newspapers published under the Bulgarian regime, it is impossible to forgive the short-sightedness, ignorance and irresponsible generalizations of Western correspondents, who follow the well-trodden official itineraries through Bulgaria, eating and drinking at the expense of the Bulgarian government. It is more than clear that their dependence on the authorities and the official translators as intermediaries has cut them off from real contact with ordinary Bulgarian citizens. They could not possibly perceive the biting irony of the noncommittal inhabitants of Dragalevtsi, nor are they able to hear the popular joke question often asked outside cinemas: 'Is the film good or is it a Soviet one?', or take part in conversations which reveal the real attitude of Bulgarians towards 'Big Brother'. It is certainly a mystery where and how the foreign authors of such reports on Bulgaria have encountered the love of Bulgarian people for the Soviet Union. At best, they can point to a few historical monuments. It is even more upsetting that this litany about the Bulgarians' eternal love for the USSR has become one of the most mendacious, misleading clichés used by Westerners to characterize Bulgaria.

'You Bulgarians love Russia,' these people say with the same certainty with which they claim that Turks and Greeks hate each other to the death. I cannot refrain from expressing my amazement, to put it mildly, that a whole nation gets labelled with feelings which even the most fanatical supporters of the USSR in Bulgaria might have reason to doubt. That is why I would like to take a closer look at this famed Bulgarian love for the USSR which I would not even have known about were it not for the above-mentioned newspaper reports.

To begin with, in the West people do not differentiate properly between the concepts of Russia and the Soviet Union. On the front pages of many leading Western newspapers we read: 'Russia decided ...,' 'Russia declared ...' 'Russia ...' when clearly the Soviet Union is meant. Whereas for many Western citizens the word 'Russian' is a near synonym for 'Soviet', the Bulgarians are among the few inhabitants of the world who really know the difference.

Certain historical links between the Bulgarian and Russian peoples exist because of their common Slav origin, orthodox Christianity and the similarity of the language. But links of this nature do not in any way imply love. From a historical point of view, Russia owes its linguistic and cultural development to medieval Bulgaria. However hard Soviet historians try, they cannot suppress the fact that the Cyrillic alphabet which they use originated in Bulgaria, nor that at the time when Bulgarian literature was in full bloom, their Prince Svyatoslav was little more than a barbarous chieftain. The historian would have a hard task trying to prove that before the nineteenth century the name of Russia meant anything in the life of Bulgarians or inspired any feelings in them. The legend of the Christian 'Dyado Ivan'* who would come to the aid of his enslaved Christian brethren was born only in the last century and grew particularly after the Crimean War. There was also the influence of the new post-Pushkin Russian literature and culture which penetrated Bulgaria at about the same time. Indeed, the eyes of many Bulgarians under Ottoman domination were turned hopefully towards Russia. This hope was founded mainly on the idea of the Christian faith acting as a bulwark against the Muslim conqueror. Of course, many young Bulgarians were educated in Russia at that time and later became a living link between the two countries. But the more far-sighted among them, especially Botev† and Karavelov,† had a profound understanding of the illusory nature of the Christians' hopes in Russia. They saw clearly that the Russian people, who lived in wretched poverty and ignorance, deprived of human rights, were indifferent to what was happening beyond the Danube. Botev, who was in touch with the Russian revolutionaries of that time, perceived that the tyranny in an almost feudal Tsarist Russia was equal to the oppression in the Ottoman Empire. Feelings of compassion, sympathy and commiseration towards the Bulgarians were expressed by representatives of the Russian intelligentsia, especially in Panslavist circles, but they were certainly not shared by the Russian masses.

Bulgaria's liberation by the Russian army in 1878 is a significant historical fact. But let us not be blind to its real meaning. Love is the most neglected feeling in the world of politics. The liberation was not the result of a Russian outburst of humanity, compassion and love for the unhappy Bulgarians, but the fruit of a rational imperialist policy. No one could take seriously the pathetic descriptions of Russian generals allegedly deeply moved by the fate of the Bulgarian insurgents

* Grandfather Ivan: a Bulgarian nickname for Tsarist Russia.

impaled by the Turks in the April uprising of 1876. Indeed, Bulgaria's liberation was not even the aim of the 1877–8 Russo–Turkish war, but only its result. Despite this chilling truth, the gratitude of the Bulgarians towards Russia was very great and widely expressed. Many monuments testify to it. This, however, did not stop the Bulgarian army from fighting against the Russians in the First World War some years later.

The essential relationship between Bulgarians and Russians is not some mythological love between citizens of two countries unknown to each other, but instead reflects the influence of Russia's creative genius at the end of the nineteenth and the beginning of the twentieth century. The emancipation of Bulgaria coincided with a remarkable flowering of Russian literature, music and painting. The country took its first steps while Dostoevsky was still alive, shared many decades with Tolstoy (who in his last days wanted to run away to Bulgaria) and Chekhov, and responded to the energy and excitement of the Russian progressive intelligentsia. It is easy to trace many fertile Russian influences in Bulgarian culture. These continued to exist later, despite the different political courses of the two countries.

Many contemporary accounts testify to the genuine, realistic attitude of the Bulgarian towards the Russian state and vice versa. Perhaps this relationship is best chronicled in Simeon Radev's book *The Builders of Contemporary Bulgaria*. The description of the events following the liberation suffices to show how quickly enthusiasm for Russia evaporated and even gratitude withered. This was because Russia attempted to treat the young country as its puppet; and all the ploys, machinations, interference and ceaseless intrigues of the Russian administration now appear as a portent of what was to happen after the Second World War. From Simeon Radev, Zachary Stoyanov and other sources we learn that the anti-Russian feeling in Bulgaria was very widespread, sometimes exceeding the former anti-Turkish feeling.

Because of this, Simeon Radev's book was not reissued for many years after the Communist take-over. When it was finally published, it became – according to a recent article by a well-known Bulgarian critic – the favourite reference book of almost every Bulgarian home. And yet, it is in essence an anti-Russian book. So what is this pro-Russian love in Bulgaria that Western correspondents prattle about?

Let me re-emphasize that a fundamental distinction should be made between the attitude of Bulgarians to the Russian state, on the one hand, and their attitude towards Russian culture on the other. As regards the attitude to the Russian people, this does not differ from their attitude towards other peoples the world over, and has always been characterized by tolerance and respect.

If one had to single out one clearly defined healthy tendency in the Bulgarian way of life, it would be precisely the feeling of genuine sympathy, tolerance and respect for people of all other nationalities. I think that today, as in the past, the Bulgarians are some of the most tolerant people in the world. They do not know racial or religious pogroms, they do not commit chauvinist outrages – not even in the days of great patriotic fervour. The Bulgarians have always lived in harmony with the minorities in their own country, including the Jews, Armenians, Greeks, Turks and gipsies. Even in Ivan Vasov's novel *Chichovtsi* (*Uncles*) one is aware of that friendly disposition towards other nations which seems to be the hallmark of an inquiring spirit. Bulgarians past and present have always admired the positive aspects of other countries, irrespective of the state of international relations. Thus one cannot talk of any special relationship between the Bulgarians and the Russians. Perhaps there was a special relationship among politicians or pro-Russian officers of some limited Russophile circles, but the ordinary Bulgarian has hardly ever let himself be drawn into such a close relationship. His native wisdom, realism and fairmindedness have made him impartial towards all nationalities: from Americans to Arabs, from Germans to Chinamen. Looking at it purely from the standpoint of folk psychology, we see that it is impossible, and always was impossible, for Bulgarians to single out any nation for special preference.

Neither I, nor any other writer I know, would relish the task of having to decide for whom the Bulgarians harbour friendlier feelings: Serbs, Greeks, Turks or Romanians? The most truthful answer would be that their feelings are the same towards all of them, irrespective of this or that historical fact.

The gratitude of the Bulgarians towards Russia for the liberation and their respect for the thousands of Russian soldiers who died for their freedom have found expression in many historical monuments and the immortalization of certain names. But the idea of some sentimental feeling of eternal love and attachment (at the expense of other nations) is a tasteless figment of literature, suitable only for official declarations of loyalty from one regime to another.

All the same, if the attitude towards Russia can be examined in the

light of historical gratitude and cultural influence, the attitude towards the USSR, Soviet culture, the Soviet regime and Soviet man
take us back inexorably to the square in Dragalevtsi and the loaded
irony of the village commentators.

THE JUSTIFICATION

I wish to emphasize that in the years between the Hungarian Revolution [1956] and the Prague Spring [1968], the most discussed theme in Bulgaria was the steadfastness of one's convictions: the chosen position. It may sound strange and illogical, since in my judgement there were very few really consistent people, but all those who had demonstrated their inconsistency felt obliged to offer some excuse. I am told that it is no longer so: that my friends and acquaintances, whose inconsistency helped them to further their careers, no longer think it necessary to explain anything away. But in those days it was a burning topic, the unavoidable real thread of all conversations, perhaps because the whole atmosphere was still dominated by a shadowy question-mark to which the majority felt obliged to respond. An explanation was necessary because many people, either openly or secretly, had previously declared their position of basic disagreement with the Party's current policies and criticized the regime, only to find themselves in time the champions of the policies they had criticized and the defenders of its defects. I must have heard hundreds of justifications, without asking for them, without anyone being obliged to justify himself to me. Everyone explained to everyone else why he had accepted certain things, why he thought like this now, why he had changed. Tragically, or comically, everybody represented at one and the same time the innate conscience and its individual violation. Everything was in such an unbelievable muddle that even ministers complained about their own government, secret servicemen criticized their institution, and writers their own books. In a normal society, this would probably have been regarded as a positive phenomenon. But, with us, it was merely a game, part of society's ritual. Oh, how often people concluded naively that 'if everybody knows and recognizes his betrayal, this is bound to bring about some change!' In reality, the end result of all the explanations, justifications and confessions was – nil.

If I had to summarize all the excuses proffered, I would reduce them to two basic themes, with all sorts of variations. The first and most popular motive for a change of position, for the acceptance of a corrupting proposal, for the whole process of climbing up the ladder of success was: 'everyone else does it'. In other words, the most popular justification was – the others.

'I'd be crazy to refuse! Anyone in my place would have done the same! Why should I be a fool?'

And the comrade in question, who only yesterday had been a self-declared rebel, telling brave jokes against the militia and referring to the regime as 'they', suddenly appeared in the guise of a strict disciplinarian and loyal executive of some governing body. Some more flexible characters even had the audacity to come and pretend to ask advice beforehand: 'Look here, I've been offered this job. . . . You may find it odd – but I think, why not accept? In the end I might achieve more if I accept. . . .'

Here we come to the second basic motive, which the more adaptable characters used as their personal platform: 'I accepted because, from within, I shall be able to be a much stronger influence for change.' As a plan of action, this sounded quite convincing. Such people often said: 'We shall achieve nothing if we remain outside. Nothing depends on us. We have left the power in the hands of the sycophants. Can we wonder why things are going the way they are? If we are all on the inside, if we all take up positions of power, we could influence the entire policy.' Similarly, there was insistent canvassing of the idea that all of us non-Party citizens should join the Party, because this was the way for us to secure responsible positions.

Though at first sight this justification looked plausible, a person had to be very simple-minded to accept it. First, the regime demanded that the conforming comrade play the game by strictly observing the rules. Second, once his foot was on the ladder of power, this new servant of the establishment not only lost his sensitivity to justice and injustice but also developed, to a high degree, his own instinct for self-preservation: in other words he strove with all his might to cling to his position and to climb higher. At best, one could sometimes count on a certain tolerance from the new chief, who might remember his past as a dissident in the capital's cafés.

However sad it makes me, I must accept the fact that most of these rebels had actually rebelled for the sake of the power they coveted. Once they had received it, their rebellion was at an end. Nothing in public life changed, everything proceeded as before: there were absolutely the same outrages, distortions, unscrupulousness, demagogy, public and private villainies; only now our heroes were on the other side. In the literary circles in which I moved, examples abounded. Perhaps the most vivid was the case of my one-time friend, the poet Lyubomir Levchev.† [...] I should stress that I am not talking here about 'compromise' – which everyone accepts to an extent in the name of something, and which at times can be justified, at others not – but about a fundamental change of position, about renouncing one faith and adopting another. Most of those who, in the 1960s, struggled against the domination of the Writers' Union by Karaslavov's† group (which was regarded as a creature of the regime) in time turned out to be far more disagreeable, reactionary and dogmatic managers of our culture than the most extreme representatives of dogmatism. There is proof enough in the brilliant careers the 'anti-Karaslavovs' made. [...] The change of guard merely served to perpetuate the system. In fact, I sometimes think that all these rebels who protested so loudly had chosen rebellion as the surest claim to ... a decent slice of cake. Excuses like 'everyone else does it' or 'I'm doing it for the sake of change' turned out to be lies or self-delusions. In both cases, the real motive was personal prosperity.

But one of the most interesting cases of a person justifying his actions entirely by invoking the actions of 'others' was that of comrade M*, a highly placed favourite of the regime who wielded considerable influence in the cultural sphere. Once, under the influence of drink and nostalgic memories of innocent youth, on the terrace of the Lucky Dog restaurant, high on Mount Vitosha, I listened to his story, which made a profound impression on me.

Somewhere during 1950–1, M was a student at Sofia University. By origin and convictions his family were well placed in the new social order. But, out of pure idealism, in response to the Stalinist terror and the outrages of the Bulgarian dictators, M took part in a conspiracy of university students and older pupils who planned to publish an illegal dissident bulletin. Ironically, most of the participants in this conspiracy came from the neutral middle class or from Communist families. There were no 'class enemies' amongst them. Despite the courageous intention of the young people to stand up against the raging terror, despite their vow to fight with all their strength for 'the good of the people', matters did not progress very far because of lack of funds and opportunities. They were unable to secure the necessary duplicating machine and, while they were still looking for it, someone betrayed

* This is believed to be Markov himself.

them. Of course, the Stalinist State Security rounded them up mercilessly and, in the summer of 1951, they all found themselves in the left
wing of the Central Prison, where detainees were questioned.

M told the story of how he had been arrested on the street and taken
to the prison at No. 21, Stoletov Boulevard; how he had been kept
standing a whole day with his nose to the inner wall of the prison cell;
and how he had been grilled about the ramifications of the terrible
enemy conspiracy. Once, in a corridor, he glimpsed for a moment two
of his fellow conspirators, both sixth-form pupils. The palms of their
hands were badly swollen and blood dripped from them. At this sight,
M's hair stood on end. Afterwards, locked in one of the cells of the
seventh division, he listened all night to the groans and wails of youths
who had tried to be men.

He was surprised when, at midnight, he was taken down to Room
No. 7 for interrogation. The interrogator was a young man with an
intelligent face who, as M learnt later, was the only examining official
who was a graduate. There had been two other graduates amongst
the secret servicemen but they had left.

The interrogator, who had the rank of captain although he wore
civilian dress, started to question M carefully in a most friendly way.
He seemed less interested in a confession of the required facts than in
the motives, the psychological basis of this 'childish' conspiracy, as he
referred to it. The conversations between the two continued for a long
time – in fact several months – and not once did the captain raise his
voice or threaten M with beating or other tortures. Only once, a
certain Major Stanko burst into the room and shouted from the door:
'Why are you wasting your time with this bastard?'

But the captain did not drop his friendly tone and, more often than
not, the interrogation took on the character of psychoanalysis. Long
excursions into the individual experiences of M were followed by
literary or philosophical discussions. But, at the same time, the relentless prison regime continued. M was kept in solitary confinement,
often only on water and a small piece of bread, and, what was hardest
to bear, amidst the terrible cries and wails of people being tortured.

'I didn't know what to make of this interrogator!' he told me. 'On
the one hand, I knew that there was no genuine sympathy in his
attitude, however polite he was; and on the other, I imagined that he
understood me and even felt for me. If he had behaved like Major
Stanko, things would have been quite clear, but as it was, everything
was veiled in mystery. I wrote reams and reams of papers, some of
them on subjects like "Why I like Dostoevsky" or "If you were a

writer, what would you write?" But meanwhile I grew weaker every day, both in body and in spirit. Sometimes I felt like hitting him, provoking him so that we could end this interminable, idiotic dialogue: I wanted to wipe out his eternal smile. But, at certain crucial moments, his face took on a particular expression. This happened every time I tried to explain that if we had plotted to do something, it had been for the sake of the people. I even remember that I used the expression "the happiness of others" which somehow seemed to offend him. From time to time I had the impression that he hated me, because I was touching on his personal problems and he badly wanted to hear another more congenial answer. After about a month of questioning, he said to me one evening:

'"Listen, if I go on bothering with you, it's because I want to help you. And I want to help you because you're an intelligent person and our society needs people like you. The trouble is that your head's filled with sentimental rubbish, which I want to get rid of! You see, I could transfer you to Major Stanko and have the whole thing over and done with, but I think that you can be saved. Do you understand me?"'

M was at a loss to understand the drift of the whole interrogation. Abruptly, there followed a night of confrontations during which he saw almost all of his friends reduced to a state past recognition – beaten up, bearded, dirty. And at the end of this all-night parade of horrors, the captain said with a sinister laugh:

'And you imagine you are doing something for the people, that the people need the likes of you! The people haven't even noticed you! Nor will they notice you!'

A few mornings later, at 8 a.m., M was brought to the captain's office. His inquisitor received him in a very kindly way and said:

'Today is 9 September Day. And in order to show you and others like you that, in spite of everything, we believe in behaving properly, we have decided to let you go home for the holiday. But the day after tomorrow, the eleventh of September, at 9 a.m. exactly, I want you back here at the gate. Go and have a shave and clean yourself up. ...' And with a sudden grin, the captain added: 'I'm sorry, but you'll have to walk: all transport has been stopped because of the political rally. You live outside Sofia, don't you? Well, from Macedonia Square you can take the No. 5 tram, but you'll have to walk along Pirotska Street to Christo Botev Street ...' – and there followed detailed instructions about the journey home.

When M found himself outside the prison gates, he could not believe that he was free. He walked slowly because he was very weak, but eventually he turned left into Pirotska Street. It was already 9.30 a.m. and the whole street was packed with demonstrators waiting for their turn to march. There was a veritable sea of people, all dressed in their Sunday best, adorned with flowers, bearing multi-coloured slogans. Orchestras were playing and people were joining in the folk dancing. The weather was superb, the sun was shining brightly, everything seemed steeped in happiness and jubilation. Fathers were throwing little children into the air and loud-voiced propaganda groups chanted their slogans until totally exhausted: 'STALIN - CHERVEN-KOV! STALIN - CHERVENKOV! Eter-nal friend-ship!'

The contrast between this picture and the prison was annihilating.

'I felt my throat tighten suddenly,' M told me with visible emotion. 'And as I wound my way through the jubilant crowds, I could not stop my tears; I sobbed like a child and I remembered the bleeding faces of my friends, their palms hideously swollen from the rubber lashes, our hellish nights, the horror we had lived through, and I kept repeating as if in a trance: "Was it for the sake of these people ... for these people. ..." With difficulty I reached Macedonia Square, where my own university faculty had joined a huge folk dancing group; drums were beating, clarinets screamed, and the people were chanting "STALIN - CHERVENKOV!" I wanted to throw myself under the tram. And then a terrible anger exploded in me, which really saved me from going crazy.... I almost shouted aloud: "All right, dear people! If that's your game, you no longer interest me! I shall look after myself! I shall lead my own life! And you, mercenary and vile creatures, you live your own and don't dare complain to me that you are suffering! You just don't interest me!" '

The shock of this walk on 9 September Day was so profound that M subsequently had to undergo treatment. However, on 11 September, at 9 a.m., at the Central Prison, the captain met him with a long searching look.

'I think that you now understand a few important things,' he said. 'I was following you and I saw everything.'

M remained dully silent. He felt indifferent. He received a conditional sentence, and, over the next fifteen years, he pursued a remarkable career. And on that night in the mountain restaurant he told me: 'It was from this point on that I became what I am now, and I think that I'm right.'

That was his justification. I am not sure, however, that it satisfied him. Because he knew that he was one of those who conveniently justify their own sins by the sins of others.

IV

In 1961 Georgi Markov published two collections of short stories and then, in 1962, his first novel *Men*. It received the highest literary award and that same year Markov was elected a member of the Bulgarian Writers' Union.

A MEMBER OF
THE WRITERS' UNION

One evening in late June 1962, Christo Fotev, a young poet from Burgas, and I were sitting in the journalists' club on Count Ignatiev Street awaiting our fate. A hundred yards from us, at No. 5 Angel Kunchev Street, the Executive Board of the Writers' Union was holding a meeting chaired by Georgi Karaslavov.† The meeting was examining the applications of new union members and deciding on the annual literary awards, which were almost as important as the coveted Dimitrov Prizes. Both Fotev and I were on the list of proposed members and we were extremely nervous. In later years I would often reflect that, in the final analysis, membership of the Writers' Union had taken more from me than it had given. But at that time, on that particular evening, I felt like so many other young writers; I longed for official recognition of my literary calling. I want to emphasize that all the young authors I knew, without exception, were striving with almost hysterical persistence and obsessive ambition to obtain official recognition as writers and poets, dramatists or screen writers. But one of the ugliest paradoxes of our situation was that recognition was not the expression of the readers' or the nation's appreciation, but a red membership card handed out by the Party through its relevant institution, the Writers' Union. It may sound absurd, but Bulgarian society as a whole, the readers and the general public, had accepted this administration of literature as something quite normal. Whereas elsewhere in the world membership of a union of artists might signify simply the recognition of talent or a certain profession, in our situation the membership card was almost the only criterion for being considered a writer, a painter or a composer. Outside the Writers' Union you were no writer. Through this institutionalization, Party and regime effectively took over the natural right of the public to discover, accept and recognize talent. Who was a writer or not, and consequently who had talent and who did not, was determined on the same basis as promotion in the army, that is, through the judgment of senior officers. And the evaluation itself was made exclusively on the basis of whether a given literary work served or could serve the current needs of Party propaganda.

From the standpoint of real writing and the greatest achievements of world literature from Homer to our day, such administration of literary art is absurd. Shakespeare, Tolstoy, Dostoyevsky and Christo Botev were never members of any writers' unions, let alone bureaucratic ones. Not one respected literary name in the West today would accept the humiliation of being a member of such a body and wearing its repulsive grey uniform.

I do not know and I cannot explain convincingly how we, mostly rather sensible young authors, were possessed by this Party absurdity to the point of believing that membership of the Writers' Union would make us into writers. I think that there were two reasons for the nonsensical importance of the building at No. 5, Angel Kunchev Street: first, the vain hunger for distinction in an unequal and unjust society, the desire to be recognized as somebody in a world where the regime had no regard for anyone; and, second, practical calculations that were a result of the general corruption. Not a few young authors lost all sense of proportion when their attempts at membership of the Writers' Union were unsuccessful. There were people, Vassil Popov for instance, who were placed on the list of candidates every year but failed countless times and took this as the blackest personal tragedy. Many young writers lived with one obsession, one cherished dream – to become members, which at that time was very difficult. As we shall see, circumstances largely explained, and even partly justified, this almost pathological aspiration to acquire the red membership card.

On that June evening when Fotev and I were waiting for the results, we were both conscious of the falsity of our positions and tried to laugh at ourselves. When I asked Christo Fotev whether he thought that membership of the union would change his life in any essential way, he replied with the sincerity for which he was known as a poet: 'Well, the militia won't be able to arrest me after drunken brawls, and I'll be able to borrow money from the Union cashier.'

I feel ashamed to this day when I remember how excited and proud I was when, shortly before midnight, the deputy editor of the newspaper of the Writers' Union, *Literaturen Front*, came into the club and was the first to inform me that, as a mark of exceptional recognition, I had been elected directly as a full union member, which in those years was unprecedented. My novel *Men* had won the award for the best novel of the year. I nearly went out of my mind with joy. This was not merely recognition, but recognition with distinction. I had been elected in the most triumphant way possible. Previously – and subsequently – I hated titles, laureates and awards because I believed that they were part of the corruption of Bulgarian art, but during that memorable night I was a victim of the general madness. Fotev, who had been elected an associate member, was in seventh heaven. We wandered all night through the streets of Sofia and it seemed to us that the world was ours. A little later we were to laugh at a young author who, on being elected an associate member, shouted across the club to another young author: 'Hey, Vassko, now we too have become writers!'

And so it was. The red card with Karaslavov's signature was a document certifying that we were writers, that we were accepted on that inaccessible and strange Parnassus which is how people imagine the writer's world. Our vain pride and delight may have been fully justified by the longing of every young man to receive this coveted public recognition, but I very soon understood not only that this had nothing to do with literature, but something more important – *that the Writers' Union exists to hinder the creation of real literature.*

The day after our election, countless people congratulated us because they, too, accepted that the votes of the twenty-seven members of the Executive Board had made writers of us.

As I have already said, it was very difficult in those years to become a member of the union. Later on the procedure became much more democratic. The Party believed and still believes that literature is a vital propaganda instrument; hence the Writers' Union is considered the most important of all the unions of artists. Its staff included ten members of the Party's Central Committee and even a Politburo member, and where importance and influence in the country's ideological life were concerned, the Union was crucial. As we shall see later, in contrast with the writers' unions in Hungary, Czechoslovakia and Poland, the Bulgarian Writers' Union was the regime's spoilt child and at the same time the most narrow-minded and dogmatic of bodies. It was directly answerable to the Politburo, thus by-passing the various departments of the Central Committee and the Committee for Art and Culture. The attitude of our Union to the other unions of artists was that of an arrogant *prima donna*. Great power was concentrated in the hands of the Writers' Union and its executive, and almost all publishing of any significance was controlled by the writers. The union's role was even more important if one takes into account the personal connections and influence of eminent individual members, whose words carried weight with the first Party secretaries. The influence of the union's chairman, Karaslavov, in the Politburo was a more important factor in our cultural life than all the government decrees put together. The close personal friendship of Georgi Dzhagarov† and Todor Zhivkov was the tuning-fork which gave the pitch to our official cultural life, not to speak of the crushing authority of Todor Pavlov,† another union member.

The Writers' Union, a highly privileged dragon, was set up immediately after 9 September 1944, replacing the existing union. Copying the Soviet model to the letter, the Party strengthened its propaganda work by recruiting to the union people with obvious literary ambitions who had proved to some extent their loyalty to the regime. The task of the union was twofold: to produce the kind of literature needed by the Party, and, much more important, to prevent at all costs the emergence of any literary activity outside the Party's ideological framework. Since all means of publication were in the hands of the regime, it was not difficult for the Writers' Union to become the only organization which could offer a writer any professional outlet. Thus, every writer in the country saw membership of the Union as the necessary password to open the doors of publishing houses and editorial offices. Moreover, in time, Party propaganda managed to transform writing from a purely individual calling into a public office with its own set of rules. In the past, only a handful of the representatives of classical Bulgarian literature dared to call themselves writers. Bulgaria had only one national writer – Ivan Vasov.† Now there are two dozen 'people's writers' whose scribblings are an insult to Bulgarian literature, and over three hundred citizens who appear on various platforms, stick out their chests, lift their chins and listen proudly when they are introduced by their obscure folksy names: 'Comrades, we have before us today the writer XYZ!' We shall see later how an overwhelming majority of the union's members not only are no writers but also lack a normal sense of humour which would save them many an embarrassment. Even those who are quite intelligent take themselves and their writing seriously and consider themselves the direct counterparts of Leo Nikolaevich Tolstoy or Johann Wolfgang von Goethe. Heaven knows how many naive and ludicrous performances I have attended in which an author of doggerel would strike a pose like Pushkin, or at least lay claim to equal immortality. The madness works in two ways: on the one hand, the pen-wielders themselves have come to believe that they are writers; and, on the other, official society has declared them to be, and insists that they are, writers. There are few indeed who understand that the literary production displayed is far removed from real literature. Paradoxically or not, the Party has succeeded in identifying the Writers' Union with Bulgarian literature and this is one of the tragic desecrations of our time. A bureaucratic institution, which in form and content has nothing in common with creative activity and the creative process, which in every way negates the art called literature, which persecutes and stifles every natural expression of literary talent: this institution has become a synonym for proven creative ability, a synonym for the literary life of a whole nation. I think it must be acknowledged that the Communist Party has one astounding gift: its knack of organizing and imposing its substitutes – pseudo-institutions, pseudo-activities and pseudo-artists – in place of real ones.

We saw countless cases when the Party machine produced not merely one or two of its pseudo-creatures, but a whole chain that would strengthen them. For instance, first the Party declares that the pseudo-author Monchov is a writer. After that the Party organizes the pseudo-critic Ponchov to write articles in praise of Monchov. Then it appoints the pseudo-producer Tonchov to screen the pseudo-novel of the pseudo-writer. And finally it sets up a whole group of hacks in newspapers, radio and television who endorse the genius of comrade Monchov. Once he has been promoted to 'genius', this comrade himself starts handing out similar promotions, naturally to pseudo-authors like himself. From a normal viewpoint, this whole tragi-comedy directed by the Party resembles a lunatic asylum, where the inmates declare that they are Napoleon or Alexander the Great, wave their arms about and command invisible armies. To no other society is Andersen's tale of 'The Emperor's New Clothes' more applicable, and one can only hope that one day a child's voice will be heard shouting: 'The Emperor has no clothes!'

A friend of mine, the author of cheap little novels, confessed to me one day: 'I know I am no writer, but it gives me the greatest pleasure when I pass Slaveykov Street and hear people say: "That's the writer who wrote that novel about the man who walked in the rain" ...'

Angel Todorov had the sense of humour to tell the following story on the radio: he went to the swimming pool at the public baths. Another naked man was sitting next to him and they started talking to each other. 'What do you do?' asked the stranger. 'I'm a writer', replied Angel. 'Oh!' exclaimed his questioner and looked closely at him. 'And what is your name?' 'Angel Todorov!' said Angel, self-confidently. The face of the naked stranger expressed complete puzzlement. 'Angel Todorov?' he repeated. 'I know of a few writers – Ivan Vasov, Yordan Yovkov, Elin Pelin, Dimiter Talev* ... but Angel Todorov ...? There is no such writer! There just isn't!'

I think that these words 'There is no such writer!' can be applied to most members of the Writers' Union. But it would be even more apt to say: 'There is no such union!' because a state organization of talented people who create literature is an impossibility.

Unfortunately, however, because of the needs of the regime, Angel was a writer, a Writers' Union existed and I ... was its member.

*All these writers are recognized as masters of Bulgarian literary prose. Talev is the only one amongst them who became known after the Communists came to power.

WE MADE YOU INTO
A WRITER

When it came to recognition of my literary career, I was very lucky. After long years completely devoid of literature describing contemporary life, my novel *Men* was one of the first works to appear during the thaw under Khrushchev's regime. Perhaps for the first time in a contemporary Bulgarian novel disagreeable and cruel truths were told openly, with guilt being ascribed not to the 'personality cult', as Party fashion demanded, but to the actions and characters of the people themselves. Despite my merciless exposure of the failings which had become typical of our situation, without my intending it, the central ideas of my novel provided the Party with a much needed defence. In it, the weaknesses of the system, the regime and the Party were blamed on individuals or shown to spring from individual human defects. This was precisely the line that the Party was propagating: individuals can make mistakes, but never the Party or the system. There were times when many of us, keen to cling to some hope of salvation, proclaimed with naive optimism that if certain, human, individual vices could be eradicated, then the whole dark side of our lives would disappear. Sometimes we deliberately closed our eyes so as not to see the ugly, bestial face of the system, the humiliation and shame that it never ceased to produce. Every unprejudiced witness of our period can see clearly that the responsibility for everything evil, repellent and reprehensible in Bulgaria today is shared more or less equally between the weaknesses of the system and the weaknesses of individual people. What is so bad and depressing in today's Communist world is that the system rests on individual human shortcomings and therefore encourages, develops and perfects them. Even the most fanatical Party member would have to admit that never before in Bulgaria has there been so much deceit, baseness, adultery, dishonesty, denunciation, betrayal and, particularly, larceny. But that is another major theme.

The Party critics found in my novel exactly what they needed. From there on, a wide avenue with its traffic lights permanently green opened before me. When the Party machine starts working for someone, everything goes smoothly. After the publication of my novel, I was deluged by the most flattering reviews. Apart from serialization in the monthly literary journal *Septemvri*, there were two further editions of the novel and many translations into foreign languages, as well as a dramatization for radio, an adaptation as a play, and a film. I had been richly rewarded for my efforts.

Early on the morning after my election as a full member of the Writers' Union, Pavel Matev, then the union Secretary, called at my home to offer his congratulations. At that time I lived in an attic not much bigger than a wardrobe, exactly opposite the Universiada Hall. The housing situation in Sofia was desperate. But as a fully-fledged union member, that is, a writer recognized by the Party, I quickly noticed a happy change. Soon I was given a new apartment in a block shared by privileged comrades. Membership of the union not only satisfied vain ambition but also provided official access to a privileged category of people. According to the unwritten but firmly established rules of our existence, I passed from the world of the ordinary Bulgarian citizen deprived of his rights into the world of those who, in a phrase much in use in Dragalevtsi, had 'set up a state for themselves'. Indeed, as Christo Fotev had indicated, the red membership card had a magic effect on the militia. But that was by no means its greatest importance. While as an ordinary citizen I had to wait for the duration of whole five-year plans to obtain a home, as a writer it was easy. Indeed, not a few of my colleagues acted like temperamental *prima donnas*, changing one apartment for another, taking advantage of the goodwill of the relevant authorities. As an ordinary citizen I had to fight ruthlessly for a more or less decent job; as a writer I had the choice between a dozen good editorial posts with an official four-hour day. Much later, as an editor in the publishing house *Narodna Mladezh* (Nation's Youth), I uneasily remembered that when I was an engineer the working day was never less than twelve hours, while in the editorial office one worked in effect only a few hours weekly. While ordinary citizens wanting cars had to wait for about two years, having already paid for them (at an interest fixed by the state), I and many of my co-writers got our cars within a few days. Those of us whose works had been translated abroad enjoyed additional privileges. While ordinary citizens could only dream about foreign travel and spent lifetimes fighting for passports that would never come, we, the more active writers, received our passports in a day or two. Some of my senior colleagues had their own way of using the special supply shops reserved for the cream of the Party establishment. The journalists' club, and later the writers' club too, had a privileged status where supplies were concerned, and so their food was much better than the fare provided in first-class restaurants. Every writer had the right to six months 'creative leave', which he usually spent in one of the union's rest homes or in one of the holiday homes for artists, paying nominal prices. Most of the union's members were able to receive long-term subsidies from the union which were either not repayable or merely linked to a promise to write something. In addition, one could obtain special loans guaranteed by the outline of a book, play or film. By contrast with other artists' unions in Poland, Hungary and Czechoslovakia, the Bulgarian Writers' Union was exceptionally rich. On the strength of a government decree, the union's fund received percentages from every book published in the country, irrespective of whether the author was a union member or not, whether he was a Bulgarian or a foreigner. This meant that the writers had huge annual subsidies at their disposal. The Polish writers' union was in a wretched financial situation, the Hungarian writers had difficulty in making ends meet, while the Bulgarian writers' fund had plentiful resources enjoyed by few organizations of this kind in the world. I am convinced that this form of bribery was one of the most successful devices of the Bulgarian regime, which displayed a far shrewder practical approach than any of the other East European regimes. This explains to a large extent the relatively harmonious relations between our writers and the regime. If a Polish writer is expelled from his union, he loses little, for his situation is already difficult. But if a Soviet or Bulgarian writer incurs expulsion, he must face a painful change and a considerable loss. Many writers from other countries can only dream of the advantages of their Bulgarian counterparts: the richly subsidized so-called creative field-trips (where usually nothing was created), the magnificent rest home in Varna, the former Royal palace in Sitnyakovo, now a Writers' Union residence, the hostels in Hissarya or Sozopol, the club-restaurant in Sofia, the manifold free comforts offered by different councils and committees, the sums generously made available by various ministries and organizations such as the Komsomol, the Trades Unions Council, the Ministry of Defence, the Ministry of the Interior, the Committee for State Security, the Forestry Ministry and many others.

The official union membership card had the value of a university language degree, so that every member of the Writers' Union was entitled to occupy a teaching post at the University. But the main advantage of membership was the opportunity it offered to mingle with powerful literary colleagues and use their connections and influence. In short, for a young author, joining the Writers' Union meant entering the magic circle. From this point on everything was easy, provided he observed the rules of the game. It flattered me that whereas as an engineer my public importance had been nil, as a writer I became the centre of public attention. This was more than the normal popularity that every writer in the world enjoys amongst his readers, or the sensationalist attention commanded by fashionable names. I am talking of a single-minded attention on the part of the country's rulers. As an engineer I could view the Minister of Light Industry from a respectful distance. As a writer I could dine with the Prime Minister or various high Party or State officials. Being included in the register of the privileged, even at the bottom of the hierarchical ladder, led to the useful attendance at all sorts of official meetings. Everything that I have enumerated so far could hardly fail to influence the thinking and the work of anyone who had experienced such a momentous change in his life. The delicacies on the Bulgarian writers' table were too many and too enticing not to have tempted the great majority of my fellow writers. They explained the frantic efforts of all sorts of pen-wielding citizens to gain entry into the union, because for them literature did not mean tenacious, difficult, harsh labour, sleepless nights, the denial of entertainments and pleasures, bitter doubts and anguish engendered by the consciousness of the disparity between desire and possibility – but simply a convenient way of life.

'What do you want to write for, surely you're not lacking anything, are you?' said a writer I knew, when I complained that I had not been getting on well with my writing.

And here I come to the inevitable, cold and unpalatable conclusion: all these luxuries were put at the disposal of the writers for one reason only – to prevent them from writing. That was precisely the purpose behind the sweet life offered us – to stop us writing. It was designed for those who could write, for those who were gifted but had to deny their talent, bury it deeply and try not to remember it. Because talent, as I have said many times, meant independence, and consequently inevitable conflict with the totalitarian forces of organized society and the norms established by it, and hence the pointing of a new way for many others.

And yet, the delicacies were not for everyone in the Union. Out of roughly three hundred members, only about eighty writers actually took part in the game, since some of them were sacrificed for the comfort of others. Of these, not more than twenty were persons with some literary talent. Amongst this group of the elect, the law of mutual dependence applied with special force. The gospel of the existing friendships was: 'Do as you would be done by.' Each of the writers on the special register knew that behind every other man like himself there stood a mysterious, terrifyingly fickle power. We spent long hours guessing who protected whom and what was the relative importance of the Union's various members. There was usually a huge disparity between a writer's talent and his official position, despite the regime's policy of wooing the talented and popular names. For instance, the mediocre poet Vlado Golev was the leader of the union orchestra, while the talented poet Ivan Peychev counted for nothing. The best poet Bulgaria has today, Konstantin Pavlov, was not even accepted as a member of the union. A whole crowd of insignificant would-be writers and poets in effect ruled the union and largely determined its official face. I refer to the writers by appointment, who by any true literary criterion cannot be included in literature. They were the most fanatical, zealous conveyor belts for the Party line and their alliance was invincible. Try to make a union out of really talented people and you are bound to fail, because every one of them pulls in his own direction, has a different opinion, and feels independent from and, to some extent, even intolerant towards the others. But with the mediocre, the solder is perfect. They have only one objective – to be in power. Most of them realize that they do not deserve the positions they have acquired, that they have won them, so to speak, in the Party lottery and that is why they fight so hard to retain them. I cannot bear to draw up a list of such pseudo-writers, appointed by the Party to administer literature. I even find it painful to remember the whole of this cheap masquerade. But these hacks are the citizens to whom the banal phrase 'We made you into a writer' applies exactly. Many times and on various pretexts, numerous writers have been told menacingly: 'We made you into a writer!' However absurd this may sound, it was the pure truth as far as the hacks were concerned and they had to abide by it. At every tense moment, at every hesitation between conscience and action, at every important vote, before every concerted Party move, a warning red light would appear, flashing the words: 'We made you into a writer'. I very much doubt that any of these 'made' writers could have won literary renown in any normal society. On the other hand, everybody knows that it was not the regime which made Yordan Radichkov† into a writer, or Konstantin Pavlov and Stefan Tsanev into poets. They are what they are and will remain so under any regime and in any circumstances. A few are in an intermediate category, like Lyubomir Levchev,† in whom I detect a painful struggle between the 'made' writer and the natural, independent poet.

I must say that of the young authors of my generation who gained entry into the Writers' Union, all, with hardly any exception, had an ambiguous attitude towards it. On the one hand, we accepted the comforts, the hand-outs and the money which membership made available to us; on the other, we felt open contempt for the union management. We never got used to their literary pretensions and our relations with them remained highly complex.

When I stepped over the threshold of the Writers' Union, I perceived that a violent battle was raging inside between two almost equally powerful groups; heavy literary guns belched out hatred against each other, and every post in the Party and state hierarchy was fiercely contested while respected and despised names were defiling each other under the Party's benevolent smile.*

---

* In Vol. I of Markov's original, this chapter is followed by two others - 'Divide and rule' and 'The literary swamp' in which the internecine battles of the Bulgarian writers are described in detail. (This section, about 6,000 words, is not translated.)

AT THE FOOT OF
MALYOVITSA

I was invited to meet the students of the brigade who, during the summer, worked on the new road to Malyovitsa [a peak in the Rila mountains].

These organized meetings for authors and their readers, or simply the public at large, were and are a very commonplace form of compulsory socializing for propaganda purposes. Both sides were constrained. The writers were obliged to leave the exclusive and friendly club atmosphere which was their element and to meet those who were supposed to read their books. Only the vainest and most mediocre literary figures accepted this chore with pleasure, because it gratified their vain desire to be big popular names. The simpler and more naive of my colleagues took pleasure in the posters and newspapers which announced their arrival in a village or town, graciously accepted the bunches of flowers, signed autographs in a florid handwriting and posed for photographs with the public in order to immortalize the moment. Sometimes they jotted down in their notebooks the address of a local lady teacher with beautiful dreamy eyes who would haunt their dreams as a proof of their powerful talent.

For their part, various organizations representing factories, offices, districts, the military, women et cetera were often expected to invite writers either for a public reading of their works or for a meeting with readers, as part of their social and political activity. Thus, the confrontation between the writer and his public was not due to genuine interest on either side, but was simply a variation of the general rule of 'getting it over with'. Both sides knew that this cultural event would be chalked up in their favour and thus it was worth the trouble of suffering a few boring hours. It was because of this lack of genuine mutual interest that the conversation had to be organized beforehand. A few victims chosen from the public were obliged to read the works of the invited writer (or writers), to look up a few reviews and to prepare some questions. Usually, the conversations which ensued were unbearably artificial and were often demeaned by quotations from the speeches of the Party's First Secretary. There was no genuine dialogue, since both writers and readers recited the same monologue. The proceedings were weighed down by a feeling of meaninglessness such as two prisoners would experience if asked by the warden to discuss last year's snow. 'Well ... it was white,' the first one would say. 'Too true. It was really white!' the second would reply.

People were too wise to ask awkward questions, and the visitors were too artful to provoke them. The safest questions concerned the prototypes of certain literary characters, but the discussion very seldom ventured into the dangerous zone of issues like the truth of life and its travesty in literature, which, in my opinion, should be the main theme of every serious literary discussion in Bulgaria.

And yet, despite the instinctive caution which prevailed at such meetings, from time to time a bomb would explode. At such moments, the rigged lesson of meaningless questions and answers would count for nothing and powerful voices seemed to cry out: 'Can't you see that the Emperor has no clothes?'

I arrived at the student camp by car early one afternoon. It was a beautiful sunny day. Looking at the motorway which stretched towards the inaccessible pure mountain altitudes, I thought sadly that the fate of Vitosha would soon overtake Rila, that within a few years there would be no trace left of the marvellous rich solitude of its peaks, that the lush pastures would soon be strewn with empty tins and newspapers, that the noble trial of the mountaineer pitted against the steep slopes would be abandoned on the seat of a Moskvich chugging uphill. The student who met me seemed to have read my thoughts, for suddenly he said: 'We're turning the mountain into a lavatory!'

His biting voice was full of irony and clearly he expressed something to which he could not resign himself. He was very blond, with clear blue eyes and a handsome face. His movements were clumsy and from time to time he gave me a searching look. Evidently he was trying to size me up.

'I haven't read any of your works,' he said as we walked across the meadow towards the shed in which the meeting with the students was going to take place. Then, he added, without the trace of an excuse:

'I don't read today's Bulgarian literature! Don't think I haven't tried – endlessly. The girls mention the name of one writer or another and one doesn't want to be out of it, but,' here he stopped, turned towards me, and looking straight into my eyes, said: 'I simply don't understand what you write.'

This was a warning that my meeting with the students was not going to be the usual performance, with everything fixed beforehand. At the same time, I noticed the glances which my brand-new BMW was attracting and I fervently wished I had come instead in some battered van. In the shed, which also served as the students' canteen, the atmosphere was unfriendly. There was no table with the usual red table-cloth and regulation vase of flowers and, quite unbelievably for Bulgaria, there were no portraits or slogans on the walls. I was offered a chair and the students sat down on the surrounding tables. As they arrived one by one in their faded dungarees, my guide told me that if I wanted I could sample something rare after the meeting – meat-balls made from fresh donkey meat. I thought they were joking. Immediately I also noticed the complete absence of the servile politeness with which the organizers of such meetings usually surrounded us. The boys and girls looked at me with severe, serious faces and even the few jokes with which I began did nothing to soften the mood. There were about a hundred people in the shed and more kept arriving. My fair-haired guide introduced me with the ominous words: 'Today, we welcome Georgi Markov, the author of *Men*, for a ... manly conversation!'

Trying to disarm my future assailants, I chose a well-tried safe theme: 'The existence of cowards is no reason for us to behave in a cowardly manner.' It was my deep conviction that in Bulgaria social responsibility was used for washing individual dirty hands, that most heinous crimes and base actions were committed in the name of Party, people and country, and that the only standard that made sense was the standard of personal responsibility. I have never been able to accept justifications like 'the Party gave me the order', 'I didn't want to, but I did it because I was ordered to.' It is in this substitution of general concepts like Party, people, country, for concrete personal responsibility that I see individual villainy thriving and legitimized. I spoke for about half an hour. I felt that they listened to me with critical attention, that unexpectedly I had presented them with a wider battlefield than they were looking for. I even had the impression that they liked my strict delineation between personal responsibility and Party responsibility. When I finished, there was no applause. Instead, I heard a voice say:

'And how do you reconcile your convictions with the privileges you enjoy? With the expensive Western car outside? There would seem to be a contradiction here?'

My questioner was a thin young man with a squint.

'When you call for individual responsibility in others,' he continued shrilly, 'it is to be assumed that you yourself have an individual conscience! Or, perhaps you too will say, "You must make the sacrifices; we'll just enjoy ourselves."'

I could see that everyone approved of what he said and eagerly awaited my reply. I felt very embarrassed and tried to explain that my car was not necessarily a privilege; but, hearing my own unconvincing voice, I hesitated and fell silent. They were absolutely right. To a greater or lesser degree, at that time I belonged to the generously remunerated élite and it was stupid for me to claim (as some of my colleagues did) that I deserved everything that was given me. But the discussion was only beginning.

'Would you tell us how much you earn a month,' was the next question.

All eyes were on me, expecting that I would be evasive. I told them the approximate figure: so much from books, so much from films, from television, from radio, from various newspapers and journals.... They reacted with noisy surprise, and a few whistled.

'That's what my father earns in a year and a half!' someone exclaimed.

'Do all writers earn as much?'

'No ...', I said. 'No ... only a few....'

I had spared them. I had been tempted to tell them that writers existed who were little more than factories for making money; that they earned ten times what I did; that some of them had more than a million stashed away in the bank; that the greatest rogues more or less divided the available printing paper among themselves; that in a paper factory on the road to Gorna Banya I had seen unsold books being reduced to pulp, only to be published again a month later. I wondered what effect the exact figures for the income of so-called commercial writers – many times higher than any conceivable socialist income – would have. And what the students would have said about other very rich colleagues of mine whose wives (or mistresses) went to market on Fridays in London or Paris, who bought large quantities of hard currency on the black market, built themselves expensive villas and had an entourage of paid hacks. It would have been too much for them.

'And what are these fees paid for?' asked my guide, obviously pleased at the turn of the discussion. 'I told you that I've tried to read this literature, but it's unreadable. . . . It simply has nothing to do with me.'

'It has nothing to do with anybody!' shouted a cheeky student.

'When I read all these works . . .' began a third student who was trying to express himself more fluently, 'I don't know why they've been written . . . If they're meant to reflect life as it is, then I must say that either you writers don't know life, or you lie. If they are meant to pose a problem, then their general level is so abysmally low that the problem vanishes without trace. But even if we accept that they are merely an instrument of current Party propaganda, I must inform you that they are so cheap as to be counter-productive.'

'The Party must hate itself to pay such hacks!' piped up yet another.

Then, several of them started talking at once, so that I had difficulty in following their arguments. But their discordant chorus was clearly a spontaneous protest against Bulgarian contemporary literature and put my colleagues and myself into the unenviable category of wealthy and frivolous aliens who visited Bulgaria occasionally.

'Don't the critics see these things?' asked a student, who had quickly analysed a third-rate novel.

'The critics are just as bad as the writers!' someone else replied.

I thought about the hopelessly corrupt state of our literary criticism. Ninety per cent of the critics were minor officials of extremely limited intelligence, with even less heart. The remaining 10 per cent were either crafty ambitious political acrobats, who traded their talents shamelessly, or a few other intellectuals isolated from both life and literature. I badly wanted to tell the students how the writers themselves organized their critics and their notices, how they would do anything for good reviews. I also wanted to tell them about the hapless critic, Maxim Naimovich, who had approached an editorial office with two different reviews of the same book: in the left pocket, he carried the favourable review; in the right, the unfavourable. The point of the story was that the fellow did not know the editorial attitude to the book in question and had played safe by offering a choice. All Sofia had laughed at this story, forgetting that Maxim Naimovich had in fact merely acted out the general unwritten code of behaviour.

I wanted to tell them too how most of the critics strained to ascertain opinion 'at the top' and then immediately conformed to it, either by attacking a book, or praising it to the skies.

But I did not say anything. I waited for them to calm down and then asked them: 'In spite of everything, what do you like in our literature, if you like anything?'

Someone managed to be the first to blurt out: 'Konstantin Pavlov!' after which the name was repeated many times, followed by the names of Radoi Ralin,† Nikolai Kunchev, Yordan Radichkov,† Georgi Mishev and Stefan Tsanev.

'Is Konstantin Pavlov rich?' asked a girl student.

'No,' I replied.

'And Radoi Ralin?'

'He can hardly get by. You can see him at lunch-time when he crosses Slavevkov Square carrying mess-tins of food for his children. . . .'

'What about Nikolai Kunchev?'

'I think he's paid less than a student grant.'

The students became animated. I could see that my answers were exactly what they wanted to hear. They would have been horrified if Konstantin Pavlov had turned out to have had a fat bank balance, or if, following the fashion of the richest writers, he had had a private chauffeur. The poverty of Konstantin and Radoi filled the students with optimism and hope, assuring them that not all writers were factories for churning out money, that not all of them sold their talents or traded with them. The writers they had chosen as their own were even poorer than themselves. Their faces lightened, as if I had brought them some very good news. . . .

The uproar quickly subsided. I felt with embarrassment that once more all eyes were on me, harder and more insistent than before. I tried not to see them and fixed my gaze on the middle distance between them and me, bracing myself for an even more disagreeable question. But they kept silent, clearly expecting me to talk and say something about myself, as inexorable logic demanded. For a moment I thought that I could not bear it. Then, in the continuing silence, against the wooden background of the shed, all these faces surrounding me, with their most diverse and distinctive characteristics, gradually merged into a single face which asked me with a knowing smile: 'And what about you, comrade Markov?'

The voice belonged to the student with the squint.

THE DIALECTIC OF CENSORSHIP

Although Stalin's death altered little as far as original literature and art were concerned, there was some relaxation towards Western culture. Khrushchev's travels around the world led to the opening of a few narrow chinks in the Stalinist prison walls.

First of all, the classics began to be published again. Very timidly, the publishing houses started printing Western writers of whom it was known with certainty that they had been published in the Soviet Union already, or that they had a 'healthy, progressive outlook'. Very rarely, the cinemas showed carefully selected Western films which painted life in the bourgeois capitalist world in the darkest colours of misery and hopelessness. In their attitude towards Western culture the party censors behind the scenes often made themselves utterly ridiculous.

As a result of the Marxist definition of literature and the arts as an expression of the class struggle, which states that they are created and exist in order to be a weapon in the hands of a given class, the spiritual and intellectual climate in Bulgaria was changed beyond recognition. In only a few years, the gentle, sunny atmosphere of old in which anything interesting could blossom was replaced by a polar Soviet frost. The second half of the twentieth century found Bulgarian culture not very different from that of the Soviet Republics of Tadzhikistan and Uzbekistan.

But even the blindest Party fanatics soon perceived that the strict application of the Marxist discovery of the class nature of art was leaving the 'class enemy' in possession of more than 99 per cent of world literature. The Party could not accept a line which made it the equal of Attila's barbarians. A way out of this predicament was offered by the Party's dialectical method, which consisted in examining every development according to the Party's needs at any given moment; or, more precisely, the needs of the leadership, which – by the same dialectical method – could turn out eventually not to have been in the least representative of the Party. One of the most telling examples was the fate of the Bulgarian painter Alexander Zhendov. Dialectically, he began by being the personification of militant progressive art under a bourgeois regime. According to the same dialectic, he became [under the Stalinist regime] a symbol of the enemy of progressive art and a victim of reprisals which led to his death. After that, once again according to Party dialectics, he was metamorphosed into a martyr and an angel of progressive art. And to complete the dialectical picture, his spiritual heir, Bogomil Rainov,† instead of being punished, was showered with honours.

What dialectic in fact proved was that, in practice, neither established aesthetic criteria nor long-term assessments existed for the Party.

This is why the Red *auto-da-fé* of the first period under Communism had to be replaced by continual assessment and reassessment of developments and personalities in the arts. Through the years, we witnessed such dialectical somersaults that our heads spun.

I remember, at the very beginning, an absurd example. Radio Sofia's music then consisted mainly of Bulgarian and Soviet Party songs and folk music. Classical music was played comparatively rarely. Nevertheless, at a lecture on music, a vigilant comrade asked: 'Why does Radio Sofia play Beethoven when it is well known that he wrote music at the bidding of Austrian aristocrats and consequently has nothing in common with the working class and the struggles of the Party?' The lecturer gave the following reply: 'Although Beethoven's music was commissioned by the aristocracy, it reflects the revolutionary progressive spirit of his time and therefore we accept it;' and here the lecturer raised his voice to deliver the clinching argument. 'Comrades, Comrade Lenin liked to listen to the *Appassionata*!'

Clearly, in the ideological revaluation of Beethoven, the composer was saved by the myth that Lenin loved the *Appassionata* – which, so far as I have been able to check, is not even true. By contrast, Johann Sebastian Bach had to be amputated. After all, the man had only written church music. The decision was really quite simple – only Bach's instrumental music was to be allowed. For many years, not one of Bach's choral works could be broadcast on Radio Sofia.

If such things happened in the relatively abstract realm of music, it is more than obvious what the fate of literature would be.

With the establishment of the Communist dictatorship, the American Communist writer, Howard Fast, was extolled by the propaganda machine as the greatest living American writer. His novel *Spartacus* was considered a major work of art and became a subject of compulsory study by readers' groups and seminars. But when Howard Fast turned in his Party membership card as a protest against the Soviet invasion of Hungary in 1956 and the suppression of the Hungarian revolution, the dialectic again performed its abracadabra. Fast was pronounced a renegade, his books were thrown out of the libraries and it was explained to us that the works of this lackey of American reaction were artistically worthless. So much for Howard Fast!

A similar fate befell the eminent American writer, John Steinbeck. At first he was considered the living embodiment of American literature. His novel *The Grapes of Wrath* was described as a revolutionary work depicting the miserable lot of working people in the United States; and his other works as indictments of the capitalist world of high artistic merit. But when Steinbeck made his famous declaration about the Vietnam war, he was liquidated as a writer and as a person at one dialectical stroke. In the most recent edition of the Bulgarian encyclopædia you will find the names of neither Howard Fast nor John Steinbeck. They simply do not exist. Translations and new editions of their works are proscribed. Some time will have to pass before the dialectic discovers that both were 'misled by the reaction' and that 'we should not judge them by their mistakes but by their art which belongs to all progressive people throughout the world'....

The older the work, the easier it is to make re-reassessments. For instance, Balzac at first caused some difficulties with his firm Royalist views. But when it became known that Karl Marx had said that he had learned more about conditions in France from Balzac's novels than from history books, the great Honoré was forgiven by a certain Vulcho Vulkov Vulkanov and returned to Bulgarian libraries. But Balzac's countrymen – Beaudelaire, Verlaine and Rimbaud, who were supposed to symbolize decadence and decay and to divert people's minds in the wrong direction, were not allowed access to the builders of socialism. The same ban affected Marcel Proust, although he could count himself lucky that his pre-War editions were not destroyed. [...]

Kafka was considered right from the beginning as the most vivid representative of the corrupt human spirit which sees no way out and whose pessimism is a cleverly forged weapon of the bourgeoisie aimed at undermining progressive thought. Many years had to pass before the dialectic discovered that Kafka had had in mind only the bourgeois capitalist world and that the allegories *The Castle* and *The Trial* were in fact his judgement on the doomed world of the bourgeoisie. And yet, no paper could be made available for reprinting Kafka. Neither he nor Joyce fitted easily into the struggle of Bulgaria's chief ideologist and defender of Socialist Realism, Academician Todor Pavlov,† against the insidious effects of implied meaning. 'Impossible! How can one write about one thing, while meaning another! That's not the way we do things!' – another quotation from yet another Vulko.

But it was Jean-Paul Sartre who offered the greatest possibilities for displaying the Marxist dialectic. In the first years [of Communism], he was the great French anti-Fascist; thereafter he became the Satan of reactionary existentialism and all who negated the reality of existence; then, when he joined the peace movement and became a member of the World Peace Council, Sartre was transformed into a passionate fighter; after which he changed into an anti-Soviet hireling, paid by world reaction, only to degenerate into a Maoist or Trotskyite, until, in the end, the epithets seemed to run out and he was, in the final analysis, proclaimed to be a subjectivist and a pessimist but also a critic of bourgeois reality. It is impossible not to laugh at the definition which Bulgarian academics gave him in the encyclopædia: 'gradually the humanist tendencies in him gained the upper hand'. It was as if a hardened criminal were being discussed! However, even while Sartre was changing in a trice from devil to angel, quick-witted editors managed to publish some of his works.

Eventually, the Marxist dialectic applied its abracadabra to Albert Camus, who, from being a 'nihilist', became 'controversial' so that we were able to read *The Outsider* and *The Plague*. André Malraux, however, had to remain entrenched for a considerable time in his unenviable Gaullist position. Of the British, the school of Angry Young Men had their works translated immediately, since the vituperations of John Osborne against the English class system were the very sounds that the Party propaganda wished to hear. But as soon as the anger of the angry men subsided and the invective ceased, nobody bothered to translate any more of their writing. Alan Sillitoe alone continued to weep bitter tears over the miserable fate of the unfortunate English under the indignant eyes of the fortunate Bulgarians.

If I were to enumerate all the games of the dialectic censorship in Bulgaria, I would need more space than *War and Peace*. William Faulkner and Louis Aragon, Rainer Maria Rilke and Ezra Pound, T.S. Eliot and Edgar Allan Poe.... Yet, it must be admitted that the general trend was towards the forgiveness of sins and the opening of doors. Again as a result of the dialectic, it suddenly transpired that purely bourgeois writers like Scott Fitzgerald or Alberto Moravia were far less dangerous than Communist writers like Aragon, since Communism spawned many heresies. In the last decade or so, the chief criterion for publishing the works of a Western writer has been reduced to whether or not he was a critic of bourgeois society or, failing that, whether he took a 'controversial stand'. Gradually, books which attacked the horrors of the capitalist world began to disappear; in an era of expanding tourism it became awkward to talk of the wretched life of Frenchmen, the privations of Americans and the lack of privilege of Germans. But this did not prevent the removal of inconvenient pages or the doctoring of various passages, as happened to Hemingway.

To this more optimistic picture was added another, very strange, criterion, which dominated Bulgarian culture: publishing houses scrambled for authors who were known either as having been published or as about to be published in the Soviet Union.

'The book has already appeared in Russia' was a very strong argument which, at first, the censorship watchdogs did not dare contradict. In this way, for instance, we had access to almost all the works of Heinrich Böll. But a time would come when the dialectic of censorship would produce its most astonishing trick: 'It may be all right for the Soviet Union, but not for us!'

Unbelievable though it may seem, during the 1960s Bulgarians were subjected to the censorship of Soviet works which Bulgarian dialecticians found insufficiently 'Soviet'. Soviet films dealing with this or that not particularly praiseworthy aspect of Soviet reality, or deviating from the clichés of 'socialist realism', were released in the Soviet Union but not shown in Bulgaria. For instance, at a special screening for the film industry, we were able to watch a very interesting Soviet film about sexual relationships between Soviet pupils, which was never released in Bulgaria. Once again we were acting out the old saying: 'More Catholic than the Pope, and more Turkish than the Sultan'.

'We cannot allow Soviet works to lower the prestige of the Soviet Union, of Soviet man!' one of the ideological watchdogs in Sofia used to say. Shortly before the Prague Spring of 1968, the well-known drama critic Stefan Karakostov attacked Soviet art for having let itself be contaminated by foreign influences, declaring: 'Comrades, the most dangerous ideological sabotage is coming to us via ... the Soviet Union!'

Clearly Karakostov, who had close links with the most extreme Stalinist group among the Soviet writers in Moscow had been instructed to open fire against certain Soviet works, so that his Soviet friends would have a pretext for going on the offensive. When I visited Moscow at the end of 1967, Soviet writers indignantly discussed a speech which Karakostov had made at a conference there in which he had fulminated against some young Soviet writers [...] as well as bitterly attacking several Bulgarian writers, including myself. [...]

Until they hit on the explanation that jazz was the music of the enslaved and underprivileged American negroes, one could not hear even the most innocuous jazz compositions on Radio Sofia. However, in all the battles waged by the Party ideology, it was precisely Western pop music and jazz which caused its most serious defeat. I doubt if any other artistic genre has ever generated more passion, fanaticism and mad addiction in Bulgaria than pop and jazz. I don't know whether Bulgarian listeners tune in regularly to political broadcasts from all over the world, but I am sure that, where the latest fashion in jazz is concerned, tens of thousands of tape-recorders up and down the country secretly record the newest records issued in the West. This reminds me of a true story worthy of the pen of Aleko Konstantinov.*

In the middle of the 1960s when the ideological climate in Bulgaria was at its mildest, feeding our illusions about normalization, Louis Armstrong and his orchestra set out on a tour of Eastern Europe. His last stop was Bucharest. The Bulgarian concert management knew of the huge interest in Armstrong, who was an idol of Bulgarian youth, and so decided to invite the great musician to give a few concerts in Bulgaria. It was explained to the top Party leaders that Armstrong was black and that his music should be understood as an expression of the wretched condition of negroes in the United States. The leaders nodded in agreement and everything seemed in order, until someone remembered Armstrong's hoarse seductive voice and said: 'All right, do invite him - but only on condition that he plays and doesn't sing.'

And, to justify himself, he quoted the writer Emilian Stanev who once said (I was present) that when he heard Armstrong's voice, he had the nightmarish feeling of terrible hands stretching out in the night to grab him by the throat....

Of course, Armstrong declined the invitation. And the puny throat of the writer was saved.

---

* Aleko Konstantinov (1863-97), one of the best-loved Bulgarian comic writers.

WHERE ARE YOU,
DEAR CENSOR?

'In socialist Bulgaria, there is no censorship!' The regime's representatives often repeat this in answer to questions from foreign journalists. Bulgarian journalists do not ask such questions. They have no time; for the main concern of everyone who attempts to write on a serious theme is how to get his material accepted, how to safeguard it from the cavalier encroachments of hundreds of censors.

Certainly, the classic image of the vigilant censor – Cerberus holding a thick red pencil and fiercely crossing out all that he judges to be wrong – does not exist. There is neither an institution nor a man whom an author can hold responsible for the mutilation of his work. But censorship has not only remained, but has created one of the most important laws of survival. Censorship forms an integral part of the life of every thinking 'builder of socialism'; it has entered the bloodstream as a permanent instinct, whose first signal is a sinking feeling in the stomach. [...] Perhaps for some people the censorship of others is a necessary compensation for their own distress and humiliation.

The regime can, I think, be very proud of its dialectical conjuring trick – the shifting of the functions of censorship from an outdated, historically compromised and ineffective institution to a multitude of private voluntary censorships established inside individual people. The official duty of the old censor has been successfully transformed into an active personal interest, and even a passion, for censoring life and the world. In other words, the Communist Party discovered and developed the principle of censorship lodged in the breast of many of its members and followers.

'Why should we censor journalists, writers, critics and artists, when they can censor each other far more effectively!' is the maxim underlying the Party's great innovation on the path towards the 'all-round development of man'.

In this way, censorship has been established on a general, or, to use the newspaper cliché, 'nation-wide' basis. Of course, we are talking here about political censorship. But what in the Communist world is not political? Whether the problems are ethical, religious, commercial, scientific, military or paediatric, they are all reduced essentially to political issues. When the late highly talented illustrator, Alexander Denkov, was doing the illustrations for my fantasy *The Victors of Ajax* and drew one of the heroines with her skirt slightly raised above her knees, a special conference was held in the central committee of the Komsomol, at which the immorality of the girl's symbolic knees was discussed and serious political conclusions were drawn. Poor Sasho had to lengthen the skirt – otherwise things would have gone badly. If, however, we take a closer look at this little story, we can see that it is typical of the 'nation-wide' method of censorship. It would hardly have occurred to the secretariat of the Komsomol Central Committee to concern themselves with a skirt a shade too short. From what I knew of its members at that time (1958), they seemed to have nothing against skirts being raised even higher. But here we come to one of the most characteristic words in Bulgarian socialist reality – the *signal*. This word was created by the regime as an acceptable synonym for the hateful *denunciation*. Thus, if you made a denunciation – open, underhand or secret – your action was not called 'denouncing' but 'signalling'. In such cases, the person to whom you addressed your report did not say 'a report (denunciation) has been received', but always 'signals have been received'. This use of the plural is intended to mask the single source of the signal and also to give the impression of a popular initiative.

Indeed, nobody would ever have thought Sasho Denkov's most innocent drawing morally provocative if a 'signal' had not been received. The person who gave this signal was an impotent editor, who had appointed himself the keeper of the decent appearance of socialist youth. His idea of aesthetics in relation to labour went no further than the uniform of the youth brigade teams – a quilted jacket and dungarees. Seeing the bare knees in the drawing, the editor had run to people who more or less shared his views (such people are always united in a kind of unregistered union) and a few hours later Sasho's drawing was labelled 'a dangerous vehicle for bourgeois-capitalist decadence, representative of the putrid morals of the degenerate West'. Who among the Central Committee secretaries would have dared ignore such a purely political *signal*? The drawing had to be altered or scrapped. Of course, the superiors did not reveal the identity of the author of the *signal*; they presented the matter as a spontaneous consensus of opinion. In this way the artist was confronted not by one responsible person, the censor, but by a thick fog that mysteriously veiled numerous censors. Our attempts to find somebody in charge with whom to argue it out failed. The immediate superiors in the *Narodna Mladezh* publishing house told us that an order had come 'from above', while the secretariat of the Central Committee insisted that this opinion had emerged 'from below'. Meanwhile, Sasho and I remained suspended somewhere between 'above' and 'below'.

What is so terrible in Bulgarian reality is that once you are stamped with a black mark, it is difficult, if not impossible, to rub it out. You can spend your life in explanations, declaring that even though you may have made a mistake you never intended any political or ideological implications, that your error should not be interpreted in such an arbitrary and absurd way – but the black mark remains. This is because you never meet either the author of the *signal* or the person who has given the order for censoring or banning your work. If you go to the highest officials, the answer is never: '*I* think so', but always: 'the comrades think so'. But if you want to find out who these comrades are, how they came to think in this way, how they failed to notice (in this case) that the girl in the drawing had fallen out of a car and that therefore it was perfectly normal for her skirt to ride up a little ... there is nobody to answer such questions. Can you question fog?

Suddenly you feel totally helpless, as if under the influence of some magic, or as if you are the hero of some Kafkaesque nightmare.

I experienced this feeling much more precisely and frighteningly in connection with the stopping of my play *Let's Go Under the Rainbow*. I say 'stopping', which is a synonym for censorship or ban. In Bulgaria, nothing is censored and nothing is proscribed. Some works are merely 'stopped'. Although the effect is one and the same (the works do not reach the public), the word used is different, well bred, thoughtful and implies that there has been no peremptory order behind the action, but that the times, society itself if you like, have put on the brakes....

When my play was stopped at its thirteenth performance in Sofia's Military Theatre, I asked the First Secretary of the Party, Todor Zhivkov, to read it. He readily agreed and really did read it. When he returned the text to me in his office in the Party Central Committee, he told me that he saw nothing reprehensible in the play and that, barring a few minor remarks, nothing in it could be criticized.

'This only applies to the political part', he said. 'Artistically, I'm not an expert judge, but if you want my personal opinion, I'll tell you that I don't like it, because it is very pessimistic, gloomy. . . .'

'But if there's nothing wrong with it politically, why has it been stopped?' I asked.

'I don't know anything about stopping,' he replied. 'It is merely that the theatre has changed its schedule and, as a certain feeling has developed against the play, the comrades have decided to drop it. . . . What do you want from me? I can't order them to put it back on again. . . .'

Once again, I found myself in a fog. Since the play was not politically incorrect, but had been stopped precisely for political reasons, to whom could I appeal for an explanation? What was this public opinion? Who were these comrades? All the same, Zhivkov was polite. Only a few months after our conversation, the Party newspaper *Rabotnichesko Delo* printed a leading article which claimed that the play was alien to Bulgarian audiences and that they had discarded it of their own accord.

But how did the censorship of the play really come about? It must be admitted that in both form and content this play was very different from what was required by socialist drama. The theme, in short, was the betrayal of ideals, or the betrayal of oneself. For me, and I believe for many others, this was one of the most burning issues of our time. The play had been accepted by the theatre before it became known as the Military Theatre. At that time it called itself 'Popular Stage' and it had the best male actors in the country. This was important for my play, in which all the main characters were men. But even at the start of rehearsals (the producer was Assen Shopov) it transpired that, from a purely technical point of view, our production had the best team available and so stood in the way of other productions, including two military plays by military authors, who were obliged to wait until the next season. Their chagrin, as often happens in our country, turned into spite, and spite provided the energy for a campaign. The authors mobilized their friends and started to go through my play with a fine tooth-comb in order to prove its ideological dubiousness. Certain remarks were taken out of context, others were completely misinterpreted, various innocent actions were endowed with a sinister allegorical meaning and the seven unfortunate heroes suffering from tuberculosis were declared to represent the Bulgarian people, while the tuberculosis itself turned out to be a symbol of Bulgarian life. At the time a colonel was director of the theatre, and, seeing that he was very keen not to lose his post, the conspiracy managed to frighten him into believing that he was taking great risks with my play. And so, just as full dress-rehearsals began, with only three weeks to go before the first night, we were confronted by an utterly hostile artistic council which put strong pressure on us to stop work. All the authority of Assen and our friends had to be mobilized to enable us to continue. Meanwhile, the campaign proceeded in a purely political direction. Having convinced themselves that this was a 'hostile' play, our adversaries professed to believe that it was their duty to stop it.

Sofia was full of rumours that the play was about to be banned and friends telephoned me to express their sympathy. At the final dress-rehearsal and the first special preview on 27 March 1967, the play was performed before a packed audience, because as soon as people hear that something will be stopped, they hurry not to miss it. But the stronger the opposition against the play, the more ambitious and inflexible became those who were involved in it. Meanwhile the actors begged me to bring the most influential Party and State leaders to the première. This was the pitiful unwritten law of theatrical success: every playwright and producer tried with the greatest servility to ensure the attendance of some Politburo member, Central Committee secretary, or even Zhivkov himself at the performance of their works. The presence of such high-ranking people always guaranteed official acceptance of the production, and was sure to be followed the next day by notices in the press. Without it, everything hung in the balance. This is why it had become standard practice for writers to try at all costs to lure the First Party Secretary to their performances. The theatre staff knew that I was able to invite the 'heavy guns' for the occasion. But I chose not to approach anyone at the top, so that the first night took place in front of empty government boxes. On the second night, however, three generals with the Chief of Staff at their head turned up in one of the boxes. About forty minutes into the performance, a stout military voice resounded in the tense silence: 'This cannot be watched any longer!'

Then the door of the box was slammed dramatically and the three generals left in utter disgust. The next day, at the Co-operative Farmers' Congress, they openly branded the play a mockery of the Bulgarian people and reality. From this point on the play's fate was decided. But who took the decision and on what grounds we never knew. Nevertheless, how does one 'stop' a scheduled performance? The first indication was the reaction of the press. Not one of the better newspapers published a notice of our production, which had been performed at one of the foremost Bulgarian theatres by a first-class cast.

Neither good, nor bad, simply nothing! The second indication was the suspiciously poor attendance. Later we found out that, again anonymously, all planned group visits to the theatre had been cancelled. Thus, only one hour before the performance was due to start, about a thousand tickets were released which up until then had been reserved. I was stunned when I heard that the factory where I had worked as an engineer some years before had asked for six hundred seats and had been refused on the grounds that everything was sold out. As a result, we played to almost empty houses. Nothing is more demoralizing for actors than to have to perform in front of empty stalls. It was difficult for them to suppress their disappointment and frustration and to act only for each other. And yet, with every performance, the acting rose to new heights. Paradoxically, our only consolation came from foreigners. A delegation of Greek theatre artists from Athens said very gratifying things to us. But the most moving reaction came from the visiting group of famous Soviet artists who, after the performance, climbed on to the stage, embracing and kissing our actors. . . .

The thirteenth performance was our last. Owing to financial and organizational considerations (so the directors of the theatre said), they could not afford the luxury of running performances without audiences. Nor were we able to bring more people to fill this great auditorium: all our friends and relatives had already seen the play, some even twice. The production was taken off, and a wave of reprisals followed. Five people were sacked from the theatre. The producer, Assen Shopov, the wonderful actor Naum Shopov and his wife were banned from Sofia for two years.

This is how the personal ambition of a few managed to create the blackest 'public opinion', to provoke numerous letters of protest against the production, to label the play as well-nigh subversive and – disregarding any aesthetic considerations – to stop it.

My efforts to discover who had been at the bottom of it all were in vain. The theatre director washed his hands of the matter by saying that the decision had been 'quite proper'. At the army's chief political directorate, under which the theatre came, they said that the play had been stopped due to lack of public interest; while at the Central Committee I was told that public opinion had been against it. All explanations were phrased in the past tense. Who had punished these people? Who had exiled them from Sofia? The Committee for Culture and Art? No! State Security? No!

In the surrounding fog, my mind's eye clearly perceived a ghost. And thinking about this ghost whom I could neither meet nor question, I missed, for the first time, the old censor who could be visited, seen and spoken to.

'Where are you, dear censor?'

Unfortunately for me, there was no censorship in Bulgaria.

SODOM AT THE TOP

Friday evening. I am at the flat of a friend and colleague. He does not write well and is not even a member of the Writer's Union, but everything he produces gets published and he earns a fortune from pseudo-historical, pseudo-adventure novels and from film scripts. He is the exact equivalent of the Western commercial writer. Many envy him his knack of selling his work and say all sorts of things about him. Otherwise, he seems a good and well-mannered man. His apartment at Vladimir Poptomov Street is amazingly well furnished: a very effective combination of contemporary Western furniture and goat-skin rugs from the Rodop region. We arrange to play cards tomorrow, Saturday. Just a few hours of friendly poker. I drink the whisky he has generously poured for me and am preparing to leave when his telephone rings. A well-known voice booms from the receiver. I cannot help overhearing the whole conversation.

'Listen, man,' says the voice, 'I'll need your place tomorrow night. I'm sending you two tickets for the opera. It's the first night, of course. ... After the show take your wife to the restaurant, but be sure to reserve a table beforehand.... The same as last time, you understand me?'

The voice is off-hand, as if it owns the apartment. My host feels rather embarrassed that I have overheard the conversation and clearly wants to hang up quickly. He mutters something about everything being in order. 'All the same, try not to break another vase!' he says, with a faint show of resistance. The other responds with loud laughter.

Now that the secret is out, my colleague comes over to me and says placatingly: 'What else can I do? I've got to do him a favour – after all, he's helped me so much.'

I understand him. The voice belongs to the man who is in command of the whole world of Bulgarian literature, all the arts, the newspapers and so on. It is not easy to refuse such a small service to a secretary of the Party's Central Committee. He does not want to take his clandestine mistress to one of the numerous guest-houses for Central Committee or Politburo members near Sofia where he would be seen. Even if they do not tell his wife, they will make a note of it and some day, if necessary, they will use it against him. That is why the private apartment of a friend like my host is by far the safest arrangement. A friend whose silence will be generously remunerated. And should he talk, he can be mercilessly destroyed.

Obviously, our poker arrangement is cancelled. 'Only, please, not a word to anyone. You could cause a lot of trouble for me,' says the host, seeing me to the door.

He is afraid of gossip which might harm his highly placed patron. In fact, the agreement between them is that if anything untoward happens, he will take the responsibility by claiming that the mistress is really his own. At other times, he personally receives the lady who arrives earlier, having first sent his wife out. Altogether every precaution is taken. The high-ranking comrade never comes in his own limousine but in a borrowed battered old Moskvich which he parks several streets away. But despite all the safety measures, one day the gossip starts and it becomes known that this comrade is very crafty and a great lover. He is perhaps the most famous sex hero at the top. According to reliable rumour, a considerable number of the better-looking women of Sofia have passed through his bed. He has a soft spot for actresses, but does not disdain others. An acquaintance of mine, a well-known Sofia beauty, was unemployed. Then some obliging go-between led her to the office of the important comrade, who took a liking to her and invited her out to dinner. Afterwards they spent the night together and the next day she found herself in an editor's post, which neither her education nor abilities merited.

At an official reception, he asked a promising young actress to dance. Her colleagues, who were standing next to me, commented maliciously: 'Well, well! Our Danka is about to take the plane for Paris!'

And that is exactly what did happen. After some time, the actress in question was sent to Paris on a six-month official trip. Nor was she the first or the last young Bulgarian whose paid stay in Paris was the outcome of comrade K's sexual escapades. At one time, the wits in Sofia's coffee-houses used to call Paris the 'concentration camp for former Party mistresses'. Nevertheless, in the interests of variety, some of the intimate lady friends of the comrade in question were sent to London. Whatever else was said about him, nobody could accuse him of ingratitude or failing to pay for his pleasures. The man was thoroughly honest. The trouble with the whole matter, as with the cases of other high ranking citizens, was that they never paid out of their own pockets, but always out of the pocket of the State.

Later, when this tall, athletic, strong middle-aged man – with a not particularly attractive face – was dismissed from his important post and sent into ambassadorial exile, one of the reasons for his punishment was believed to be his loose morals. But it must be said that he was in no way an exception in infringing the Communist moral code: on the contrary, he was a typical representative of a large group of Party and State officials who used their position to extract more pleasure from life.

Quite near the house where K's secret adventure was to take place, there was another home used for the same purposes by another high-ranking citizen. One evening there I met General Z, a member of the Politburo who would become a minister. He had a wife and two daughters, but had suddenly fallen madly in love with an ambitious music editor. She was expecting his child and was clearly trying to prise him from his family. As the pregnancy advanced, in order to avoid adverse publicity and rows he sent her to the United States, to Los Angeles I think. A little boy was born – an event which filled the General, who had hitherto fathered only two girls, with great joy. Eventually his mistress returned to Sofia with the child. He received her with great solicitude, bought her a lovely apartment in the best neighbourhood, and was happy to have a son. However, a fierce war began between his wife and daughters on the one hand, and his mistress on the other. The family, which belonged to the most powerful group of the Party aristocracy, tried to destroy the mistress and her child. On the other hand, the music editor possessed tremendous energy and dauntless tenacity. Caught in the cross-fire, the General manœuvred skilfully, trying to bribe both sides. Thus his daughters were often sent to London, Paris and other tempting destinations, where they lived with all the comforts of Oriental princesses, with plenty of hard currency at their disposal. When they returned, it was the mistress's turn to see the world. She travelled frequently on all kinds of pretexts and always stayed at the best hotels. Sometimes, so that she should not be alone, the General would arrange for a companion to go with her.

Looked at as a human story, the love and family drama of the General was probably not a wicked or criminal deed for which he should be castigated. Indeed, the very fact that he had fallen in love when already well advanced in years, makes him appear quite likeable, at least in my eyes. But as with the case of his colleague, comrade K, the real question was who paid for the whole drama. Whose account was charged for the trips abroad and the plentiful hard currency? The salaries of Bulgarian ministers and generals are relatively modest and would not stretch to such extravagance. I know for sure that in his capacity as one of the most important persons in charge of secret intelligence, the General used to send his mistress abroad on the pretext that she was entrusted with an intelligence mission. The large amounts of money which, in reality, were used for the relief of General Z's family problems came from secret service funds. It was understandable that he was devoted to his illegitimate son and more than generous to the baby's mother, but the bill for all this was being settled by the State. On top of it all, he tried to raise money in an unorthodox fashion. His mistress, who worked as a music editor in television, was also an amateur painter. She produced hopelessly unsophisticated and mediocre pictures, which I have seen in their home, and which could not be taken seriously on any level. However, under pressure from her, and with a view to securing her future, the General organized a full-scale official exhibition of her work. The exhibition was immediately visited by buyers from various ministries, Party committees and government departments, who bought up the pictures at the highest prices. I ought to add that neither Ivan Kirkov, Georgi Bozhilov, Georgi Banev nor any other talented Bulgarian painters have never had such a successful exhibition as the amateur painter mistress.

In other words, the exhibition of these artistic failures was a clever subterfuge for legally supplying the mistress with money. To top it all, out of solidarity, the Politburo members themselves visited the exhibition – an honour which few real painters have enjoyed. It is possible that the General's subsequent dismissal from all his posts was linked to some extent with this clandestine love affair. I should also mention in passing that as Minister of the Interior he revealed himself to be a fanatical soldier in pursuit of the 'enemy'.

Be that as it may, the General's love affair possibly cost the Bulgarian State much less than comrade K's many sexual adventures.

I was told about an event which occurred in the corridors of the television studios at No. 2, Todor Strashimirov Street. The General's mistress had just returned from Paris. In the corridor, a group of girls employed in the studios had surrounded her and she was proudly showing them everything she had bought for herself in the Paris shops. Among other things, she boasted that she had stayed in a hotel which

cost eighty dollars a night (I believe it was the Crillon), where everything had been unbelievably luxurious. Listening to her, one of the
women fainted. Later it transpired that it had been from exhaustion:
she had to support three children, and the traveller's tales of Paris had
proved altogether too much for her.

No doubt many careers started their swift rise in the secret circles of
the Sodom at the top. Hardly a week passed without gossip spreading
about new appointments or dismissals taking place for purely sexual
reasons. This in no way applied only to the world of the arts, but more
often concerned the sudden elevation of a district Party secretary with
a pretty face or a Komsomol activist with a trim figure. A woman's
beauty began to be generally regarded by our superiors as a good
Party asset. Did gossip exaggerate? Did a few cases provoke unwarranted generalizations?

Unfortunately, the cases were not few and not isolated; we were
witnessing a powerful wave of fashionable sexuality which was en-
gulfing life at the top. The whole of Sofia was amazed when, in only
twenty-four hours, the husband of an alluring lady made a headlong
leap in his career. From having been comrade Nobody, he became
the director of an important cultural institute, chairman of his own
trade union and a member of important bureaux and committees. A
little later, he was elected a deputy in the National Assembly. Everyone who was aware of his modest talent and his lack of connections
was astonished at this meteoric rise. Perhaps because I was close to his
family, with whom I was linked by memories of student days, I refused
for a long time to believe this story, and tried to explain things as a
rare play of coincidences. At the same time as the career of the husband
prospered, the wife began to travel widely in the West and showed
several times that she had powerful protection behind her. Nevertheless, she did not seem too happy at what had befallen her and suddenly
gave up all pretence. I had the feeling that she wanted to punish
herself for what she had done. One evening when she was drunk, she
poured out a lurid confession about her secret life and her husband's
career to a mutual friend. Generally, she had to see her high-ranking
lover once a week. For the sake of decorum, she used to go alone at the
appointed hour to one of the comrade's residences. At the door an
officer was waiting for her; he always smiled knowingly and remarked
with irony: 'Oh, comrade! You're late again!'

Then he used to lead her inside, where he delivered her to another
officer, who in turn took her to the bedroom.

'What I found most humiliating was that they knew what I was coming for and led me to their chief's bedroom with cold contempt, as if ashamed of what they had to do. There is nothing more awful than being publicly led to perform intimate functions. They didn't even pretend not to know and ordered me not to be late the next time!'

This report of her confession, which I remember well, made a profound impression on me. Subsequently, when I met her, I discerned in her two opposing feelings which she found hard to control. The first was a mad desire to escape from everything that had happened and to punish herself; the other was the impulse to throw herself recklessly into the riches and pleasures offered by her position as a highly placed courtesan. In any event, she hated her husband bitterly and tried to take her revenge by cruelly humiliating him whenever she had the chance.

If this was the tune set by the highest ruling circle in the country, one can imagine the sort of music played by the middle and lower ranks of the Party establishment.

V

'Zhivkov's unerring instinct told him that the only people who could seriously disturb his quiet reign were the members of the creative intelligentsia.'

As one of Bulgaria's leading writers, Markov met everyone of importance in the Party, including the President, Todor Zhivkov.† Here he describes a series of meetings with Zhivkov which, when they were broadcast, enraged the President and astounded his audience in Bulgaria. What delighted them was that Markov had managed to break through the personality cult Zhivkov had encouraged around himself; what seems equally remarkable to the Western reader is the sympathy and humanity of the writer's approach. But it was after these particular broadcasts that Markov was first threatened.

MEETINGS WITH TODOR ZHIVKOV

October 1964. It had rained for almost a whole week and when the sun finally came out over Dragalevtsi it was too faint to drive away the damp and the cold. Everything around was waterlogged and the cars had difficulty in making their way through the mud on the rough road between the village and the Cinema Centre. I came home towards evening, fed up with the weather because only a few days earlier the mud had made me fall and break my left arm. They had put me in plaster at the Red Cross hospital and I was holding my arm in front of me like a ledge. There was nobody at home. My wife, as usual, was somewhere in town. She was either playing cards with other bored wives of Sofia's high society, or she had gone to a special film show [reserved for Party people].

As I climbed the stairs, I heard the telephone ringing above me. I hated it when the telephone rang while I was out of reach and I slowed down to allow it to stop. But whoever wanted to speak to me was clearly determined, and, when I realized that he was prepared to ring until all hours, I decided to give in.

'Is that Georgi Markov?' asked a curt unfamiliar voice, strongly reminiscent of a militia chief on duty.

'Yes', I said.

'The writer Georgi Markov?' he asked again, as if reading from some script.

'Yes', I replied, somewhat irritated.

'You're not the University lecturer, are you?' he persisted

'I am not', I said and added: 'The lecturer Georgi Markov is without a leg, while I am merely without an arm, but there is yet another Georgi Markov, who has no head!' I had the General Secretary of the Union of Soviet Writers in mind, but the unknown telephone voice did not understand what I was talking about.

'This is Colonel Zhelyazko Kolev of the Party Central Committee', he said.

I realized immediately that this was a well-known partisan from the 'Chavdar' brigade. He was, in fact, a Colonel of the Ministry of the Interior, but I had never encountered him before.

'Do you think you can walk for any length of time?', Zhelyazko Kolev asked me.

'Well, I don't really walk on my left arm!' I replied, still none the wiser about the point of this conversation.

'I am asking quite seriously whether you are able to walk?' he repeated.

'It depends what the object of the walk is!' I said. 'If you mean to invite me to take part in some mass tourist march – count me out, but if you know of some nice restaurant renowned for its grills . . . I might come.'

'You are invited', he said, slowly and distinctly, 'from the very highest quarters for a walk!'

'If you say that this invitation comes from the highest quarters . . .' I repeated, trying to guess who could be behind this joke. I had several times taken part in such wicked practical jokes, despatching suitable victims to non-existent meeting places, banquets or cocktail parties with imaginary big shots.

'Put on suitable clothes', he continued. 'If you like, we can send a car to fetch you, or, if you prefer, come in your own car tomorrow morning at 7 a.m. to the 'Levski' monument.'

By then Zhelyazko Kolev sounded so authentic that I decided that even the king of such telephone pranks could not have imitated him.

I replied that I would be at the monument at 7 a.m.

'Be punctual!' Zhelyazko Kolev ordered.

As I put the receiver down, I remembered that some time ago Lada Galina had told me that Todor Zhivkov wanted to invite some of the younger writers to meet him and that my name had been mentioned. She even asked what I thought of Zhivkov – a question I could not answer.

Nevertheless, my immediate reaction after my conversation with Kolev was very negative. I felt that there was something unfriendly and offensive in this whole invitation, in the way it had been made, and in the flat and cold tone of Zhelyazko Kolev. Next I imagined that I personally had been invited as part of the daily amusement of some big shot, who would play the host with condescending smiles. I was angry with myself because I had been gullible enough to accept. After all, I had such a good excuse to refuse – my arm was in plaster.

My wife came home later and when I told her about it all she was seriously alarmed, thinking that because of the unusually early hour this might be a trap. There had been insistent rumours about plans to arrest two hundred representatives of the intelligentsia and send them goodness knows where.

Be that as it may, the next morning I rose early and went into town. I parked near Alexander Nevski Cathedral and in the cool morning air made my way to the Levski monument. On the other side of the monument, near the beginning of Vladimir Zaimov Boulevard, a Soviet-made Chaika limousine was waiting. I advanced cautiously towards it, when suddenly the rear door of the car opened and revealed the face I knew so well from countless photographs and from a distance at public meetings – the face of the country's Number One. He was dressed in ski trousers and a sports jacket of a light brown colour resembling the old army uniforms, and he wore a cap.

'Come on, Georgi! We're all waiting for you', he said affably, and with the self-assured manner of a host who knows his job he beckoned me to my place in the car. Inside, already seated, were the painter Zlatka Dubova, the authoress Lada Galina and the poet Anastas Stoyanov. Next to the chauffeur sat a young man with a dark, attractive face. A little later I discovered that he was one of Zhivkov's personal bodyguards and that he was called Pesho. As I sat down in my appointed seat, Zhelyazko Kolev appeared. Clearly he, too, was coming with us.

The car moved off smoothly in the direction of Poduene, keeping to the middle of the road, easily overtaking all other cars which observed the speed limit. It was the first time that I had ridden in a Chaika and I was surprised by its spaciousness. Small blue curtains hung over the back windows and I remembered the expression of a friend who used to say: 'on the other side of the little curtains', meaning the privileged world of the Party aristocracy.

Jokingly, Zhivkov gave up what is meant to be the traditional seat for a head of state – the one at the back diagonally across from the chauffeur's (as he explained to us) – and seated himself in the middle so that we faced each other. When one meets someone face to face whom one has seen before in a photograph, on the screen, or at a distance, one almost always discovers some physical difference. At close quarters, Zhivkov's face appeared to me more symmetrical and even somehow more spiritual. At any rate, it was a very mobile face with an attentive self-confident air that I did not find disturbing. His eyes gave the impression of quiet energy and keen observation.

He immediately asked me what had happened to my arm and, in

passing, remarked that my shoes were not particularly suitable for our excursion.

During the first few minutes the atmosphere in the car was a little stiff, as if there was a clearly defined distance between our host and ourselves. Each of the people present was sufficiently quick-witted to avoid the banalities which it is customary to utter in such circumstances and, at the same time, each left the initiative to the host. And here I am bound to say that Zhivkov showed a surprising skill in handling the situation. Without undue preliminaries, he provocatively asked Anastas who, in his opinion, was the greatest living Bulgarian poet.

'Is it Mladen Isaev?' enquired Zhivkov with a knowing smile.

Anastas was embarrassed. He evidently wanted to reply in a way that would please Zhivkov, but at the same time his own preferences lay in another direction; he mumbled something about different poets having different qualities, that Mladen Isaev had possessed something which he had now lost and so on. Anastas's evasiveness forced us to join in the conversation and before long we were all engrossed in argument while Zhivkov remained on the sidelines and listened to us with interest.

This was the first thing about him which impressed me, and which I was to see many more times. He knew how to listen. In comparison with almost all the other Politburo members and senior ministers whom I had met, Todor Zhivkov alone, I believe, was capable of listening without interrupting, without commenting, without showing what he was thinking or feeling. [...] In Zhivkov one could find a patient and good listener. Later I was told that many others who had talked to him had also been struck by this quality. But there are many ways of listening. People can listen to you in such a way that all your desire to talk evaporates, or they can listen so that you feel encouraged to go on and on talking. In my opinion, Zhivkov's talent for listening was of the more inviting kind and perhaps because of this it was the more misleading.

The second discovery I made while the Chaika took the highway to Vitinya was his desire to be as natural and spontaneous as possible. Personally I find it difficult to be at ease with new acquaintances, but in the car I had the definite feeling that Zhivkov and I had known each other quite well for some time. Perhaps this impression came not so much from his own attempts at spontaneity, as from his simple origins, his peasant blood. If I had not known him at all and was meeting him for the first time somewhere without security guards and official entourage, I would have taken him for one of the typical inhabitants of a contemporary Bulgarian village or small town, situated not far from the capital – say, the local postmaster, or the teacher in the preparatory school, or perhaps one of the council clerks or the local agricultural expert.

Although I followed the conversation closely, I could not detect in Todor Zhivkov any trace of that pomposity which is so typical of the Bulgarian Party *prima donnas*, no self-assertion, nor any withdrawal behind a veil of mysterious inaccessibility. He appeared normal, sincere and sociable, and treated us as equals, without making visible efforts to appear other than he was. And so the atmosphere in the car gradually became relaxed and friendly. In all the other faces I read the same feeling of vanishing suspicion and tension, as if we did not have the most powerful man in the country in our midst, but a good old friend.

So far, all this strongly contrasted with my memories of the occasions when I had seen Zhivkov on the public platform. There he kept a kind of official distance and I (and I am sure many others) had classed him as an alien and remote speaker. What I found particularly irritating in his speeches was the cheap, pseudo-popular rhetoric, which seemed to be obligatory for all public speakers in socialist Bulgaria. Sitting opposite him, I was thinking about that Zhivkov who in the preceding year, in the spring of 1963, had assembled all of us members of the arts unions at Party headquarters to harangue us about our deviations from the Party line. There he had exhibited a repulsively second-rate sense of humour and, at the same time, had not hesitated to threaten us crudely like a policeman. He attacked the modern trends in our literature, accused us of worshipping foreign idols and repeated for the umpteenth time that we must above all serve immediate Party interests. This address to the 'cultural and artistic workers' was merely an ideological plagiarism of Khrushchev's earlier speech in Moscow on the same theme. But the most offensive thing in this speech of bombastic empty phrases and outworn clichés was its tone, which reflected a complete lack of understanding of complex phenomena and the impudence of a not very intelligent minor dictator presuming to give orders to spirits far above him intellectually.

Thus the natural question which occurred to me while the car was climbing the mountain road was: which one is the real Zhivkov? This rather courteous, agreeable interlocutor, who listened to us with interest, or the other one, who unceremoniously took it upon himself to decide the fate of the whole intelligentsia and dared decree what was true art and what was not with roughly the aesthetic equipment of a former sergeant-major.

I reminded myself that in fact I knew very little about him. He had appeared almost from nowhere. Although Party propaganda in the 1940s and 1950s had succeeded in popularizing the names of certain leaders, and people had become used to hearing about those whose official portraits hung on the walls of offices and factories, although gossip touched even the private lives at the Party's apex, Todor Zhivkov's name meant nothing. In those years, the famous biography of all but the greatest leader of a so-called Bulgarian national revolution and the moving spirit of the 'Chavdar' partisan brigade had not yet been composed, and hardly anyone knew of it. I remembered that when Chervenkov† was forced to relinquish his post as First Party Secretary and Zhivkov stepped into his shoes, rumour had it that Chervenkov had chosen the most obedient and meekest of his collaborators to succeed him so that he could continue to run the show. Later, when Chervenkov was definitely eclipsed and Zhivkov's name began to gain ground and to be associated with the changes after April 1956,* those from both left and right considered him a temporary figure. The Stalinists and hard-liners mocked him openly, while the liberals looked upon him with suspicion and mistrust. It was constantly said that this or that politician would soon supplant him. However, the way in which Zhivkov got rid of all his enemies and overcame all obstacles showed that the popular opinions about him were arbitrary and superficial. Obviously he enjoyed the confidence of Khrushchev – and that was no small matter in a particularly stormy period in Eastern Europe. I thought that perhaps I, too, had been wrong to judge him solely on the basis of his attitude towards culture and the arts.

The Chaika stopped at Vitinya, not far from the petrol station. We got out and Zhelyazko Kolev led us into the woods to the left of the road.

The sun caught up with us in the middle of a young beech wood not far from Vitinya. It was damp and still rather cool. The fallen leaves had obliterated all traces of a path and we walked freely through the

*The reference is to the ninth Congress of the Bulgarian Communist Party, which mirrored the decisions of the twentieth Soviet Party Congress.

trees. Zhivkov strode ahead of us as if he wanted to force his accelerated pace on the whole group, which gradually began to disperse. From time to time Zhivkov stopped to wait gallantly for the ladies who often lagged behind.

'We have quite a way to go!' he warned.

'Are you sure we're going in the right direction?' I asked him, being far from certain that he knew his way about in these deceptive woods.

'I really don't know!' Zhivkov replied in a tone which suggested the exact opposite. And he added: 'I have a very poor sense of direction.' Whereupon he told us how once during the War he had been obliged to go on a mission somewhere north, but had found himself going in exactly the opposite direction – far south. As he ended his story, he smiled with a very deliberate self-irony and remarked: 'What do you say to that, a First Party Secretary with no sense of direction!'

We responded with smiles expressing disbelief. Later I noticed that Zhivkov liked to throw out self-mocking and self-deprecating comments; this was obviously a well-rehearsed technique for putting people at ease.

We trudged on. After a while, we left the woods behind us and began to walk through alpine meadows. The sky was clear and all around us the Balkan autumn displayed its rich, many-coloured beauty. From far away there came the muffled bells of invisible flocks of sheep, and the damp air was filled with the strong smell of decaying vegetation.

I noticed that nowhere, during our whole walk, had we seen a living soul. Somehow it was unnatural not to meet any people at all, whether forestry workers, woodcutters, peasants or other mountain dwellers. At the same time, I had not seen any sign of security arrangements.

Anastas, who eventually caught up with me, seemed preoccupied with similar thoughts.

'Do you think that the road is unguarded and that we have no protection apart from Pesho?' he asked.

'I don't know, but I can't believe we're all alone on the mountain,' I replied.

'Strange!' he shrugged his shoulders. But a little later he approached me again and told me he had sighted a jeep among the trees.

Thinking about this, I recalled the huge security precautions which once upon a time used to accompany Zhivkov's predecessor Chervenkov wherever he went: the procession of cars and the constant changing of the limousine in which the dictator rode. All this was the expression of real paranoia, since it was clear to every sensible Bulgarian that the murder of the Soviet-appointed Bulgarian leader would not have brought about any substantial change in Bulgaria's situation. Zhivkov's realism had clearly led him to abolish this armed retinue of security men and to replace it with a less numerous but more efficient and well hidden guard. His several appearances in public places without a visible security guard around him had made a good impression on the people.

And still none of us four guests knew beforehand where we were going. It was only when we reached the mountain meadows that we were told our destination was to be Mount Midjur, where we were supposed to lunch. [...] Pesho was carrying a bulging rucksack which, besides a flask of coffee, contained a modest picnic for us all. We stopped in a meadow and Pesho opened the rucksack.

Anastas meanwhile remarked to the First Party Secretary that he still remembered the accusations which he had thrown at him last year in his speech at Party headquarters. Anastas Stoyanov had said in one of his poems that the forest smelled of incense, meaning the fragrance of the pines. Zhivkov had thundered from the rostrum: 'Comrades, our forests, our partisan forests, can never smell of the Church.' One must point out that the rebuke directed at Anastas had been very unfair and that Zhivkov had clearly been influenced by some of his advisers. Anastas was precisely what is described as 'a Party poet'. All his poetry was imbued with that unbearable cheap Communist pathos which was always highly valued by the Party.

'Well, and what are you going to tell us now?' asked Zhivkov benevolently, after the question of the incense had been dealt with and it had been established that the forest had never represented a church for Anastas. Our poet did not wait to be asked twice and immediately started to recite verse about the Party. These were the same high-flown, inept and false words about the Mother Party and her loyal children which invariably turned my stomach. I looked around. Zhivkov was listening attentively and was clearly pleased by what he heard. Zhelyasko Kolev was transported. Lada Galina was smiling equivocally, Zlatka Dubova, flushed with indignation, kept her eyes fixed on the ground, while Pesho imperturbably packed his rucksack. Anastas had lifted his gaze towards the distant horizon and rhymed word after word with inspiration: 'ta-ta-ram, ta-ta-tam....' I thought that he was posing in front of the highest leader in the country as the kind of contemporary poet Zhivkov most desired. No doubt at this moment the blot left by the incense vanished for ever from Anastas Stoyanov's biography and, indeed, after this he rose quickly in the administrative hierarchy of the writers' world.

Looking at Zhivkov, I asked myself whether this poetry of hollow, banal phrases was to his taste. Was his human feeling for beauty really completely subordinate to party and state considerations? Somehow I hoped that I might be able to detect some difference between Zhivkov the man and Zhivkov the First Secretary of the Party and Prime Minister.

But I detected nothing. [...]

We set off again. Now somebody asked Zhivkov about the country's economic situation. He replied that after the reorganization of agriculture things were going in the right direction, and he announced the good news that huge manganese deposits had been discovered in Bulgaria. 'The third biggest in the world', he said, adding that Bulgaria had already received interesting offers from abroad for the joint exploitation of this mineral wealth. Someone else asked him whether there was any point in the development of international tourism, which was beginning to grow in the country. Zhivkov replied that tourism brought great economic advantages and even quoted a rather impressive sum in foreign currency which Bulgaria had apparently earned from tourism in the preceding year. Precisely in connection with tourism, I asked him what he thought of the free travel of Bulgarian citizens abroad, and, more generally, whether he approved of the restrictions then in force. Without any hesitation, he replied: 'I personally am for the free travel of all Bulgarian citizens, with the exception of highly-qualified experts.'

And he told us how, some time ago, two Bulgarian experts from the textile industry, I think, happened to be in Italy, where they had been offered large sums if they stayed. The experts, however, had been real patriots and had returned home. The sums offered had been so considerable that it had been extremely difficult to resist.

'Why on earth should the Italians need our experts?' I asked.

'They tried to buy them,' Zhivkov said, 'not because they needed them but because we need them. It is not that easy to produce a good expert!'

Next I asked him why, then, travel was difficult for ordinary citizens too. Zhivkov replied that the difficulty lay with currency regulations and formalities rather than in anything else. Then he turned suddenly towards us: 'And why should our writers be pining to go to the West? Their work is here, let them tour our own country, learn to know life here and describe it. Writers have no business going to the West!'

He said all this very categorically, leaving no doubt about his conviction. Even so, one of us mumbled that writers needed to travel to the West to broaden their cultural horizons and to familiarize themselves with world literature.

Zhivkov shook his head in disagreement and repeated: 'Our writers must travel in our own country!'

And now, in order to change this rather disagreeable subject, he asked if it was true that there were many divorces amongst writers. He accompanied this question with a knowing smile which implied that he was well informed about quite a few details of the writers' personal lives, but merely wanted our confirmation. Clearly, he was interested in the amusing gossipy side of the writers' extra-marital adventures.

I said that I did not think there were more divorces amongst writers than in any other professional group in the country, but, because the writers were naturally in the limelight, people exaggerated. He said that perhaps I was right, but that people were impressed by the frequency of writers' divorces.

Our conversation followed a pattern of free association, as do most desultory conversations. Zhivkov knew that we would have liked to ask many more questions, but that we hesitated. And could we really question everything? It seemed to me that he managed quickly and very skilfully to establish the proper limits of the conversation, which could not be transgressed. These limits excluded the large and dangerous issues of the day, while leaving plenty of room for personal, private talk. It was more than clear that Zhivkov's invitation to this excursion was motivated by his desire to form his own direct impressions of us, not so much as representatives of the so-called 'creative intelligentsia', but as individuals. We continued on our walk.

The higher we climbed towards the top of Midjur, the more our group became scattered. Zhivkov and I were walking at least half a kilometre ahead of the others. I was astonished by his endurance. He explained that he loved walking and that every day he covered a certain distance, while on weekends he went on long excursions like this one.

'What about work?' I asked. 'When do you attend all those meetings? When do you meet all those people? I imagine that being First Party Secretary and Prime Minister leaves you no time for anything else'.

'On the contrary', laughed Zhivkov, 'the higher you go, the easier it is!'

He looked at me and, when he saw that I did not believe him, he said that he left ordinary work to his deputies. For instance, he only rarely attended the meetings of the Council of Ministers. This prompted discussion of the change in the style of the top leader. Zhivkov said that, for him, the model of a real Communist Party leader was Khrushchev. Here I must mention that only two days after our walk Khrushchev was toppled, but it was all too clear that Zhivkov had no idea of what was happening in the Soviet leadership. I am convinced that, had he had even the slightest inkling, he would not have permitted himself – even in front of me – such unqualified admiration for Khrushchev.

He expressed enthusiasm for the Soviet leader's speeches and thus confirmed my feeling that in his own speeches he tried to imitate Khrushchev. Furthermore, he also admired Khrushchev's verve and even his eccentricity. Zhivkov's whole attitude towards Khrushchev was that of a company commander towards the commander-in-chief: the attitude of a man conscious of his subordinate position. This impression was borne out by the story Zhivkov then told.

With obvious pride, he told me that he had twice had serious disagreements with the Soviet leadership. The first time was over the most recent reorganization of Bulgarian agriculture, when the Soviet model had been discarded; the second time was over the improvement of our relations with Greece.

I remember his words exactly: 'Twice Khrushchev gave me a real dressing-down!' he said, and added: 'But I was proved right!'

I was very struck by his use of the expression 'dressing-down' which in Bulgaria is used only by very junior officials to describe how they have been reprimanded by their superiors. This expression, it seemed to me, characterized with great precision the real relationship between the Soviet and the Bulgarian leaderships, and clearly shows up the complete dependence of the Bulgarian leaders on the Soviet ones. For a sovereign and independent country cannot be subjected to 'a dressing-down' by another country. In the Bulgarian vocabulary, it is the chief, the superior, the master who gives a dressing-down: the man who is in command and to whom one owes unquestioning subordination.

Zhivkov might have said that Khrushchev had got angry, made a scene or lost his temper, which would at least have preserved the equality of the Bulgarian leader. But the fact that he chose the very unequivocal expression 'dressing-down' showed me how deep was his blind obedience to the Soviet leader's will. Khrushchev's right to administer a dressing-down could not be challenged, it seemed.

The picture of Zhivkov's utter subordination was further completed by the undoubted pride he felt at having dared to do something on his own initiative. Moreover, that something had turned out to have been the right thing: Zhivkov was proud that, in the whole of his career, he had managed to act twice in accordance with Bulgarian interests, which were different from Soviet ones. What more can be said?

At the start of our walk I had intended to ask Zhivkov about our relations with the Soviet Union, particularly about the claim of some of our ministers that without Soviet aid our economy would quickly become bankrupt. After what he had said about Khrushchev giving him a dressing-down, I sensed that my question was superfluous. Since one could not talk of Bulgaria's political sovereignty, it was absurd to enquire into its economic independence. Nor did I question whether Zhivkov really had improved relations with Greece on his own initiative or had embarked of his own accord on such an important measure as the reorganization of agriculture. [...]

In all fairness, I must say that during the same conversation Zhivkov repeatedly referred with unmistakable irony to the Soviet example. Thus, for instance, I fiercely attacked the institution of Dimitrov Prizes for literature and the arts, giving examples of how the distribution of these prizes had led to veritable wars between Bulgarian writers, painters and artists and how, as a result of these awards, people had come to hate each other for ever and the whole cultural atmosphere in the country had become poisoned for a long time by malice and envy. The same could be said of all the other titles and decorations.

'All this is very alien to our national character', I said. 'It has never been our tradition to display our titles like peacocks or to lavish magnificent awards on each other. What is the point of these Dimitrov Prizes?'

Zhivkov looked at me, laughed and said: 'We have them only because they exist in the Soviet Union!'

I may be mistaken, but at that moment I had the feeling that my scepticism about the so-called Soviet experience had made him like me better. For after that he started saying that the mechanical aping of Soviet models in the past had caused great damage to Bulgaria.

'We have our own, very valuable experience' he said, with the fervour of a genuine patriot.

A little later in our conversation, he suddenly complained of the inertia of the Politburo, which he clearly despised. He said: 'We have Politburo members who are there for no good reason. Nobody knows of anything useful they've done. They just sit there being members of the Politburo!'

Later some of my acquaintances explained to me that the Politburo had scuttled many of Zhivkov's important initiatives and that he could not stand the older members whom he had inherited from Chervenkov's era. Yet the members he disliked so much were precisely the veteran trusted stalwarts of the Soviet Union. Thus his outburst was indirectly addressed to the Soviet leadership. [...]

He went on to say that many of the offspring of the Politburo were dissipated, capricious, and changed their various privileged posts as often as they liked.

'My children', he said proudly, 'are not like that! Lyudmila works seriously at her speciality!'

He also said categorically that he would never push his children into a public career. Zhivkov seemed completely sincere when he envisaged his daughter's future as a research worker. What later impelled him to make her into a Minister for Culture, so that she too followed the path of other children of Politburo members, is still not quite clear to me.

From all that was said or alluded to concerning life and relationships in the Party élite, I formed the impression that Todor Zhivkov did not enjoy wide support, that at the very core of the Party powerful forces were at work against him. Perhaps that is why he was trying to distance himself from the other Politburo members and to suggest that he was quite different.

It was after one o'clock when we started the climb towards the mountain lodge at the summit of Midjur. The others were still quite far behind us. Only Pesho followed closely with his rucksack.

But on the slope immediately below the lodge a rather unpleasant surprise awaited us. We were suddenly confronted by two men. One of them had a greying, almost white forelock over his ruddy face and the other younger one, an imposing giant, was holding a film camera. I recognized the first as the director of the State Studio for Documentary Films, Nyuma Belogorski, of whom I can say with a clear conscience that he was one of the greatest bores in contemporary Bulgaria. For many years he had lived by touring the world, earning a small fortune by making films about Georgi Dimitrov.† [...] The giant was his camera-man.

Nyuma leapt towards us while his camera-man, without any warning, started filming Zhivkov and myself. (I wonder where this film is today?)

When he saw the clicking camera and Belogorski running down the slope breathless and smiling, Zhivkov looked at me significantly and sighed.

'Comrade Zhivkov', Nyuma exclaimed, shaking hands with us. 'This is what is called luck! If you only knew how I need you! When we heard you were coming, we dug ourselves in here and have been waiting for you for two whole hours! All I need is one shot of you, just as you are, climbing Midjur.... Nothing more.... Such luck ... and the sky is exactly as I want it! If you only knew how well this film is coming along! This morning I was looking at the rushes, and, do you know, that moment when you are standing up surrounded by the partisans of the brigade, you have no idea how realistic it is of you. ...'

Nyuma rattled away like a machine-gun, spitting with excitement. I can still see his rapturous face and hear his enthusiastic unctuous tones. He reminded me of those elderly sales assistants in the clothing shops along Pirotska Street who go into rhapsodies at the sight of a client trying on a new suit.

It transpired that at that very moment, in mid-October 1964, the cunning Belogorski was making a film about the skirmishes of the Chavdar brigade. This was to be a kind of documentary about the exploits of the partisans, based on a screenplay which Zhivkov was obviously familiar with. It turned out, too, that an actor had been chosen to impersonate Zhivkov himself.

Zhivkov did not reply to the effusive flattery of the film director, but let himself be filmed, while I withdrew. [...]

The meeting with Nyuma made a great impression on me and a rather painful one. This was the first time I had been a direct witness of such an open, repulsive display of servility, obsequiousness, false love, and even worship by one human being for another. Moreover, I have to admit that nothing in Todor Zhivkov's bearing encouraged such behaviour. It would have been far more usual for the film director to have discussed his particular problems with calm and reserve, or to tell stories about the making of the film. Where did it come from - this servility, this cloying sycophancy, this lackey's enthusiasm?

'Your image, comrade Zhivkov!', he exclaimed at one point, as if it was a question of the ikon of St John the Baptist.

I was more than sure that the very filming of the story of the

Chavdar brigade (and not another brigade) was Belogorski's own idea. Probably he had left no stone unturned in an effort to persuade Zhivkov and his cronies that their 'glorious' past should be immortalized. And probably he had succeeded in inspiring them with a feeling for the exceptional historic value of what were, objectively, very modest historical facts.

But if it were solely Belogorski who had played a part in this old, transparent game, one need not have been concerned. The trouble was that he was only one of the keenest among a huge, muddy wave of sycophants, who, during the following decade, would seek to persuade Bulgaria, the Party and Zhivkov himself what a great and wise statesman he was. Up to about that time, Todor Zhivkov was just one of the country's leaders. Thereafter he would be enthroned on a burlesque Olympus of Party history and his every word or step would be extolled as the most pregnant manifestation of a demi-god.

Meanwhile, as we were descending the mountain, I looked at the First Secretary and asked myself: 'Does Todor Zhivkov believe in this charade? Does he really believe that his image can move people like Nyuma to such ecstasy?'

The answer would come with time. [. . .]

Gradually the group fell apart again and Zhivkov and I found ourselves once more in the lead. For a long time we walked on in silence as if we had nothing more to say to each other. Then, after a while, he asked me what, in my opinion, was most lacking in our literature.

'Passion!', I replied. He did not seem to understand, so I explained that bureaucracy ruled our literature and that the writers had a formalistic attitude not only towards their own subjects but towards the whole life of the country.

He was listening attentively but I sensed his mistrust of what I was saying. He evidently had such a good opinion of contemporary Bulgarian literature that I risked finding myself in the role of an unwelcome critic. So I told him about the report of Lyuben Dilov, the writer, who had visited West Germany to publicize Bulgarian literature with German publishing firms. He had called on some of the best-known publishers and shown them German translations of extracts from the writings of nearly every contemporary Bulgarian writer. He had been particularly impressed by the serious approach of Rowohlt Verlag, where the editorial board had taken the trouble not

only to read the submitted samples of contemporary Bulgarian literature but also to analyse them in writing. Most humiliating of all had
been the publishers' comment that they would like to translate and
publish genuine Communist literature, but that the contemporary
Bulgarian writing which had been offered was not in the least Communist, but (I quote from memory) 'an anachronistic petty-bourgeois
literature devoid of interest'. The representatives of Rowohlt Verlag
had explained in detail that neither the content nor the form of the
Bulgarian samples bore the marks of that innovative approach which,
in their opinion, should distinguish Communist literature. Instead,
they had found tedious circumstantial detail, sugary romantic characters and superficial dialogue; in all these works there had not been one
convincing portrait of a Communist.

This verdict of Rowohlt Verlag had been passed on by Lyuben
Dilov to the Writers' Union secretariat. When we heard about it, we
asked Lyuben for more details. My personal view was that the German
publishers had been absolutely fair in their assessment.

But Zhivkov, who had a close interest in writers' affairs knew
nothing of this report and was rather taken aback.

'So they say that there is nothing Communist in our socialist literature?' he asked.

'That is what they say.' I replied.

'I want to see this report!' he said, striding ahead. After a few paces
he turned round and asked me what I thought of the German verdict.
I told him that in principle they were right and that we had to give
some serious thought to the problem of what kind of literature we
were producing. I did not proceed further in this criticism because I
had the feeling that he either did not understand me or did not want
to listen to disagreeable things. After all, had he not himself spoken
many times about the remarkable successes of our socialist literature!
And now to have to be told that this was no socialist literature at all,
but merely petty-bourgeois retrospection!

We continued to walk in complete silence for quite a time. Zhivkov
was striding energetically ahead of me and seemed absorbed in his
own thoughts. A few paces behind, I asked myself for the umpteenth
time: what was he really like? What kind of a man was leading
Bulgaria? I was trying to put my own impressions of him into some
sort of order and not to lump together the many different aspects of
his nature and my reactions. But I had to admit that for me he
remained an enigma.

What I had heard about him up and down the country was not

flattering. The intelligentsia, which probably judged Zhivkov by his speeches, thought him crude. In Sofia there were at least a dozen people who could imitate him very well: especially his voice and his laughter, which seemed to tumble down several flights from its highest level. If this was the attitude of the intelligentsia, who went as far as to claim that Chervenkov had been highly cultured, the reaction of the ordinary people was open mockery. The whole country was inundated with jokes about Todor Zhivkov in which he was invariably portrayed as common, uncultured and limited. Moreover, as I have already mentioned, he was regarded with disparagement even in the Party itself. Of course, all these popular opinions could have been mere prejudice, as so often is the case.

My immediate impression of him, during this long excursion, was that he definitely rose above these popular notions and that, for me at least, he was undoubtedly superior to any of the other high Party leaders. Admittedly, Zhivkov was far removed from the intellectual world. Admittedly, he had not read many books and his education was rather limited; even his vocabulary frequently showed the uneasy combination of simple peasant language and pompous phrases. His aesthetic judgements, too, could be questioned. But none the less he had undoubted natural intelligence, quick wit and a magnificent memory. Many people were amazed by Zhivkov's memory. What I thought he lacked, above all, was imagination, but instead he had a well developed intuition. I believe that after this excursion he classed us, his four guests, faultlessly. His attitude to me, albeit friendly, remained to the end full of suspicion. No doubt he loved his power and basked in it, but with a well disguised vanity which did not irritate. At first I doubted if he had a realistic picture of life in the country, of the suffering of the people, of their insoluble problems. I had often found that highly placed party officials did not have even the most elementary idea of the conditions in which the people lived. They seemed to retreat to a kind of island of their own and not to care about anything outside. Zhivkov, I discovered, knew quite well what things were really like, certainly much better than his colleagues. And I imagined his answer in precisely the words that I was to hear him utter many years later: 'It's not up to me!'

He was like an actor who had accepted his role, had learnt it well and acted it out with pleasure, without any pretensions about interfering in the work of the stage director or the playwright. That he was conscious of his allotted part could be seen from his ironic attitude towards himself.

This brings me to the most interesting incident of our excursion. As we were following a narrow mountain pass, we came to a large puddle right across our path. It was about two and a half metres wide. We looked around for a rock we could use as a stepping-stone but found nothing.

'We'll have to jump!' said Zhivkov.

I was the first to take a run and jump across. Zhivkov followed and would probably have made it had he not stumbled. He fell on his hands, but with such a splash that he was covered in mud. And then suddenly he stood up, looked at me, smiled and said in a very peculiar voice: 'Well, you've probably never seen a muddy First Party Secretary before. Now you have!'

He stressed the word 'muddy' in an ambiguous way which implied: 'I know quite well what I am and don't need others to tell me!'

Maybe I was exaggerating, but at that precise moment I felt that, for the first time, I was making real contact with him. Whenever, later, I used to tell the story of Zhivkov falling in the mud and his comment about the 'muddy First Secretary', few believed that he was capable of saying such a thing. The prejudice against him was so pervasive that it deprived him of the right to have made such a profound remark.

I reached out my hand to pull him out of the puddle but he refused and got up by himself. With the help of his handkerchief he cleaned himself up and we continued the descent without further comment. Gradually the mud on his clothes dried out.

The sun was setting when we reached the wooded plain. Just then I suddenly heard a loud military command: 'To greet the Prime Minister of the People's Republic of Bulgaria, all heads – to the right!'

In the clearing ahead, a strange sight awaited us: standing to attention in two long lines were former gendarmes from the time of the Second World War in navy uniforms with German tommy-guns, and partisans, armed with old rifles and carbines. It was an incredible picture. What we were seeing was obviously the military unit taking part in the filming of Nyuma Belogorski's documentary. And the commander of this unit, himself kitted out in the uniform of the bourgeois past, lifted his hand in a salute to the Prime Minister to whom he reported. This was too much for me and I hid behind a bush, leaving Zhivkov to deal with the ceremony on his own. But he stopped and called out after me: 'Hey, Georgi, why are you running away?' And, turning to the formation, he interrupted the whole ceremony to point at me and say: 'Look at those writers! The moment they smell danger, they vanish into thin air!'

I had to go back. Zhivkov presented me to the soldiers as the author of *Men* and joked about gendarmes and partisans standing in the same line.

Soon afterwards we were back on the highway, where the Chaika awaited us.

When we parted, Zhivkov said that he would like us to have many more such meetings. He added nothing further, and refrained from any official phrases about the need to maintain contact between the Party and the young intelligentsia; he simply said that he would like to see us again. One of us remarked that it was our turn to invite him, to which he immediately replied: 'But nobody invites me!'

'We'll invite you, but you won't come,' I said.

'I'm sure to come. Whatever work I have, I'll come.'

Our meeting with the Party's First Secretary had left us elated. The light in which he had shown himself outshone all our expectations. We thought that since the highest leader in the land could treat us with such tact and attention, since he had indicated that he fully understood the problems not merely of literature and the arts but of our whole society, since he had listened patiently to our long representations, it was possible to believe that Bulgaria was in good hands. We quickly forgave him his atrocious speech of the previous year, and easily accepted his good manners as evidence of good intentions. But when we told our fellow-journalists at the club of the meeting, my own enthusiasm was clearly regarded as ill-founded, for from all sides I was met with sceptical smiles. That same evening one of my friends took me aside and said: 'If you have any illusions that you need only tell Zhivkov about abuses for him to act, you are very much mistaken! Your excursion was nothing but a flirtation, which will not bring about any significant change.'

When, soon after our excursion, Khrushchev fell from power, it was rumoured everywhere that Zhivkov's days as Party Secretary were numbered. But every time the question 'Who will replace him?' was asked it was left hanging in the air. It transpired that in the whole of the Politburo and the Central Committee there was no serious contender for the succession. The only possible candidate, Mitko Grigorov, was extremely unpopular among writers and artists.

The years which followed showed that the Soviet leadership, too, had not come up with anything better than Todor Zhivkov. [...] Moreover, during those long years he won for himself the reputation of a Communist leader who had caused the minimum of trouble for the Soviet Union. Not once, not for a moment, did he have illusions about being able to defy the will of the leaders in the Kremlin. Even when provoked to strong and perhaps quite sincere patriotic outbursts, he never forgot that the Soviet Union came first, and only after that Bulgaria.

Thus, after Khrushchev's fall, while the dust was settling in the Kremlin, Todor Zhivkov had already taken the necessary measures to survive, whatever the upheavals. He surrounded himself with young and loyal men. The Central Committee and its secretariat were packed with newly formed cadres who looked on Zhivkov as did the Roman legions on Caesar.

This explains why not only the new, but any Soviet leadership, even one consisting of extreme Stalinists, would always prefer Zhivkov to other candidates. He was the toughest, the most quick-witted and above all – the most loyal. One can say that he served the Soviet Union more zealously than did the Soviet leaders themselves: he was in the forefront of the struggle against the Chinese, he was the first to support Moscow at the time of the invasion of Czechoslovakia, the first to express hostility to Eurocommunism, and so on. As a reward for his loyalty he was permitted to say that when the Soviet Communist Party made mistakes, the Bulgarian Communist Party did not.

It was clear to both Zhivkov and the Soviet leaders that they were bound together by the closest mutual need. Without the Soviet Union, Zhivkov would have become the easy prey of his enemies, now lying low in the Party. Without Zhivkov, the Soviet Union would lose an excellent and, probably, not easily replaceable servant. This relationship could be compared to that of the classic English lord and his butler, who have grown so accustomed and attached to each other during many years spent together that a separation would be most painful for both. In this long process of interchange between the master's benevolence and the servant's loyalty, there has grown mutual confidence, a particularly rare commodity in politics. The greatest happiness in a butler's life is to know that his master cannot do without him. In his turn, the master is happy in the knowledge that the butler depends just as much on him. In the times in which we live, it is probably more difficult to find good butlers than good masters. [...] That is why it stood to reason that Khrushchev's successors would accept with relief and joy the loyalty of such a tried and true servant, who was offering them, neatly parcelled up, a whole country and a whole Party.

In the years following our meeting Todor Zhivkov made considerable efforts to establish direct contact with almost every important social group in Bulgaria, and especially the intelligentsia. What he was doing was in stark contrast to the gloomy alienation and inaccessibility of his predecessor, Vulko Chervenkov. In fact, even after Khrushchev, Zhivkov was following quite closely the pattern of Khrushchev's public behaviour and particularly his sociability. The better known figures in Bulgarian cultural life, who had not lunched, dined or had a private conversation with the First Party Secretary, could be counted on the fingers of one hand. The people whom he invited ranged from his most consistent critics to his most obsequious admirers. Sometimes I wondered how he had the time to meet and talk to so many people. He went hunting with writers keen on the sport; he organized dinners with poets and playwrights, he visited painters' studios, he assembled musicians, he sought the company of popular actors, and so on. It wasn't a case of surrounding himself with a narrow clique of favourites, but of activity on a mass scale. Of course, the small clique of favourites existed, but few amongst the wider intelligentsia could accuse Zhivkov of neglecting them. Almost every day in clubs and cafés one heard that Zhivkov had met Nikolai Khaitov,† that he had at last received Yordan Radichkov,† that he had spent a hilarious evening with Kaloyanchev and Neicho Popov, that he had danced with the wife of Bogomil Nonev† and that he had personally praised Ivan Kondov. I know of no other political leader who indulged in such an all-embracing flirtation with the whole intelligentsia. Since it was known that in his youth Zhivkov had aspired to be an actor, it was perhaps understandable that he liked to be surrounded by the world of the arts.

At the same time, his unerring instinct told him that the only people who could seriously disturb his quiet reign were precisely the members of the creative intelligentsia. Every one of the Communist Party's troubles - in Poland, in Czechoslovakia, in Hungary and in East Germany - had been stirred up by the intellectuals, artists and writers, or had occurred with their significant participation. In Bulgaria, attempts at military *coups* were condemned to failure in advance, not so much because they lacked the support of the masses but because they were not supported by the creative intelligentsia. That is why Zhivkov took this intelligentsia under his personal protection and entrusted its management to his closest associates.

When Zhivkov's cronies claim that they would never allow a Solzhenitsyn to emerge in Bulgaria (implying a criticism of mistakes made by the Soviet leadership), they are thinking not only of the possibility of quick reprisals by the State Security, but chiefly of the whole Zhivkov atmosphere. As soon as the name of a Bulgarian Solzhenitsyn rose above the permissible height, instead of creating an outcry and attracting general attention, all sorts of pressure would quietly be applied to persuade him to climb down of his own will. I am utterly convinced that Zhivkov would send him an invitation to lunch or an excursion like ours; that he would listen to him carefully, promise him many things and concede many except the most important – the right to publish his works in their original form. Perhaps even that would be granted, but in so tortuous a way that most of their impact would be lost. If anyone doubts me, they can ask Radoi Ralin, Christo Ganev, Konstantin Pavlov, or so many other Bulgarian potential Solzhenitsyns, whose influence, popularity and significance were adroitly restricted and reduced to below danger level.

It is precisely in Zhivkov's complex and rather widespread relations with Bulgarian writers and artists that one can see the special qualities which helped him to retain power for so many years. But if, on the one hand, the result was the consolidation of his personal position, on the other, it was the certain extinction of all dangerous intellectual sparks and the transformation of the restless creative spirit into a fattened foster-child of the state.

In my opinion no one else in Bulgaria has had a more disastrous and destructive influence on literature and the arts. I have tried in these reports to portray in detail different facets of the life of the Bulgarian intelligentsia now, and to explain, as well as I can, the reasons for its remarkable artistic anonymity. I have stressed over and over again that the principal evil in the life and work of Bulgarian writers, painters, composers, actors and so on was interference by the Party, which imposed the most mediocre standards and did all it could to strengthen the power of the untalented.

When I said that we were all paid *not* to write, rather than to write, I was thinking of the deathly hand of the Party which destroyed almost all dedication to work. And behind the Party's interference stood its chief organizer and executive – Todor Zhivkov. No important step affecting the life of the intelligentsia, no major appointment or dismissal, no punishment or reward could occur over the head of the First Secretary. Indeed, many of these measures could be traced back to his personal initiative. Thus one has to conclude that what at first sight looked like a very positive interchange with the intelligentsia was, in reality, the source of its great misfortunes. The fact that Zhivkov knew everybody, that he had his own contact with people, that he was able to obtain their commitment without really committing himself, was very useful to him. Under his direct supervision real assaults against cultural organizations and institutes were perpetrated. The break-up of the Writers' Union and its transformation into a faceless bureaucratic machine was accomplished by Dzhagarov† under the direct observation and guidance of Zhivkov. The ruin of the National Theatre by the appointment of an artistic nonentity like Philip Philipov was Zhivkov's own achievement. The rout of the powerful group of film makers who had dared to rebel against mediocrity was the work of Venelin Kotsev† under Zhivkov's personal supervision. The promotion and demotion of editors of newspapers and periodicals and directors of radio and television – all these things happened with the direct participation of the First Secretary. [. . .]

As a result of Zhivkov's general, arbitrary and often quite unwarranted interference, Bulgarian cultural life became permeated by an atmosphere of insecurity and chaos and the abandonment of elementary artistic standards, and all this was cemented by the establishment of a bureaucratic structure. Seen from a distance, Zhivkov's flirtation with the intelligentsia brought magnificent holiday homes, well endowed arts funds, a profusion of medals and titles, increased salaries, consumer satisfaction and the gratification of vain ambition for posts and privileges. But in fact all this was part of the means which the First Party Secretary used generously to halt and undermine the independence without which no creative spirit can exist, to isolate the intelligentsia from any real contact with the ordinary people, and to keep it in the position of a spoilt Party creature.

This flirtation ran parallel with the gradual but massive development of a new 'personality cult' – that of Todor Zhivkov. [. . .]

When it became clear who would call the tune in Bulgaria, Zhivkov was literally swamped by a huge wave of self-interest, careerism and cupidity. Figuratively speaking, he woke up one morning to find himself surrounded by people whose backs were bent, who whispered flattering words to him, admired and applauded him and offered to serve him. The same Bulgarian citizens were already studying his speeches, selecting quotes from them and loudly declaiming them at Party meetings.

'As the comrade teaches us...!'

In all honesty, I must say that in those years Zhivkov did not order anybody to worship him; he did not send out a Party directive asking people to admire him nor did he select quotations from his pronouncements for them to cite. All this came from below, quite spontaneously, in line with the corrupt nature of the Party and the regime. I could send Zhivkov a long list of people who at that time called him all sorts of offensive names, but who today are his greatest admirers and vie with each other to shower compliments on him.

It is probably very difficult for a normal person to withstand such a wave of flatterers, admirers and followers, even if he knows that all this is nothing but self-interest and show. I imagine that it requires great moral strength to slap the faces that offer ingratiating smiles, to disband the chorus of flatterers, and to stamp out all sycophancy. We are so strangely constituted that we do not only like, but actually encourage, people to regale us with pleasant untruths.

As for Zhivkov, who longed for popularity, who had been nurtured within the Party leadership in an atmosphere of unquestioning worship of the cult figures of Stalin and Dimitrov,† he instinctively wanted the same for himself. In the end, was he not as good as they? If the legend of Dimitrov was based on the exaggerated reputation of his 'heroism' at the Leipzig trial, why should the legend of Zhivkov not rest on similarly inflated accounts of his own 'heroism' in the Chavdar brigade? If Kolarov† and Chervenkov could lay claim to popularity, despite ruining the country's economy and despite the sinister reputation of their armed State Security detachments with their notorious blue peaked caps, why should Zhivkov, who had abolished them and considerably improved the standard of living, not also taste the fruits of such popularity? Objectively, he inherited from his predecessors a country crushed by terror and brought to its knees by misery and destruction, but he changed the whole picture for the better. All improvements in Communist Bulgaria are linked exclusively with his name and actions. Why, then, should those who admired Dimitrov and Chervenkov not also admire him? Why should those who quoted them not quote him too? Why on earth should Dimitrov and Chervenkov have their writings published and not he, who had achieved so much more? I imagine that these were the powerful inner reasons why Todor Zhivkov not only accepted but also encouraged his admirers – all the more so as Party and leader had always been identified. Consequently enthusiasm for Zhivkov was enthusiasm for the Party.

Because the Party was Todor Zhivkov!

But here I must emphasize one of the most striking features of the Todor Zhivkov cult, or rather the motives of his admirers. The difference between them and the admirers of Stalin and Dimitrov was considerable. While the cult of Stalin had its roots in Party fanaticism to a great extent, the cult of Todor Zhivkov was based exclusively on careful calculation of the benefits to be gained from it. In other words, the enthusiasm, the admiration, the mania for quoting him and the prostration before him – all of these were the result of having been given a bigger slice of cake. Almost without exception, Zhivkov's admirers have all been rewarded by him. If the First Secretary wanted to see through the hollow hypocrisy of his entourage of loyal followers, he need only take back from them what he gave. Then he would see how quickly their enthusiasm for him would evaporate.

I think that Todor Zhivkov himself saw through the insincerity of the people around him. Several times he would say in public with bitter mockery: 'Who knows what you will say behind my back after I have gone?'

And so, the cult for Todor Zhivkov was built upon purely mercenary foundations. [...] Zhivkov's merit was to help the mercenary spirit establish itself, not only in relation to himself, but as a simple clear code of conduct in Party and society.

In the years which followed our first meeting, I saw Zhivkov several times on official occasions. He continued to invite people from the world of culture and the arts to grand dinners or banquets in honour of various occasions. For instance, the yearly writers' meetings were accompanied by a special dinner attended by Zhivkov. In the course of these rather crowded meetings, he somehow found time to exchange a few words with most people. I noticed several times with amazement that he remembered very clearly the things I had told him and treated me with great courtesy and kindness – perhaps because I belonged to the few who had never asked him for a favour.

Watching the manner of those people present towards him, I was the witness of the disagreeable mercenary attention with which he was surrounded. From the moment he appeared, writers, actors, painters – both men and women – and generals, with their wives, surrounded Zhivkov with the happiest smiles their faces were able to produce, with the over-anxious desire to make a good impression on him and, if possible, to have him to themselves for a minute or two. How I wish that I had a tape of their syrupy words; how I wish I had a film of their unctuous phrases, the spurious shine of their eyes, their servile gestures, their envious glances at those to whom Zhivkov talked. I felt that I was not in Bulgaria in the second half of the twentieth century but in the world of Gogol's provincial officials I should add that this infection of servility spread also to serious and undoubtedly gifted artists, which made the scene even uglier. While it was possible to accept the obsequiousness of some cultural function- ary, it was difficult indeed to swallow the servile behaviour of a good painter, actor or writer.

I still shudder at the memory of one of the last dinners with Sofia's cultural élite, which took place in the Party headquarters, because of the sycophantic oriental picture it presented.

'Ah, comrade Zhivkov, when will you come and see us?' cooed a well-known actress next to me.

'Comrade Zhivkov' – drawled the oily voice of a fat writer, 'only you can understand me!'

'Comrade Zhivkov, will you help us?' chirped another eager crea- ture, joining in the game with beguiling dark eyes.

'Comrade Zhivkov! Comrade Zhivkov!' They barred his way, tried to lead him aside, to escape from the others, to ask him quickly for something, or at least to express their enthusiasm and their love.

Clearly, all this gave him pleasure. It seemed that he needed all this attention: an attention for which he had paid dearly but had the right to enjoy. Perhaps these were for him the moments of real triumph, when the élite of intellectual socialist Bulgaria was cringing at his feet.

But definitely – not everyone. At that last reception my nerves gave out half-way through the evening. I made for the door, where I was stopped by one of Zhivkov's closest followers, a writer, who asked me reproachfully if I was leaving already. I lied that I had stomach pains. He did not believe me. Walking towards the exit of the Party head- quarters, I saw another ten people or so who were also about to go. I caught up with a well-known poet. He looked at me and said: 'I have a terrible stomach ache! It seems that banquets and receptions don't agree with me!'

November 1968: it was the day on which the Americans were choosing between Nixon and Humphrey. Darkness was falling over Sofia when the Politburo car, in which the poet Lyubomir Levchev† and I found ourselves, took the highway for Samokov. We were going to dine with Todor Zhivkov at the Palace of Bistritsa near Borovets [in the Rila mountains].

I was in low spirits for several reasons. I had no desire to see either

Todor Zhivkov or his entourage. All morning my closest friends had tried to persuade me to go, saying that I should not give in to my mood, and that I had a lot to lose by rash gestures. In fact, I had no intention of staging a protest. I simply saw no point in this meeting where, at best, I would be superfluous.

'I've nothing to say to him or the others,' I told my friends.

'Shall I give you a piece of advice?' asked one of them, a 'People's Artist' experienced in such public ordeals. 'Say something about shooting or tell a hunting story; you'll see that after that they'll talk about hunting for the whole evening and forget you.'

During the four years which divided my first meeting with Todor Zhivkov from my last but one, many things had become clear to me so that I had no more illusions. The naive, unfounded but vitally necessary faith that internal changes in the Party were possible had perished with the invasion of Czechoslovakia. For many like me, the end of Dubcek was also the end of my attempts to reconcile plainly irreconcilable things, to compromise in the name of something which would never be. The truth about us and our future had emerged with such force that I would have had to be blind, deaf and dumb not to grasp it. Never before, not even during the most terrible Stalin years, had I felt with such merciless clarity that we were doomed. My memories of the days and nights in the streets of the excited Czech capital, of the liberating force of the Prague Spring, of the intoxication which the people in the East did not know and the people in the West had forgotten - all that had changed into repugnance for the regime under which I lived, for its representatives whom I used to meet, and for myself - because the compromises continued. There was something highly offensive in my going to dine with the man who had sent (albeit symbolically) Bulgarian troops into Czechoslovakia.

My disillusionment with the career of Todor Zhivkov had started long before August 1968, but the invasion by the Warsaw Pact forces was the watershed, the moment when all the masks were torn off. I understood then that all the actions of the First Party Secretary and his entire social behaviour strictly conformed to the part he was expected to take in the Soviet play entitled *People's Republic of Bulgaria*. Only in a delirium of naive optimism could one see anything more in his paltry insincere gestures of conciliation, his ambiguous phrases. [...]

I shall never forget the dinner which Dechko Uzunov, the well-known painter, gave in Borovets on the occasion of his seventieth birthday. He had invited only two writers to this dinner - Stefan Tsanev and myself. Todor Zhivkov was expected to attend, but

instead Venelin Kotsev, the Politburo member responsible for culture
and the arts, arrived. Kotsev, who was then already regarded as the
Number Two in Bulgaria, stood up to congratulate the host. After he
had conveyed the appropriate felicitations in Zhivkov's name and his
own, he suddenly lifted his arms and, holding a piece of bread in one
hand and a knife in the other, turned to Stefan and myself. 'As for the
writers over there,' he said, 'let me remind them that in one hand we
hold the bread, and in the other – the knife!' Icy water seemed to have
been poured on the whole company and Dechko's celebration dinner
was ruined. To this day I remain convinced that Kotsev would not
have dared utter such threats without Zhivkov's authority.

Todor Zhivkov's personal meetings with representatives of the creative intelligentsia not only failed to promote understanding, mutual
confidence and lasting ties, but led to the exact opposite – the division
of 'ours' and 'theirs', the growth of intolerance, the crushing of almost
everything decent and, at the same time, the encouragement of bureaucracy, mediocrity, lack of personality and corruption. The meetings with Todor Zhivkov played an important part in setting writers
and artists against each other. The few principled and honest people
amongst the leaders of the cultural front were thrown out and replaced
with unworthy but ambitious mediocrities. [. . .]

One of the directors of the National Theatre once told me in
confidence that every time he had to cast a play he was subjected to a
great deal of pressure, because many of the actresses had access to the
private telephone number of the Party's First Secretary.

A national review of Bulgarian drama was organized during the
1968–69 season. Special committees of qualified people selected the
best plays from all over the country for performance in Sofia. And at
the last minute Lada Galina, whose rather weak play had been re-
jected unanimously by the jury, happened to meet Zhivkov and
complained to him. Purely because of his immediate intervention, her
play was put on in Sofia, which, to put it mildly, made a mockery of
the jury's expertise and the review itself. Sometimes the First Secretary's interventions had an almost grotesque quality. The humorous
writer Vassil Tsonev suggested to Zhivkov that, given the patriotic
line plugged by the Party, it would be most appropriate to resurrect
and reintroduce in every restaurant those tasty old Bulgarian dishes
which had long been forgotten. At a stroke, Vassil was appointed head
of some shadowy department with special powers, and he travelled up
and down the country for two or three years searching for old Bulgarian recipes – just like one of the characters in his own *feuilletons*.

Of course, all this activity on the part of the First Secretary of the Bulgarian Communist Party cooled any good feeling towards him among the worthier writers. In certain circles in Sofia, it was considered offensive and humiliating to maintain any contact with Zhivkov or his entourage. One August I happened to be in a group of writers in a restaurant situated on the Black Sea promontory of Kaliakra. Todor Zhivkov entered, accompanied by the late General Grubchev who, at the time, was the head of his personal bodyguard. I felt very embarrassed when the whole company of writers rose silently and left the establishment, without even greeting the man whom they knew only too well. Again on the Black Sea, at the Writers' Centre where Zhivkov used to stay every year, there was a much discussed demonstration in my absence. (When I had heard about Zhivkov's impending visit, I had left the previous evening.) The following morning, Dzhagarov and other officials of the Writers' Union had knocked on every door warning the writers not to leave the building as the beloved guest was arriving. But when the official Chaikas pulled up and Zhivkov alighted and entered the courtyard of the Writers' Centre, three writers – Christo Ganev, Valeri Petrov and Nedelchò Draganov – went on chatting happily to each other without paying the slightest attention to the visitor and, walking past him, climbed into Valeri's old Moskvich and disappeared. Dzhagarov was beside himself with fury. Two days after this incident, Colonel K from the State Security service came into the television studios and told us all the details, shouting with the utmost malice: 'If I were Comrade Zhivkov, I'd teach them how to stage demonstrations! Just leave them to me, and we'll see who rules this country!' [...]

These were my thoughts as I drove to dine at the Palace of Bistritsa. Perhaps the only argument in favour of my going was the hope that I would again be able to raise the subject of the theatre director and the actors who had been banned from Sofia after my play *Let's Go Under the Rainbow* was taken off the stage. The director, Assen Shopov, one of the most talented in the Bulgarian theatre, the superb actor Naum Shopov and his wife Venche, also an actress, had been punished by being sent into exile to Burgas. The painter responsible for the sets, Mladen Mladenov, had also been exiled. Only myself, the author of the play and perhaps the main culprit, had been left unpunished, as if deliberately to make me feel guilty for the fate of the others. In an attempt to help them, I had already that summer personally given the play to Zhivkov to read to let him judge whether it was really anti-Party, as those who had banned it maintained. But Zhivkov had delayed his answer and now I was almost sure that the subject of the play would come up during dinner. I had also asked him to receive Assen Shopov and listen to his explanation, which he had refused to do. While I was making these moves, I was conscious of the absurdity of the fact that the first leader of the country had to concern himself with matters with which he was relatively unfamiliar. However, I also knew that, given the existing structure of power in the country, he alone could change the decisions that had been taken. [...]

During the whole journey to Borovets it continued to rain, which increased my disagreeable feeling of premonition.

The lighting in the hall of the former palace in the Rila Mountains, Tsarska Bistritsa, was soft and pleasant. On the walls all around hung magnificent hunting trophies, mostly deer's antlers. The whole rustic style was welcoming and cosy. The furniture and various objects had been chosen and arranged with taste and simplicity. Later I found out that much had been left as it was at the time of the Bulgarian kings. The palace had at first been offered to the artists as a guest house, but then Zhivkov had peremptorily appropriated it for the needs of the Politburo, whilst another very large and luxurious centre was built for the artists, also in Borovets. Later that same evening, Zhivkov explained that the reason why 'Royal Bistritsa' had been taken away from the artists was their 'vandalism' of the precious carvings, rugs, old pictures and furniture. According to him, some of the artists who were holidaying in the palace had gone so far as to cut out parts of the old prints and even to remove some valuable objects. On top of everything else they had started a fire. It seemed that Zhivkov was rather sensitive about being accused of taking over the guest house of the Artists' Union – so now, with a great show of indignation, he emphasized the irresponsible attitude of the former occupants. True or not, the palace, which had been converted into the residence of the Number One in the country, was now kept perfectly.

By the time we arrived, the rest of the company had already assembled. Dressed in holiday clothes, Zhivkov received us very politely, with his usual sociable public manner. Despite the dramatic events of 1968, he continued to play the role of the attentive host, anxious to share with us some of the comforts of his life. He asked me jokingly in front of all the others if I had ever slept in a king's bed. When I replied that I had not had this honour, he gave orders that the room of the former King Ferdinand should be put at my disposal.

I went up the wooden staircase to the top floor where the bedrooms were. I entered a simply furnished room with a large bed, bedside lights with old-fashioned lampshades and almost bare walls. Only the central heating was modern. Looking around, I could not help reflecting how modestly the Bulgarian monarchs had lived compared with the 'people's representatives' who succeeded them. I was reminded of the famous remark of a Politburo member about the former monarchy: 'If only they had left us real palaces! Instead, they built nothing but hen-coops!' This is probably why every Politburo member, every ambitious local leader avid for luxury, strove to outshine the Royal hen-coops.

There were two hours before dinner, which we had to ourselves. I sat down in front of the darkened window and tried to gather my thoughts. I had the feeling of participating in some pointless masquerade – so incongruous did I find this Royal room, our host who had put it at my disposal and myself who was expected to be flattered by this gesture. After a while, there was a knock at the door and Anastas Stoyanov came in. From the moment since he had been appointed Secretary of the Writers' Union, he had changed profoundly. Power seemed not only to have mesmerized and intoxicated him but also to have deprived him of all sense of reality. Oh, how greatly such modest, unpretentious, polite and sincere village lads changed as soon as the devil lowered the ladder of power before them and they placed a foot upon the first rung! Anastas, too, had undergone a metamorphosis which had severed all links between us. In fact, he would never have come near me had he been able to identify and place me correctly. But it seemed that my rather ambiguous situation confused him even more than it did me.

He now informed me pompously that he had to make a speech at the dinner and thank Zhivkov on behalf of everyone present including myself. Astonished, I replied that I preferred to express my own gratitude if necessary and did not understand why someone else should speak for me. He explained that it was not merely a matter of saying 'thank you' but that he had been especially entrusted by the Union's secretariat with the task of raising some matters of which 'Comrade Zhivkov should be informed'.

'Well, that's your affair,' I said, 'I don't see what it has to do with me.'

'It's important that we don't contradict each other', he said fiercely.

I had already suspected that our invitation to Bistritsa disguised someone's elaborate scenario, and that Anastas was trying belatedly to ensure that we remembered our parts. 'I believe', he declared, 'that some things have to be brought to Comrade Zhivkov's attention and that he'll be pleased to hear them from us'. I shivered slightly and repeated in none too friendly a tone: 'If I have to say something, I'll say it myself. What you say is your own affair.'

He blushed and left the room. But his visit contributed to the gloomy atmosphere. On my way down, I ran into the poet Lyubomir Levchev† with whom I had remained close friends throughout these years, although our relations had cooled significantly after the notorious meeting of the Writers' Union on 12 April 1968, when he had supported (albeit with a bowed head) the Party line. I asked him what games Anastas was playing. Lyubo muttered that he knew of no games, Anastas was merely making himself important.

We entered a spacious room where a long table had already been laid. Zhivkov was there, surrounded by a few elderly men and a younger one in general's uniform. He introduced us one by one. The elderly people were old partisan friends of his. I remember only the old Paunovsky, father of the literary critic Ivan Paunovsky. The General was Christo Ruskov, President of the Hunting and Fishing Union, and because of that widely known as the 'Rabbit General'. In a joking mood, Zhivkov said that he saw this evening as a bridge-building exercise between the generations. The older people nodded their heads in approval, while General Ruskov bellowed in military fashion: 'Aye, aye, Comrade Zhivkov'.

Suddenly I had the feeling that the plan for this whole dinner was the result of a misunderstanding, and that Zhivkov had perhaps wanted to dispose of two problems at the same time. Before we sat down he warmed to the theme of old ties, extolling the links between those who had shared 'the difficult years of the struggle'. Here he expanded on his own love for the members of the 'Chavdar' partisan brigade, adding something about there being no more trustworthy people. Suddenly he asked: 'Do you know what might have happened to us today?' And he informed us that recently the commander of an important military unit (a tank division if I remember rightly) had plotted a *coup*. Everything had proceeded according to plan and the danger had been acute, when, at the eleventh hour, one of the officers had betrayed his chief and exposed the plot. 'Just imagine if those tanks had invaded Sofia!' Zhivkov said, hitting the table with his fist. 'But now we have appointed a loyal Chavdar man to this post.'

For me and all present this revelation was sensational, coming as it did from the lips of the Party's First Secretary. None of us knew about this abortive plot; it must have been very recent. At the same time, we were well aware that the internecine struggle within the party continued to rage. Zhivkov was now determined to place his men from the Chavdar brigade in all sensitive positions. Despite all my efforts, I was subsequently unable to discover either the identity of the commander who had plotted the *coup* or the strength of his organization. However, from Zhivkov's tone I concluded that the danger had been real. 'With Chavdar people in charge, one can sleep soundly!' he concluded.

We sat down to dinner. My place was on Zhivkov's right, and next to me sat Christo Ruskov. Conversation dragged until I decided to follow the advice of my friend and introduce the subject of shooting. I could hardly believe how soundly I had been counselled. Suddenly there was general animation, with each guest eagerly trying to join in the conversation. In the course of it I learned that Todor Zhivkov apparently held the world record for antler trophies of stags he had killed personally. Indeed, Ruskov explained that the antlers were measured according to a special table and that Zhivkov had long ago surpassed the world record. At this momentous point, there was a pathetic argument: while Zhivkov doubted that he had exceeded the world record, the General swore that this was an incontrovertible fact. To my amazement, all those present suddenly turned out to be experts on shooting and hunting. The conversation followed the tracks of boars, ran into rabbit holes, climbed rocky paths in pursuit of hinds in the Pirin mountains and soared in the sky after winged game. As far as I was concerned, there could hardly have been a more tedious subject, but the advantage of this display of hunting fireworks was that no one paid any attention to me. Zhivkov was clearly having a good time, enjoying his own stories and laughing frequently and loudly.

Observing him, I noticed that he had become more self-confident, sharper and more cutting. His former gentle politeness had vanished. At the same time, he seemed to me more restless, there was a kind of tension in his words and gestures. At given moments, his thoughts seemed to be elsewhere. From time to time an official on duty kept coming in and whispering something into his ear. At such moments conversation quietened down, but only twice did Zhivkov hint at the content of these messages. The first time it was something to do with Romania's Party leader, Nikolae Ceausescu. Zhivkov started talking about Ceausescu with obvious contempt. He said that the Romanian leader had done unforgivable things and that now that he was asking to meet Zhivkov it was high time to teach him a lesson.

'Let this hysterical man wait at least two months', Zhivkov said categorically and, as far as I remember, he added a few more disparaging epithets about his Romanian colleague. Nobody asked any questions about the disagreements with Ceausescu, the assumption being that we knew about the latest developments. When Zhivkov called Ceausescu unflattering names, this was not done to impress us with his own power but rather because he really did have a poor opinion of him.

The second time that the hunting stories were interrupted, the pretext was the American presidential election. Some of those present tried to ingratiate themselves by saying that these elections were quite pointless because whoever won, Republicans or Democrats, nothing would change in the United States. To my surprise, Zhivkov disagreed with this opinion and said that there was some difference; he considered that, of the two evils, Humphrey was the lesser.

'Let's make a bet on who will win!' I suggested.

'All right!' Zhivkov said. 'What's the wager? Another dinner like this one?'

'No!' someone exclaimed. 'With American elections it has to be an American bet! Whatever anyone likes to choose!'

Zhivkov agreed. He bet on Humphrey and I bet on Nixon. To this day Zhivkov owes me an American bet – and before witnesses at that.

The conversation returned to Ceausescu and someone asked Zhivkov what he thought of Tito. But he merely replied with an ominous smile. It was obvious that Tito, Yugoslavia and the Macedonian question were not on the menu for dinner.

Several times Zhivkov drank a toast to 'our young creative intelligentsia', 'the old Party activists with young hearts', and so on and so forth. I noticed that relatively few bottles were being consumed and that the only one who was drinking seriously was the 'Rabbit General'. That Lyubo, who liked good wine and could hold his drink, held back showed that he was preparing himself for the moment when he had to be absolutely sober.

Orlin Orlinov had won a poetry prize. Zhivkov said he had liked the winning poem very much because it was patriotic and castigated slavish admiration for everything foreign. [...]

I had not read this poem because I have never considered Orlin Orlinov to be a poet. But listening to him now, I marvelled that such a crude and superficial composition could have won not only a prize but also the enthusiastic approval of Zhivkov. While the others applauded and either sincerely or out of politeness praised the poem to our host, I sank into my chair and yet again felt that this was 'their' dinner, 'their' company, 'their' relations, while I remained the outsider who, owing to a trick of fate, found himself where he did not belong.

And so, almost the whole dinner at the Royal Bistritsa palace in Borovets was spent discussing hunting. Suddenly, nearly all the guests were revealed as connoisseurs of game shooting and hunting and the numerous rituals which accompanied them. I listened to amusing stories about the hunting exploits of various members of the Politburo, about the passionate sportsmanship of a minister who had missed an important meeting, about an enraged boar who had been killed at the very last second, about the shooting of a man-eating bear and the tracking of an elusive stag. Gradually I began to understand what a profound impact hunting had had on the lives of the upper party aristocracy. The pastime which, before the rise of the Communist movement, had been considered the legitimate privilege of jaded archdukes and bored earls and barons, had now become the legitimate privilege of those who claimed to have sought power for the sake of the happiness of the 'working people'. 'You'll see', said my friend who had advised me to fall back on the subject of hunting, 'you'll see the triumph of the plebeians who at all costs want to pass for born patricians'.

Of course, our host and his entourage were discussing shooting in special game reserves where ordinary people were strictly banned. They described shooting parties with VIPs from abroad, shoots with all the trappings of luxury, with special guns and equipment and even music; expeditions during which every eminent Party man could give full expression to his passion for hunting and then donate whole piles of venison to the common people.

To go shooting or hunting was apparently regarded as a sign of refined taste, as a noble hobby, in the highest party circles throughout Eastern Europe. The Party leaders very often exchanged sporting visits or presented each other on various occasions with choice guns. Todor Zhivkov, for instance, had gone all the way to Mongolia to shoot. It occurred to me in passing that neither King Ferdinand nor King Boris had ever shot in Mongolia. I asked myself, 'Why does Zhivkov go shooting? What exactly gives him pleasure? Is it the stalking, or the dead game, or just the shooting itself? Or, perhaps,

does shooting distract him and take his mind off the heavy responsi-
bilities of his work?'

It seemed to me that the answer lay elsewhere. Lenin had been a
hunter, Stalin was a hunter, Khrushchev was a hunter, Brezhnev,
Walter Ulbricht, Ceausescu, Tito, Fidel Castro, Kim Il Sung, Enver
Hoxha ... all of them went hunting. Maybe hunting was part of
Marxism, although, as far as I knew, Marx himself had not only never
written anything about the hunting passion of the 'revolutionary
leaders' but had not even foreseen that, in the transition period on the
way to Communism, hunting would remain a non-transitional privilege. [...]

At last Anastas Stoyanov rose and said that he wanted to thank the
host on behalf of the whole company.

Todor Zhivkov nodded, signifying his assent that Anastas should
have the floor. I thought to myself that speeches were quite inappro-
priate for what was a fairly intimate dinner. However, this seemed to
be part of the scenario for the evening.

Anastas blushed and looked more like a Komsomol secretary preparing to deliver his first speech. There was an almost farcical contrast
between the pompous clichés with which he began and the way in
which his tense and insecure voice kept giving out. Personally, I could
never decide on which facial expression to assume when listening to
this kind of speech. I often envied friends of mine, who managed to
keep a straight face and an air of concentration even when faced with
a hailstorm of words devoid of all meaning.

Zhivkov lent back, stopped smiling and looked rather like a judge
getting ready to listen to an important witness. I noticed with amazement that most of the faces around me took on Zhivkov's expression
as people started to listen carefully to the speaker.

He began by heaping unsubtle and rather servile praise on the First
Secretary for having invited us to dinner, as well as for his unceasing
concern for Bulgarian literature and art. For their part, he said, the
writers were happy to feel the interest of Comrade Zhivkov, which
obliged them to work with even greater enthusiasm. It was precisely
because of the Party's concern that Bulgarian writers had been able to
achieve so much. Comrade Todor Zhivkov and the Party knew that
they could count on the writers, who would always remain selflessly
loyal fighters....

Clearly, all these clichés were the overture for something more substantial, which did not take long to follow.

'However' – here the voice of Anastas Stoyanov rose dramatically

– 'we cannot close our eyes to some phenomena in our literature, which I feel ashamed even to mention!' He pronounced the word 'ashamed' in almost the same tone which was usually reserved at public meetings for the word 'disgrace' (one of the Party's favourite clichés for branding enemies).

Our attention now was wholly focused on Anastas, who seemed well prepared to report on the shameful 'phenomena'. Imagining what he was about to say, I instinctively tried to stop the orator in full flood by remarking that it was not appropriate to discuss internal writers' quarrels at such a dinner. But Zhivkov nodded encouragingly to Anastas. It was then that I realized that Anastas had been entrusted with the task of delivering a carefully prepared text in front of the Party Secretary, who was keen to hear it.

This was a typical practice in the management of the country, a rule established by the Bulgarian Communist Party. Given the totally centralized regime, all principles, ideas and intentions came from 'above'. But sometimes, in order to justify such an idea from 'above', especially if it was unpopular, it was necessary to make it emanate from 'below', as a mass feeling coming from the people. To this end, somebody high-up would suggest to lesser or even quite humble officials that he would be glad to hear a certain opinion from their own mouths. Then they would meet to discuss and elaborate at length the opinion in question, presenting it as their own, which was then accepted with pleasure by the leader who had initiated the whole procedure. It seems to me that this farce epitomizes the essence of so-called 'people's democracy'. When somebody has to be criticized or dismissed, this never happens directly in the course of an explanation between an official and his boss. The manager only takes the initiative, merely hinting to his staff of collaborators that he would like a blow to be struck against a particular official. Thereafter his initiative becomes a 'collective opinion' and is followed by a farce to end all farces: the manager decides on punishment, and says to the victim that though personally he would like to help him 'it is the collective which decides'.... Pontius Pilate is a babe in arms compared with the Communist leaders. Thus, very often, opinions and proposals purporting to come from 'below' are in reality directly organized from 'above'.

The same applied to promotions and awards. If, for instance, comrade X wants to appoint his daughter or his son to an important post in a given department, he never does it directly, by signing the appointment order. No, he will suggest the idea to people whom he can trust to take it up, develop it and give it back to him metamorphosed into an irresistible desire of the collective or the mass to see this appointment made. This is usually accompanied by a piece of theatre: comrade X resists, he declares that he is against appointing his son or daughter, that this is incompatible with his principles, but ... if the collective wishes it ... if the comrades really think so ... then he is ready to sacrifice his principles.

In the same way, it was equally clear to me that the scenario for the evening had been devised by the secretariat of the Writers' Union following an idea expressed by none other than Zhivkov himself. And now this idea was served up to him as a well-reasoned speech, designed to win his approval. The result of all this would be that the Party, in this case Todor Zhivkov, would be offered the wholehearted backing of the writers' collective for action against 'certain phenomena'. If Todor Zhivkov or any other important leader had tried of his own accord to criticize a given book, film or play directly, he would obviously have run the risk of being accused of personal bias or even incompetence, as had been the case more than once with Chervenkov. However, if professional and competent writers expressed a categorical opinion about developments in their own field, not only did he risk nothing but he could, in case of an obvious error, throw the blame on them. [...]

Anastas went on to attack the 'shameful and irresponsible' attitude of writers who were trying to win popularity at the expense of the Party line. Obviously he had in mind people like [the popular poets] Radoi Ralin and Konstantin Pavlov, although he mentioned no names. It was easy but dishonest, he said, to achieve popularity by exploiting the shortcomings of society. The writer should have a constructive attitude towards the society which had created him. After all that, he proceeded to attack the main target of his 'thanksgiving' speech – the poet Vesselin Andreev,† whose strained relations with the Party leadership were common knowledge. Anastas said more or less the following:

'Comrade Zhivkov, on behalf of the Writers' Union I attended the celebrations for Vesselin Andreev's fiftieth anniversary at Pirdop [his birthplace]. Let me say straightaway that, with the exception of a few people, there was a crowd there which you'd hardly expect to see at a celebration for a Bulgarian writer. This mob of spurious admirers had suddenly discovered Vesselin Andreev's talent. After the speeches in his honour, he rose to give his own thanks. But, comrade Zhivkov, listen whom he saw fit to thank!'

Anastas's face expressed unbounded indignation while he recited his version of Vesselin Andreev's speech: "I thank my mother who brought me into this world, I thank the people amongst whom I grew up, I thank the river, I thank the forest, I thank the Balkan mountains...."' Here Anastas raised his voice to a new pitch and said: 'Comrade Zhivkov, he thanked the heavens, the sun, the sheep and the goats ... but *he did not thank the Party! He did not once mention either the Party, or your name!* This is the Communist poet Vesselin Andreev! We organize celebrations for him, we give him a prize and he doesn't even thank the Party to which he owes everything! Where would Vesselin Andreev be without the Party, I ask?'

Anastas shouted the last words with a fiery partisan passion which suggested that Vesselin Andreev should be hanged forthwith. But as he spoke, he clearly knew that he was saying things which would produce a strong reaction in Zhivkov. The face of our host had darkened and with undisguised irritation he interrupted Anastas's address: 'Vesselin Andreev should have been shot long ago!'

'He shouldn't have been let off!' said one of the Party veterans who knew what was being referred to.

I was amazed to hear the First Secretary's regrets that somebody had not been 'shot' at the time. The very word 'shot' sent shivers down my spine. As some other members of the company seemed equally ignorant of Vesselin Andreev's sins, the General and the Party veterans explained that, at the time of the partisans' struggle, Vesselin had been Political Commissar of the Chavdar brigade [with which Zhivkov likes to link his own activist career]. On hearing the news of his brother's death in the Soviet Union under Stalin's regime of terror, he had left his partisan outfit for several days and had seemed to want to end his participation in the resistance. The General and the Party veterans who clearly wanted to ingratiate themselves with Zhivkov called Vesselin a traitor, and implied that it was not too late to call him to account for his misdeeds.

This airing of old Party squabbles was very typical of Party ethics. Whenever somebody had to be attacked, crushed or liquidated, he was inevitably accused of old sins which had never been mentioned before. Suddenly it would transpire that the man had been as good as a police stooge, that he had been responsible for the death of some member of the Communist underground or that he had shirked his duty in a cowardly way. It appeared that the biography of every active Communist belonged not to the life he had led, but to the Party leadership which could tailor it to its own needs. For many years, Vesselin had been fêted as a poet-hero and showered with titles, prizes and honours, and now it transpired that he should have been shot! Why?

I knew that Vesselin Andreev did not like Todor Zhivkov and that he detested Dzhagarov's group. I knew that he had withdrawn from all public life and was living like a hermit in his native Pirdop. I knew that several times he had not hesitated to assume a position which matched his convictions and therefore had stood against the Party line. Possibly the rift between the Party and himself had now reached a dangerous climax. Clearly Zhivkov had heard from Anastas, the Writers' Union secretary, exactly what he wanted to hear. And his sullen expression did not bode well for the former Political Commissar.

None of the guests at the dinner had a good word to say about Vesselin Andreev or any of the others who were criticized. I knew that at least one of those present did not share the declared view of the Writers' Union, which had the official approval of the First Party Secretary. I found the whole scene depressing: a judgement which could have decisive consequences was being formed against people who were not present, had no possibility of defending themselves and had been given no explanation of their presumed transgressions.[...] Why had Anastas been ordered to dish up these accusations after the dessert? The fact that Zhivkov had said that Vesselin should have been shot long ago revealed that it was he himself who had instigated – perhaps indirectly – the prosecuting tone of the union secretary. All this seemed to me in tune with the intensified activity of the ideological department of the State Security in those days, in the wake of the Czechoslovak tragedy, when the atmosphere in Bulgaria was full of calls for witch-hunting. And perhaps we were just witnessing the selection of the first victims.

When I saw that Anastas was ready to continue, I bent down towards Lyubo Levchev, who sat opposite me, and whispered that if these innuendoes against colleagues and writers were to continue, I meant to leave the dinner as a protest. Lyubo seemed very worried and turned towards Anastas, who sat next to him and who had heard very well what I had said. But Zhivkov, who had been talking to someone on his left, noticed my reaction and asked me what I thought. I replied that I disagreed with what had been said about my colleagues and that, in my opinion, Anastas Stoyanov's view may have reflected divergences amongst the writers but did not represent an objective picture. I added that I thought it hardly fair to talk in this way behind the backs of those who had made a real contribution to our literature. Anastas interrupted me here and expressed doubts about the contribution of the criticized writers. I lost my temper and shouted at him: 'When you've written what Vesselin has written, then you'll have the right to open your mouth!'

My reaction had a surprising and very disagreeable effect. Had I been hoping for a future public career, I would have known with absolute certainty that I had spoilt my chances. I heard a voice on my left saying 'Nobody knows what Vesselin has written'. This was a direct allusion to the rumour that Vesselin's partisan poems had really been written by another poet, who had perished.

An awkward silence fell, which Orlin and the General tried to disguise by refilling our glasses. All the same, Anastas did not get up again to continue his speech. He was angry and glared threateningly at me, but he said nothing. In his place rose Lyubomir Levchev. With an apologetic almost childlike smile he started gently and fluently to retrieve the situation. He said that Comrade Zhivkov should not be surprised that, even at such a dinner, disagreements amongst writers were inevitable; then he spoke about the Party's tolerance towards our mistakes and aberrations, about Zhivkov's deep understanding of our problems and the complicated circumstances in which we lived. Surprisingly, Lyubomir seemed remarkably sure of himself, which attracted Zhivkov's attention. I think that this was the evening when Todor Zhivkov discovered him, because from that moment on Levchev had a meteoric career. However, despite his conciliatory tone, Levchev stated clearly that he was no mediator and, mentioning no names, he accused certain writers of being demagogic and gambling on their popularity. I have forgotten the exact words he used, but I remember that basically he defended the attitude of Anastas – that is to say, that of the Writers' Union leadership.

Levchev sounded very convincing and I saw how Zhivkov's face brightened. The First Secretary made some sort of joke and people round the table relaxed. I felt that my own expression was perhaps the only one different from the rest and I wanted to leave immediately. Suddenly I questioned what value the purest revelations, the most profound insights of a poet or an artist, the feeling for beauty of a composer or a musician or the wisdom of a philosopher had for Todor Zhivkov and his acolytes. Every reaction of our host, the entire evening, seemed to express only his instinct for self-preservation in power, while every reaction of the others was a direct expression of the desire to please the great man, to be liked by him, to impress him, to make a lasting imprint. Their response to this ruler's condescending gesture of inviting them to dinner was undisguised vanity, pleasure and the desire to make sure of many more such dinners.

Everything was false. Under normal circumstances, such a meeting could only have come about by chance; one had only to imagine that Todor Zhivkov had no power whatsoever and that Bulgaria was not a totalitarian but a democratic country, to swear that neither Anastas nor Lyubo Levchev, nor indeed any of the others, would have allowed an incompetent citizen with very different tastes and criteria to interfere in the lives of poets. Conversely, if Zhivkov had been an ordinary citizen, he would scarcely have wasted his time on people and matters which probably did not interest him. Under normal circumstances there would have been no conversation between them because they had nothing to say to each other. It was the phenomenon of power which magically changed everything so that what I was witnessing was a logically absurd evening. Todor Zhivkov felt fully entitled to distribute marks for literary achievement, which (please note) reflected not merely his private opinion, but were powerful Party pronouncements. At the same time, the poets considered this a deserved token of imperial benevolence, as if there was no more important criterion in the world than that of our host.

I was trying to divine what exactly would befall the criticized writers when the proceedings around me took a peaceful turn and the evening ended merrily.

With a tone of one announcing a pleasant surprise, Zhivkov told us to prepare ourselves to listen to a folk singer, who had been especially invited for us. The next moment there entered a rather thin man of medium build, aged anything from thirty to forty. Slung across his chest was a large accordion. [...]

'Ivancho doesn't only sing folk songs', Zhivkov explained, 'he composes them too. In fact he transforms old folk songs into contemporary texts in the spirit of our time. He has composed lots of songs about the partisans, about the building of new Bulgaria, about socialism!'

This was enough to prepare me for the ordeal which followed. I had already heard these unbearable travesties of Bulgarian folk-songs on the radio; they continued to be broadcast despite numerous listeners' protests. A wit had been heard to say that he preferred three months' corrective labour to half an hour of such 'art'.

Zhivkov clearly thought the contrary. Ivancho settled himself on the chair between me and the General. His ugly face expressed the solemn concentration of a master who knows the value of his art.

'What are you going to sing for us, Ivancho?' Zhivkov asked loudly, in great good humour.

'Whatever you like, comrade Zhivkov', Ivancho replied in a hoarse falsetto, which held out little promise of a melodious voice. 'I'll begin with a brand-new song!'

And, without waiting for further invitation, Ivancho compressed his accordion and released a strange screeching voice. Poor man! While he was singing, his bottom lip veered to the left, while his upper lip veered to the extreme right, so that his face looked comically deformed, like those of dead drunk people trying to string a few words together. Those distorted lips produced the most discordant goat-like voice imaginable, while the song was a pure copy of numerous similar folk songs. However, what was new about this song was that it was in praise of the Party. Ivancho himself had written the words, which prompted Zhivkov, much to my delight, to say to the three poets sitting opposite him: 'Ivancho, too, is a poet.'

I felt malicious satisfaction at the thought that the First Secretary actually saw no great difference between them and Ivancho.

I must confess that rarely had I been exposed to such musical torture. The accordion thundered away, almost bursting my ear-drums as Ivancho's goat-like voice bellowed about 'radiant expanses and the red flag'. I looked at Zhivkov. He was grinning broadly and his face reflected the spontaneous enjoyment of a peasant who, in the old days, would watch a bear dancing and wait for it to obey the order of its keeper: 'Come now, bow to the gentleman!'

When the song ended, everyone clapped. And now Zhivkov, in high spirits, suddenly suggested: 'Ivancho, do sing the song about my meeting with the bear!'

Believe it or not, Ivancho had composed songs about the partisan exploits of Zhivkov, who figured in the text as 'Hero Yanko'. (Yanko was Todor Zhivkov's underground name during the War.) Clearly, Zhivkov greatly enjoyed this song and wanted us to hear it too. Ivantcho immediately began to sing. I don't remember the exact words, but the man-eating bear was an allegory for fascism while 'Hero Yanko' represented the sound forces of the people. [...]

It would be an understatement to say that I was astounded. I didn't know what to think. What was I to make of the fact that the Number One man in Bulgaria could listen with such undisguised pleasure to a paean to his own exploits? For me this beat everything I had ever heard. [...]

Suddenly it struck me: 'Why am I so surprised? All this is exactly as it should be. Isn't Ivancho's art precisely Zhivkov's own ideal? Doesn't this very song about Yanko who slew the bear express most vividly the essence of the Party's directives for the cultural and spiritual life of an entire people? What do composers like Stainov, Vladigerov and Pipkov, poets like Bagryana, painters like Dalchev and Ivan Peychev represent when measured against this Ivancho? Can any of them give Zhivkov as much enjoyment as this song?' Perhaps it was the First Secretary's dream that all complex problems of artistic form and content, all great and harrowing questions concerning the essence of man and his times, should eventually be reduced merely to 'Hero Yanko vanquished the man-eating bear.'

Ivancho's song had destroyed the last of my few remaining illusions.

It was rather late when we finally went to bed. In spite of the royal bed, I could not sleep all night. Ivancho continued to stretch the huge accordion, to twist his lips and to bleat like a goat – the sole, monstrous but true answer to all my questions. [...]

On 8 November in the morning, the theatre producer Assen Shopov and I made our way to the gate of the Party Central Committee building. I felt very awkward because I had told Assen that Zhivkov wanted to see him. This was not true but I was hoping that, in the end, the First Secretary would agree to receive us both. The officer at the barrier took our passes, but said that his instructions were to admit only me. I insisted that there had been a misunderstanding and that both Assen and I were expected. He made a telephone call, probably to one of Zhivkov's secretaries, explaining the case. Shortly afterwards a security officer in plain clothes came down and, without a word, led us up the staircase. I breathed a sigh of relief. [...]

But I could see that Assen was very flustered. The meeting with Todor Zhivkov was clearly making him extremely nervous. On our way we did not exchange a single word.

Eventually we were led into the familiar spacious office. Zhivkov met us with courteous handshakes. That was another characteristic difference between him and most of the other Party bosses: while they received visitors sitting behind their desks (perhaps to emphasize the difference in social rank), Zhivkov rose to welcome his guests and saw them off personally. He invited us to sit at the oblong table in the middle of the room and placed himself opposite us. After inquiring if we would like some coffee, he quickly ordered some. In spite of his routine politeness, he seemed to me to be agitated by something which he was trying to hide. The conversation began between him and me. He said that he had read the play and handed me the copy I had given him. Then he added that he personally (Zhivkov insisted that this was his private opinion) saw nothing anti-Party or harmful in the work, although it was not the kind of play he liked. This was because it was deeply pessimistic, he explained. It was quite obvious to me that he was merely echoing the opinion of the panel of collaborators to whom he had shown the play. He added that, according to the 'comrades', the production had emphasized the pessimistic aspect of the play and so its performance was unacceptable.

We spent about ten minutes on this subject, while Assen remained silent, staring at the table in front of him. But when we passed from this specific case to the painful question of the Party's need to trust writers and artists, irrespective of their successes or failures, Assen joined in the conversation. Even now I believe that he made the most impressive speech of his life. Assen spoke with composure, with splendidly chosen words and expressed his thoughts simply. He said that the confidence of the Party, that is of the regime, was of vital importance to the artist in contemporary Bulgaria; that without full and unquestioning confidence it was impossible to achieve anything or even to embark on any artistic venture; that artists suffered from being fenced in by spurious gestures of confidence which in reality masked constant suspicion. Assen declared that he found it impossible to think, to develop any ideas for a production, to make any artistic experiments: in other words, to create in an atmosphere of constant mistrust. He demanded of Zhivkov that the Party should take a definite unequivocal decision on the matter. If he could not secure the Party's unquestioning confidence, he would prefer to change his profession.

While he was speaking, I could see that his words were making a profound and favourable impression on Zhivkov. But in his frankness, Assen did not sense that he was asking for the impossible, that in attacking the Party's mistrust towards him and people like him, he was in fact striking at the very heart of the system. Was this mistrust, constantly and deliberately fostered by the Party and the regime, not typical of all our society? Did not an enormous organization, with all its ramifications, exist precisely to sow suspicion between one person and another, between one team and another, between one institute and another? And in the world of the arts, where not even the most elementary rules of fairness operated, distrust prevailed with the most arbitrary force. Every vigilant citizen could discover and raise the alarm against anti-Party, 'ideological-diversionist', or simply dissident points of view in every single work of art. How was it possible to talk about confidence in the artists when there existed a huge ideological department in the State Security organization whose task was solely to be vigilant.

Nevertheless, Assen's eloquent appeal for confidence, addressed to the country's top leader, was so patently sincere that it had its effect.

'What exactly do you want of me?' Zhivkov asked when Assen had finished. 'To give orders that the production should be put on again, or what . . .?'

I said that for technical reasons alone there could be no question of restaging the production. Nor had we come for that. What we were concerned with was Assen's position and that of the actors who had been banished to Burgas. If it was accepted that they had been punished unjustly, it was logical to allow them to return to Sofia immediately and to restore them to their posts.

In all previous conversations with Zhivkov, he had taken the attitude that he knew nothing of any punishments or reprisals, and that this whole affair was an internal problem concerning the Ministry of Culture. But now he suddenly said: 'Let's see what can be done!' He rose and went to his desk. Without sitting down, he lifted the receiver of a special telephone and said: 'Comrade Matev, what's happening about Assen Shopov and Naum Shopov and his wife, who were sent to Burgas?'

Pavel Matev,† Chairman of the Committee for Culture, knew the situation very well and sympathized with the victimized actors: he had tried several times without success to have them returned to Sofia. It was on his advice that we had asked for an audience with Zhivkov.

Zhivkov listened to Matev's explanations, then said: 'Well, do whatever's necessary to have them returned to Sofia!' Whereupon he replaced the receiver, as if he considered the matter closed.

I was rather impressed by this gesture of his which, frankly, I had not expected. But even so, I was aware more of the whole absurdity of this unfortunate episode – the punishment of actors and producers for no other reason than that some incompetent spectators had disliked their performance. The fact that the Number One man in the country had to spend his time solving this case made me think, to say the least, of that scene in Ionesco's play in which deaf and dumb candidates enter a singing competition. The punishment of my friends was absurd. Their pardon was no less absurd. But life between these two absurdities was cruelly realistic and logical. I asked myself whether Zhivkov had ever, even for an instant, been conscious of this absurdity in which he, driven either by his own will or by circumstances, was forced to play a part. At this very moment, when the mess caused by the system had to be cleared up, did he feel that all this had nothing to do with the proper functions of a serious head of state? It should not have happened at all: for the 'anti-Party' activities of Assen and the others were no less a fiction than the 'pro-Party' activities of those who had punished them. Did Zhivkov not sense that he lived and dealt with fabrications which entangled him and carried him away from the simple and clear reality of life? Or, since the position he held in the country was absurd, did he perhaps feel quite happy to follow the absurd logic which confirmed this position?

Even so, I too was a participant in this unreal play. And according to its logic I felt that I should express my gratitude to Zhivkov for having eased the fate of my friends. Meanwhile, the First Secretary himself seemed somehow under the influence of what he had done, for he advanced towards us with puzzling deliberation, as if preparing to do something more....

'Comrade Zhivkov', I began, 'I thank you very much.... For us you are...', I wanted to say: 'a man who understands', or something of this kind, but he interrupted me in a strange voice: 'For you...? Do you know what I am for you...?' And here something quite incredible happened, the perfect culmination of this whole absurd play.

Unexpectedly he produced a small booklet, opened it quickly at a previously-marked page and almost pushed it under my nose. I saw some kind of epigram and a drawing of a pig with a funny tail. While I, completely bewildered, wondered what on earth this was all about, Zhivkov seized a sheet of paper and signed his name. Then, visibly upset, he said: 'This is me..., and this is my signature!' With trembling fingers he pointed once more to the pig's tail which, even at first sight, looked just like Zhivkov's signature.

A closer inspection made the likeness between the tail and the First Secretary's signature even greater: they were almost identical.

'That's what I am for you!' said Zhivkov with great bitterness, and, leaving the proof under our eyes, he lowered himself onto his chair.

For a moment I was dumbfounded both by the similarity between drawing and signature, and Zhivkov's violent reaction. I had never before seen him so deeply upset. I believe that his reaction came from an acute feeling of genuine mortification. He reminded me of a man who has just unexpectedly been betrayed either by a close friend or an unfaithful wife. I was also struck by the fact that in his reaction there was no trace of anger or irritation, only a painful bitterness. Perhaps anger would follow later. Clearly, the whole incident had happened very recently. I guessed that he had been shown the drawing shortly before our arrival and that we were the first outsiders invited to compare the pig's tail and his signature. Clearly, he had not meant to do this, but somehow his nerves had given way and he had revealed his hurt pride on an impulse.

This unexpected development had stunned Assen, who was sitting beside me. Zhivkov's gesture in placing his authentic signature beside the tail of the pig, his trembling hands, his altered voice, all this was too much for both of us.

In the long seconds that followed I felt that silence would be interpreted by Zhivkov as confirmation of the offensive nature of the drawing. I already knew that the sketch was Boris Dimovski's work, and that the epigrams were by Radoi Ralin. The text of the epigram itself had nothing to do with Zhivkov and this gave me the excuse to say that the resemblance was purely coincidental, and that there could be no question of a deliberate intention.

Zhivkov responded with a silent, semi-ironic smile which showed that he did not believe me and that he knew that I, too, did not believe what I was saying.

It was only then that I froze at the thought of what might befall Radoi and Boris. I turned to Zhivkov and said firmly that, from what I knew of both Radoi and Boris, neither would contemplate such a cheap joke....

But in spite of my efforts to minimize the resemblance between the pig's tail and Zhivkov's signature the bitterness did not leave his face. He listened to me attentively as if he really wanted to be convinced that nobody had insulted him. But then he said: 'When I think of how many times Radoi Ralin has been here! He sat just where you're sitting, and we've talked about all sorts of things ... and now....'

Suddenly he stood up and held out his hand to say goodbye. I thanked him once again for his decision to allow the exiled artists to return to Sofia and I repeated that I did not believe that Radoi and Boris had intended to insult him in this way.

Only when we were on the pavement outside the Central Committee building did Assen pipe up: 'I don't know how you dared try to persuade him that the tail and the signature didn't look like each other, when even a blind man could have seen the resemblance!'

A few days later, I learnt that Radoi and Dimovski had been sacked from their jobs and that there was a ban on publishing any of their works.

I expected much heavier punishments to follow, including concentration camp or prison. But this time, it seems, more intelligent people had prevailed upon Zhivkov, or perhaps he himself had sensed that he would sink even deeper into the mire if he dared impose a cruel punishment on the most popular person in Bulgaria - Radoi Ralin.

EPILOGUE:
A SENSE OF THE UNBEARABLE

This concluding chapter of my *in absentia* reports about Bulgaria was written a long time ago. In it I tried to explain why I am in exile. Then, only a few days ago, I received news that my father had died in Bulgaria. And it was the sorrow over his death and my inability to be with him during his last days that showed me, quite clearly, the main reason for my departure, which I have tried to describe with so many words, but which can be summed up quite simply as the feeling that things were unbearable.

Last Sunday, at ten o'clock, I stood separated by a distance of 2,500 kilometres from 9 September Avenue and in my imagination followed the funeral procession behind my father's coffin. I saw, as if I had been there, the faces of many people, close friends and relations; I walked in step with them and knew at exactly what moment which house they were passing. I saw my mother's tears and heard the priest's words hoping desperately that all this was only a bad dream. But when the dreadful moment came at eleven o'clock and the earth took forever the one who had given me life, I suddenly felt a crushing sense of helplessness. For the truth was that at that moment neither I nor my brother, nor our wives and children, could be there where we should have been. For so many long years, we had been unable to see him, neither had he been allowed to visit us. During all those years he lived with the hope of such a meeting, which never took place. And as I imagined how cruelly deprived he must have felt in those days before the end, a feeling that this was quite unbearable welled up in me. It was precisely while thinking about this deprivation of elementary human rights, this denial and mockery of the most understandable and respected human longings, that I recognized the same feeling which had driven me inexorably over the border. I am not talking here about ideological, political or aesthetic differences, but of the ruthless trampling underfoot of the rights and feelings of ordinary Bulgarians. My father was a typical ordinary Bulgarian, one of those millions of nameless, diligent and conscientious people with old-fashioned principles about honesty and dignity. In his own way he had tried to accept, to understand, and to resign himself to the inescapable fate of all Bulgarians like him. But what he could not explain, accept, or get used to was being forbidden to see those in whose veins his blood ran. He still remembered that he had been born a free Bulgarian, but he had the foreboding that he would die in bondage.

I began with the death of my father as the most obvious source of my sense of the unbearable, for which there were probably many other equally powerful reasons. When I lived in Bulgaria, the whole atmosphere was, for me, permeated with that feeling.

It was Sunday, 15 June 1969 – according to the astrologers a fateful year for those born under the sign of Pisces. At eleven-thirty in the morning at the State Theatre of Satire in Sofia, the preview of my play *The Man Who Was Me* was just beginning. At eleven-thirty that evening, I was at the Hotel Excelsior in Belgrade. One of the fundamental principles according to which all my plays were constructed was that they consisted of only two acts, with the second act invariably negating the first. After all that has happened since, I can say that these twelve hours were not the divide between two different plays, but were simply the end of the first and the beginning of the second acts of one and the same play: a play I would define as a 'contemporary tragi-comedy with farcical interludes'. Put more simply, it was one of those plays where the spectator often 'does not know whether to laugh or to cry'.

In spite of the long journey and the tense hours which had preceded it, I did not feel tired on my arrival in Belgrade. My agitation, compounded by the events of the morning, the parting from those dearest to me, and the strange last drive through Sofia, had been replaced by a large question-mark about what was to follow.

It was not the fate of my play at the Satire Theatre which concerned me. For me, as for everyone else, it had been obvious that it would be banned. After all, the theatre belonged to *them*. The crux of the matter was that I had never been able (despite my attempts) to identify with *them*. I had always felt with compelling clarity what was *mine* and what was *theirs*. Moreover, this difference often seemed to approach the mutual exclusion of fire and water, with only two possible alternatives resulting from their forced union – either the fire would be extinguished, or the water would evaporate.

The preview of my play before a restricted invited audience had been planned by the theatre management with two aims in view – to sound out the authorities and to seek the public's support. The director was Metodi Andonov, while the producer, Neicho Popov, had come out of hospital especially to watch our performance. Poor Neicho, he still believed it was possible to create an honest, hard-hitting satire without offending a regime which had always been against any fundamental criticism. For me, and I think for Metodi too, there were no illusions. Of all the principles that any form of art can follow, the least valid is that which, in the words of the Bulgarian proverb, wants to have both 'the wolf replete and the lamb intact'. Indeed all great literature, like all great art, has always been based on the principle of clear choice: either the wolf or the lamb.

The audience's reaction exceeded our most optimistic expectations. The actor Partsalev was magnificent and the theatre echoed with laughter. But the funnier the first act became, the gloomier looked certain faces in the hall. During the interval a well-known colonel in the State Security pushed his way towards me.

'Why have you written such a Czech play?' he said.

I retorted that the play was Bulgarian and moved on. Then came Stefan Tsanev, one of the theatre's playwrights, who told me that there would be a special meeting of the theatre council after the performance, which would include the members of its Communist committee, to decide the fate of the production. I told him that I did not wish to attend the meeting, as I had a pretty good idea of the way things would go. I asked him to represent me. The final curtain was greeted by enthusiastic applause from the audience.

Outside on the pavement, my father, who had watched the performance, said to me: 'This play will bring you nothing but trouble!'

I went to have lunch at the Russian Club. Three months earlier, I had obtained a passport and a visa for Italy, but I had been putting off my departure because of the play. Nevertheless, I had decided that one of these days I would leave. At about two-thirty, Stefan came over from the council meeting to say that things had gone very badly. The play was being taken off for the time being. He looked depressed but sounded resigned. Then one of my more important friends arrived at the Club. He took me aside and asked: 'Are your passport and visa in order?'

'Yes', I replied.

'Then I advise you to go immediately. I think you might find yourself in trouble tomorrow because of today's performance and then you might not be able to travel. Stay away for a month or two – until it all blows over.'

I went home to pack some things. My father and mother saw me to the car. I told them that we would see each other again in a few weeks. And then I left. When I reached the ring-road, the clouds had cleared after a downpour of summer rain, and the sky above Vitosha and the lovely verdant landscape shone with sunlight. On a sudden impulse I decided that instead of taking the direct route out of the city, I would drive around the whole of Sofia on the ring-road. The car sped along the drying asphalt and everything around me seemed strange and inexpressibly beautiful. Mercilessly beautiful. It was as if nature had decided to show me the priceless riches of a country that I was destined to lose. Perhaps men condemned to death meet the last sunrise with the same cruelly persistent feeling of seeing everything for the last time.

'Look! You will never again set eyes on this land, this nature!' cried a fierce voice within me.

As yet I hadn't decided on anything. One of the few lessons life had taught me was not to take preliminary decisions, but to let things follow their own natural course. This time, however, as I drove around Sofia, I felt that the decision had already been taken – by the angels or the devils who determined my fate.

Towards six-thirty I reached the frontier. All the railway and customs officials were huddled round the television set watching the Word Cup match between Bulgaria and Poland. The officer on duty recognized me and very politely invited me to join them. I made some excuse about being in a hurry. Then, on the other side of the Yugoslav barrier, I stopped by a meadow. I looked back towards Bulgaria and it seemed to me that even its natural beauty sharpened the feeling of how unbearable it was to have to live the ugly life which I and many others like me were forced to endure. It was as if nature, history and the national spirit had established a very precise standard for judging the beautiful and the ugly. I felt that I could no longer bear the atmosphere in which I lived, the work I did, the relationships in which I found myself ensnared. I had a sense of the unbearable about the outside world as well as about myself. I realized that for many years I had been unable to enjoy anything, that everything was not only poisoned in advance, but doomed to be poisoned by this sense of the unbearable. If you have entertained a certain idea of yourself, if you have imagined that you are one thing and discover that slowly but inexorably you are being turned into quite another, then the moment is likely to come when you want to smash either the mirror or your own head. In a purely moral sense, this was a feeling of two-fold treachery – towards others and towards myself. Quite apart from morals, it was a sense of an impasse.

Walking the Belgrade streets at night, I reflected that it really was impossible for me to stay in Bulgaria and remain myself. The very act of living in the country represented an endless chain of compromises. Even the struggle against compromise was not without compromise. The relationship between the individual and society was almost negligible. And it seemed to me that the ancient rule according to which man gradually acquires the features of the thing he is fighting against functioned faultlessly. More and more often I discovered in myself (even if they were directed the opposite way) the same elements of primitiveness, instinctiveness, indifference and even ruthlessness that were typical of those I hated. Unlike many others who realized that the same thing was happening to them, but believed that it was temporary, that things would get better, I had no illusions whatsoever that things could improve where I was concerned. Perhaps my feeling was more selfish, perhaps I was too preoccupied with the division in my own mind.

That is why I cannot claim that mine was a case of political courage or integrity; it was merely a matter of my own sense of the unbearable. Had I possessed real national courage and integrity, its most logical expression would have been to remain in Bulgaria and to attempt to struggle there, as do far braver and more honest people than I.

In the course of these reports I have tried very hard to paint an exact and objective picture of the life I witnessed. I realize my immense advantage over writers who live in Bulgaria – the fact that nobody directed me or placed restrictions on my writing – and I have striven to express what many of them would like to say. Nevertheless, I was an active participant in that life and perhaps that could serve as an explanation if my emotions have occasionally overshadowed my objectivity.

APPENDIX

The Staircase
by Christo Smirnensky

Georgi Markov regarded this story as the most telling allegory of a totalitarian system.

APPENDIX

'Who are you' the Devil asked him.

'I am a plebeian by birth and all ragamuffins are my brothers! Oh, how ugly is the earth and how unhappy are the people!'

The young man who was talking had a lofty brow and clenched fists. He stood at the foot of the staircase – a tall staircase of white, pink-veined marble. His gaze was fixed on the distance where, like the muddy waters of a swollen river, the grey crowds of the destitute were clamouring. They were in ferment, flaring up in an instant, raising a forest of desiccated black hands; thunderous indignation and violent cries shook the air and the echo died away slowly, like distant gunfire. The crowds grew bigger, there were clouds of yellow dust, and individual silhouettes stood out ever more clearly against the general grey background. An old man was advancing, bent close to the ground as if searching for his lost youth. A barefoot little girl held on to his ragged garment and gazed at the tall staircase with gentle eyes of cornflower blue. She gazed and she smiled. And after them more tattered, grey, emaciated figures kept coming, singing a mournful dirge. Someone whistled piercingly, another with hands in his pockets laughed aloud, and madness burned in his eyes . . .

'I am a plebeian by birth and all ragamuffins are my brothers! Oh, how ugly is the earth and how unhappy are the people! Oh, you up there, you. . . .'

The young man who was talking had a lofty brow and clenched fists.

'You hate those above?' the Devil asked and cunningly bent over the youth.

'Oh, I shall take revenge on these princes and dukes. I shall wreak cruel vengeance upon them for my brothers, for my brothers who have faces which are yellow like wax, whose wails are more eerie than the howling December blizzards! See their naked bloody flesh, hear their groans! I shall avenge them! Let me go!'

The Devil smiled: 'I watch over those at the top, and shall not betray them without a bribe.'

'I have no gold, I have nothing to bribe you with.... I am a poor ragged fellow.... But I am ready to give my life.'

The Devil smiled again: 'Oh, I don't want so much! Give me only your hearing!'

'My hearing? With pleasure....

Let me never hear anything again, let ...'

'You will still hear!' the Devil said reassuringly and made room for him to pass: 'Go ahead!'

The young man started to run, taking three steps at a time, but the Devil's hairy hand pulled him back: 'Enough! Stop and listen how your brothers moan down below!'

The youth listened. Strange – why had they suddenly started to sing so gaily and to laugh so carelessly! And again he started to run. But the Devil stopped him once more: 'If you want to climb another three steps, you must give me your eyes!'

The young man waved his hand in despair: 'But then I won't be able to see either my brothers or those on whom I want to take revenge!'

'You will still be able to see.... I shall give you other, much better eyes!'

The young man climbed another three steps and looked down. The Devil reminded him: 'Look at their naked, bloody flesh!'

'Good Lord! This is so strange: when did they manage to dress so well! And instead of the bloody wounds, they are adorned with beautiful red roses...!'

Every three steps the Devil collected his small bribe. But the young man kept on, and readily gave everything so as to arrive at his destination and wreak revenge upon these fattened princes and dukes: one step, one more step and he would be at the top! He would revenge his brothers!

'I am a plebeian by birth and all ragamuffins....'

'Young man, one more step! One more step and you will avenge them! But for this step I always demand a double bribe: give me your heart and your memory!'

The youth waved his hand: 'My heart? No! That is too cruel!'

The Devil laughed loudly, then said with authority: 'I am not so cruel. I shall give you in exchange a golden heart and a new memory! If you do not accept, you will never pass this step, you will never avenge your brothers who have faces like sand and wail more eerily than the December blizzards.'

The young man looked into the Devil's green, ironical eyes.

'But I shall be utterly wretched. You are taking everything human from me!'

'On the contrary – you will be as happy as it is possible to be! Well? Do you agree: only your heart and your memory?'

The youth brooded, a black shadow crept over his face, heavy drops of sweat covered his furrowed brow, he clenched his fists in anger and said between his teeth: 'So be it! Take them!'

And like a summer storm, his face black as thunder, his dark hair flying in the wind, he took the last step. Now he was at the top. And suddenly a smile lit up his face, his eyes shone with silent joy and his fists were no longer clenched. He looked at the feasting princes, and he looked down at the grey, tattered, shouting and cursing crowd. He looked, but not a muscle in his face twitched; it was bright, cheerful, content. Down there he saw a festively dressed gathering; the wails had become hymns of praise.

'Who are you?' the Devil asked, hoarsely, and with great cunning.

'I am a prince by birth and the gods are my brothers! Oh, how beautiful is the earth and how happy are the people!'

HISTORICAL NOTE

During the Second World War Bulgaria was formally an ally of Germany but maintained diplomatic relations with Russia. None the less, in the final stages of the war, while a democratic anti-German government in Sofia was trying to negotiate an armistice with the Western Allies, the Soviet Union unexpectedly declared war on Bulgaria. On 8 September 1944, Soviet troops crossed the Danube without encountering resistance. The following day the first Fatherland Government, a coalition of Communists and anti-Nazi 'bourgeois' leaders, took power.

Having secured the key Ministries of the Interior and Justice in the shadow of the Soviet occupation, and aided by the newly established Militia, People's Courts and State Security service, the Communists consolidated their power, suppressing civil and political rights and instituting mass terror against real or imagined enemies of the new order. Georgi Dimitrov, a member of the Party Bureau-in-exile and a Soviet citizen, arrived from Moscow late in 1945 to preside over the liquidation of all remnants of the democratic opposition. This process culminated in the arrest and rigged trial of Nikola Petkov, leader of the radical wing of the Agrarian Union and a former ally of the Communists in the wartime underground; he was hanged in December 1947. An unconstitutional 'plebiscite' had abolished the monarchy a year earlier. Bulgaria became a People's Republic, with the new 'Dimitrov' Constitution of December 1947 a virtual copy of its Stalinist model.

After Dimitrov's death in a Soviet sanatorium in 1949, his brother-in-law Vulko Chervenkov, also a 'Muscovite' and a devoted Stalinist, completed the sovietization of Bulgaria by eliminating the older generation of 'home' Communists: the best known, Traicho Kostov, was tried as a 'Titoist' and executed in December 1949. Bulgaria's 'little Stalin' himself was gradually eclipsed in the wake of changes precipitated by Stalin's death in March 1953. He ceded his position as First Party Secretary to Todor Zhivkov in March 1954, and lost the Premiership to Anton Yugov at the April 1956 Party plenum which took its cue from Khruschchev's historic denunciation of Stalin at the Twentieth Soviet Party Congress. From the ensuing ferment and protracted struggle for power within the Bulgarian Communist Party Khrushchev's protégé, Todor Zhivkov, eventually emerged triumphant. His victory was sealed by the eighth congress of the Bulgarian Communist Party in November 1962, when Chervenkov was finally disgraced and Yugov purged for crimes against 'socialist legality'.

More than twenty years later, Todor Zhivkov still rules Bulgaria. His remarkable survival is due largely to his ability to bend with the prevailing wind from Moscow.

BIOGRAPHICAL NOTES

Andreev, Vesselin (b. 1918): Bulgarian author and ex-partisan whose brother perished in a Soviet purge; Political Commissar of the wartime 'Chavdar' brigade of partisans with which Zhivkov's name is linked; associated with the literary ferment during the 1956 'de-Stalinization', elected to the Writers' Union Presidium in 1960 as part of the regime's new policy of courting intellectuals.

Blagoev, Dimiter (1855-1924): Russian-educated Marxist and revolutionary, co-founder of the Bulgarian Social Democratic Party in 1891, regarded as the 'father' of Bulgarian Communism; in 1903 the party split into the 'broad' and 'narrow' Socialists, the first remaining within the framework of democratic socialism, the second under Blagoev forming the nucleus of the Bulgarian Communist Party (BCP) which joined the Bolshevik international front.

Botev, Christo (1848-1876): Bulgarian poet, revolutionary and nationalist fighter for the liberation of his countrymen from the Ottoman yoke; killed in a skirmish after crossing the Danube to support armed revolt against the Turks; known as 'the poet of liberty'.

Chervenkov, Vulko (1900-1980): Bulgaria's 'little Stalin'; educated in the USSR; brother-in-law of Georgi Dimitrov, after whose death he became Bulgaria's second dictator until displaced by Todor Zhivkov; Party Secretary-General 1950-54; Prime Minister 1950-56; expelled from Politburo 1961 and from the Party 1962; his party membership was restored in 1969.

Damyanov, Georgi (1892-1958): A graduate of Moscow's Frunze Military Academy and a Soviet officer 1938-44, he returned to Bulgaria with the Red Army; one of the chief promoters of the reorganization of the Bulgarian army on the Soviet pattern; Politburo member and from 1950 until his death Head of State.

Dimitrov, Georgi (1882-1949): Bulgarian Moscow-trained Communist; in 1933 arrested in Berlin for alleged complicity in the Reichstag fire, won international fame for his anti-Nazi stand at the Leipzig trial; freed through Soviet intervention, became a Soviet citizen; in 1935 outlined the policy of a broad united Left front in a famous address to the Comintern; led the Bulgarian Fatherland Front during the War, returned to Bulgaria in 1945 to become

Chairman and later Secretary-General of the Communist Party; Prime Minister from November 1946 to July 1949, introduced the 'Dimitrov' Constitution and conducted the liquidation of the democratic opposition; like Lenin, embalmed and on show in a Sofia mausoleum.

Dragoicheva, Tsola (b. 1898): Soviet-educated Bulgarian Communist, sentenced for subversive activities before the Second World War; since 1940 Politburo member; much feared for her role in the purges of 1944-47, when she was Secretary-General of the National Committee of the Fatherland Front; organizer of the Dimitrov Youth Union and Chairman of the Union of Bulgarian Women; Minister of Posts, Telegraphs and Telephones 1947-1957; under a cloud after Kostov's execution; awarded the Soviet Order of Lenin and created Hero of the People's Republic of Bulgaria in 1968.

Dzhagarov, Georgi (b. 1925): Bulgarian poet and dramatist and Communist official; at first associated with the de-Stalinization thaw in literature in the mid-1950s, he later became one of the most powerful literary officials, a member of the Party Central Committee and from 1966 to 1972 Chairman of the Bulgarian Writers' Union; as a protégé of Zhivkov, he was used by the régime to win over dissident writers and restore discipline in the Union; Deputy Chairman of the State Council since 1971 and President of the Writers' Union Committee for relations with foreign countries.

Ganev, Dimiter (1898-1964): Bulgarian Politburo member from 1957, Chairman of the National Assembly Presidium (Head of State) from 1958 until his death; prominent after 9 September 1944 as Politburo member and Minister of Trade; in the wake of the Kostov trial demoted to Ambassador in Prague, but staged a comeback in 1957 and became titular head of state the following year.

Geshev, Nikola: Bulgarian police investigator before the Communist takeover; during the War, conducted the interrogations of arrested members of the Communist underground.

Ivanov, Anton (1884-1942): Bulgarian Communist, active since 1904, took part in the Communist-led September 1923 uprising for which he was imprisoned; in 1925 emigrated to the Soviet Union; member of the Bulgarian Party Bureau-in-exile; returned to Bulgaria clandestinely during the War and was elected Politburo member in 1941; arrested in 1942 and shot.

Karavelov, Lyuben (1834-79): Bulgarian writer and radical nationalist; studied in Russia; leader of the revolutionary committee-in-exile in Bucharest working for the overthrow of Ottoman rule.

Karaslavov, Georgi (1904-80): Bulgarian Communist writer and fanatic exponent of Socialist Realism; became First Secretary of the Writers' Union in the purge of deviant writers in April 1958 when Chervenkov was Minister of Education and Culture; in turn, replaced by Georgi Dzhagarov; member of the Bulgarian Academy of Literature.

Khaitov, Nikolai (b. 1919): Bulgarian forestry engineer, author of popular essays and short stories, particularly esteemed for his poetic descriptions of Bulgaria's mountains and forests.

Kolarov, Vassil (1877-1950): Bulgarian Communist second in rank only to Georgi Dimitrov; graduated in law from Geneva University; after the abortive uprising of September 1923, fled to the Soviet Union and became a Soviet citizen; prominent in the Bulgarian Party and Politburo, and in the Communist International; Chairman of the National Assembly 1945-47, Prime Minister 1949-50; ruthless organizer of the purges of the democratic opposition in Bulgaria after 9 September 1944.

Kostov, Traicho (1897-1949): The most eminent of the home-grown (as opposed to Soviet-trained 'Muscovite') Bulgarian Communists; Central Committee member before the War; as Politburo member, one of five who directed the Communist wartime underground; sentenced to life imprisonment in 1942; after September 1944 joined the Fatherland Front government; dismissed in March 1949 from Politburo and as Deputy Premier; in 1949 tried and executed as Titoist (nationalist) spy and foreign agent; at his trial he repudiated the confession he had allegedly signed in prison; posthumously rehabilitated in 1962.

Kotsev, Venelin (b. 1926): High-ranking Bulgarian Communist official; Central Committee secretary since 1966 with general responsibility for culture and the arts.

Levchev, Lyubomir (b. 1935): Bulgarian writer, poet and party official enjoying the protection of Todor Zhivkov and especially that of his late daughter Lyudmila; Editor of the Party's literary weekly *Literaturen Front* 1970-72; first Deputy Chairman of the Committee for Art and Culture 1975.

Matev, Pavel (b. 1924): Bulgarian poet and author, Editor of the literary monthly *Septemvri*; Chairman of the Committee for Art and Culture 1966-75; headed the Central Committee's department for art and culture in 1975, but demoted the following year.

Mikhailov, Ivan (1897-1982): Bulgarian Soviet-trained General, served twenty years in the Soviet Army; returned to Bulgaria in 1945 to conduct purge of the old Bulgarian officers and oversee the sovietization of the Bulgarian Army; became Deputy Minister of National Defence, Deputy Prime Minister, Politburo member and member of the State Council; in 1962 obliged to cede the Ministry of Defence to a home Communist and former partisan, General Dzhurov.

Nonev, Bogomil (b. 1920): Bulgarian diplomat and journalist; Deputy-Chairman of the Administrative Council of the Union of Bulgarian Journalists 1967-71; Editor of the review *Nasha Rodina*; ('Our Native Land') Director General of Bulgarian Radio and Television 1966-68; Head of Section in the Ministry of Foreign Affairs in Sofia 1971-72.

Panov, Yonko: Militant in the pre-War underground Communist Party and a General with the partisans; Central Committee member 1952; Deputy Minister of Defence 1954; dismissed in 1957 in a top-level purge echoing the Soviet purge of the 'anti-Party' group of Molotov, Malenkov, Kaganovich and Shepitov; in 1961 branded as one of a group of 'coffee-house' conspirators suspected of planning a putsch with dissident army elements. (See *The Truth That Killed*, p. 246)

Pavlov, Todor (1890-1977): Veteran Marxist-Leninist philosopher, literary critic and Academician; known for his ideological rigidity as the régime's watchdog over Socialist Realist orthodoxy in the arts; Communist member of the Regency Council in the first Fatherland Front government, 1944-46; Chairman of the Bulgarian Academy of Sciences 1947-1962; Politburo member since 1966.

Petkov, Nikola (*c.* 1899-1947): Leader of the radical wing of Bulgaria's Agrarian Party and partner of the Communists in the anti-German underground and the Fatherland Front Coalition Government of 9 September 1944; with other disillusioned bourgeois leaders withdrew from the Communist-dominated government in 1945 to become the leader of a united opposition; his execution by hanging on 23 September 1947 after a show trial on trumped-up charges put an end to any tolerated democratic opposition to the Communist dictatorship.

Radevski, Christo (b. 1903): Bulgarian poet and activist of the anti-Fascist movement, displaced by Georgi Karaslavov.

Radichkov, Yordan (b. 1929): Bulgarian author and journalist, works for the literary weekly *Literaturen Front*.

Rainov, Bogomil (b. 1919): Bulgarian author and philosopher; cultural attaché at the Bulgarian Embassy in Paris after 1945; Professor of Aesthetics; Editor of *Literaturen Front* 1966-70; First Deputy Chairman of the Bulgarian Writers' Union 1968-71; member of the Central Committee since 1976.

Ralin, Radoi (b. 1923): Popular Bulgarian satirical poet known for his irreverent wit, who has often incurred official displeasure; in 1960 his book *Bezopassni Igli* ('Safety Pins') was banned.

Smirnenski, Christo (1898-1923): Bulgarian worker poet of progressive ideas, accepted in the Communist pantheon although he died before the advent of 'socialism' in Bulgaria.

Staikov, Encho (1901-75): Home Communist of the older generation; Politburo member 1954-1966; in charge of the Agitprop (agitation and propaganda) Department, reputed to have been in favour of reforms.

Terpeschev, Dobri (1884-1967): Prominent 'home' Communist and wartime partisan commander; after 9 September 1944 held the posts of Chairman of the Supreme Economic Council, Minister of Labour and Social Welfare and Ambassador to Bucharest; Politburo member until 1950 when he fell from grace after the Traicho Kostov trial; rejoined the Central Committee in 1954; a colourful, folksy figure.

Trunski, Slavcho (b. 1914): Wartime partisan General who maintained contact with Tito's partisans; persecuted after the liquidation of Traicho Kostov; rehabilitated in 1954, rose to Deputy Minister of Defence and commander of the Air Force despite reports of involvement in the alleged army *coup* attempts of 1961 and 1965.

Vaptsarov, Nikola (1909-1942): Bulgarian Communist worker poet, member of the anti-Fascist wartime resistance, tried and shot in Sofia.

Vazov, Ivan (1850-1921): Famous Bulgarian poet and novelist, whose best known novel *Pod Igoto* ('Under the Yoke'), describing the suffering of the Bulgarian people and their heroic fight for freedom under the Turks, has been translated into many foreign languages including English.

Yugov, Anton (b. 1904): Before the war studied in the Comintern School of Revolution in Moscow; in 1944 became a ruthless Minister of the Interior, Major General of the People's Army, organizer of the People's Militia (police) and the notorious labour camps; known for his instigation of political mass murders; partly demoted in 1950, he was chosen to implement Moscow's 'anti-Stalin' course and the temporary rapprochement with Tito as Prime Minister in 1956; ousted by Todor Zhivkov in 1962.

Zhivkov, Todor (b. 1911): Bulgaria's highest Communist official; former printing worker who joined the Bulgarian Komsomol in 1928, the Communist Party in 1932 and the resistance movement in 1941; after 9 September 1944 he rose slowly via the Sofia City Committee; Politburo member 1951, First Secretary of the Bulgarian Communist Party 1954, Prime Minister 1962-71 and Chairman of the State Council 1971.